BELLE BOYD

Confederate Spy

Also by

LOUIS A. SIGAUD

DOUHET AND AERIAL WARFARE, G. P. Putnam's Sons, N. Y. City, 1941.
An Analysis of the Douhet Military Doctrine.

BELLE BOYD

Confederate Spy

BY

LOUIS A. SIGAUD

Former Lieutenant-Colonel, Military Intelligence Reserve, U. S. Army; Commanding Officer, Corps of Intelligence Police, A. E. F. in World War I.

THE DIETZ PRESS, INCORPORATED

RICHMOND, VIRGINIA

Second Edition, January, 1945

"I looked for Belle Boyd and found her. . . . Her cheeks were rosy with excitement and recent exercise, and her eyes all aflame. When I rode up to speak to her she received me with much surprised cordiality, and as I stooped from my saddle she pinned a crimson rose to my uniform, bidding me remember that it was *blood-red* and that it was her 'colors.' "

—HENRY KYD DOUGLAS.

Belle Boyd in Photographs

Plate 1

"THE OLD CAPITOL"
Where Belle Boyd was twice imprisoned.

Plate 2

BELLE BOYD

Courtesy of the Confederate Museum.

Plate 3

BELLE BOYD HARDINGE

Frontispiece in her own book, *Belle Boyd in Camp and Prison.*
Belle was twenty years old at the time of this picture.

Plate 4

BELLE BOYD

From an original Brady negative.

This photograph may be dated probably a decade after the preceding picture, made for Belle Boyd's book, for late in the eighteen-seventies, Matthew B. Brady, famous photographer of the War Between the States, was forced to give up his negatives. Discovered years later, they formed the basis of *Photographic History of the Civil War* in which a photograph of Belle Boyd is prominent among the secret service operators of the Confederacy.

The above photograph was made especially for this book, *Belle Boyd, The Confederate Spy*, from an original negative from the Brady collection in the L. C. Handy Studios in Washington, D. C.

Plate 5

MARIE ISABELLE BOYD HAMMOND
(MRS. A. MICHAEL)

Surviving daughter of Belle Boyd
and Colonel Hammond.
Listed on the theatre poster as
"Isabel Hammond."

Plate 6

BYRD HAMMOND

Known on the stage as "Sarah Boyd."
Daughter of Belle Boyd and
Colonel Hammond.
Died in 1932 as Mrs. H. W. Mowery.
Listed on the theatre poster as
"Boyd Swainston."

Plate 8

RUE HIGH

Nathaniel Rue High, third husband of Belle Boyd.
Famous on the stage in his young manhood for his handsome profile.

Plate 7

JOHN EDMUND HAMMOND

Son of Belle Boyd and Colonel Hammond.
Served in Battery O, First Artillery Regiment, U. S. A., in 1899.

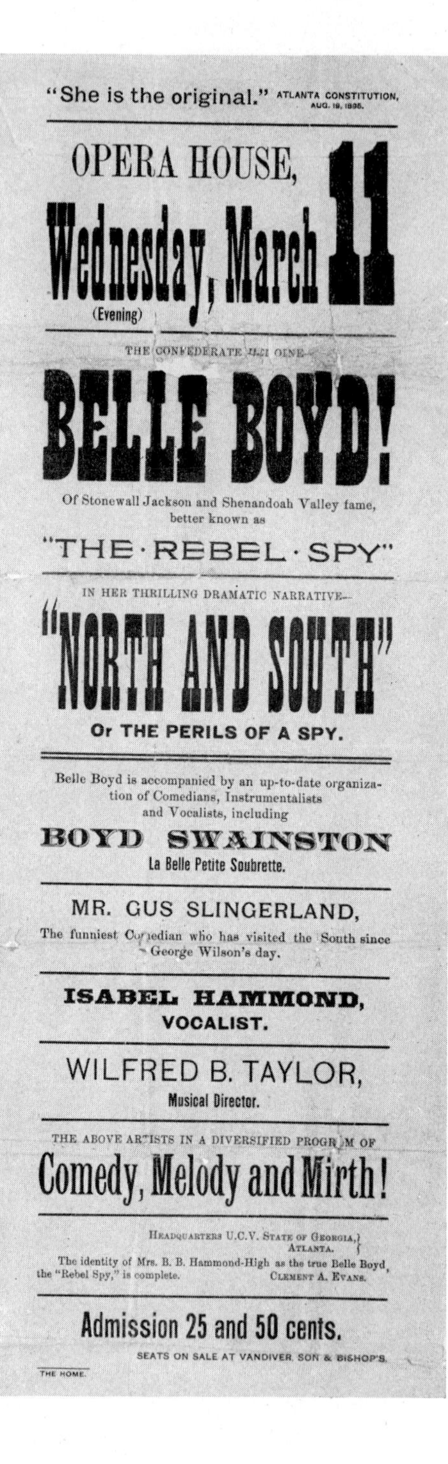

"She is the original." ATLANTA CONSTITUTION, AUG. 19, 1895.

OPERA HOUSE,

Wednesday, March 11

(Evening)

THE CONFEDERATE [illegible]OINE

BELLE BOYD!

Of Stonewall Jackson and Shenandoah Valley fame, better known as

"THE · REBEL · SPY"

IN HER THRILLING DRAMATIC NARRATIVE—

"NORTH AND SOUTH"

Or THE PERILS OF A SPY.

Belle Boyd is accompanied by an up-to-date organization of Comedians, Instrumentalists and Vocalists, including

BOYD SWAINSTON

La Belle Petite Soubrette.

MR. GUS SLINGERLAND,

The funniest Co[illegible]edian who has visited the South since George Wilson's day.

ISABEL HAMMOND,

VOCALIST.

WILFRED B. TAYLOR,

Musical Director.

THE ABOVE AR[illegible]ISTS IN A DIVERSIFIED PROGR[illegible]M OF

Comedy, Melody and Mirth!

HEADQUARTERS U.C.V. STATE OF GEORGIA,
ATLANTA.

The identity of Mrs. B. B. Hammond-High as the true Belle Boyd, the "Rebel Spy," is complete.

CLEMENT A. EVANS.

Admission 25 and 50 cents.

SEATS ON SALE AT VANDIVER, SON & BISHOP'S.

THE HOME.

Plate 9

Poster of Belle Boyd's Dramatic Recitals

Belle Boyd's success excited several women to impersonate her and she was forced to carry letters of identification.

The statement by (General) Clement A. Evans is a significant endorsement of Belle's character. A most distinguished Georgian, lawyer, state senator, and presidential elector before the War, Evans became Colonel of the 31st Georgia Infantry, Army of Northern Virginia, under "Stonewall" Jackson. Later he served under Ewell, Early and Gordon, becoming Brigadier-General in 1864.

After the War he began a ministry in the Methodist Episcopal Church, South, that lasted twenty-five years. In 1895, the date of the poster, he was Commander of the Georgia Division, and in 1908 became Commander-in-Chief of the United Confederate Veterans. He edited the twelve volume *Confederate Military History* and wrote the Introduction to Myrta Lockett Avary's *Dixie After the War*.

The significance of this is that against the vicious attacks of some writers, we have this fact: General Evans, knowing that Belle Boyd married Northerners; knowing that she placed her daughters on the stage; knowing, presumably, that as Belle Boyd Hammond-High she was divorced and her third husband was her stage manager; knowing surely that she claimed to have served the Confederacy and Jackson as a spy; he, as a minister of the gospel and a distinguished veteran, endorsed her when she appeared in his own community.

FOREWORD

Championing Belle Boyd

"She was a mystery while yet she lived, and she remains a mystery today."—Editorial on Belle Boyd, *Washington Star* (D. C.), May 8, 1943.

"Sir, will you take my life?"

Startled by this desperate plea, George Sala, the friend of Dickens and Thackeray, stared in amazement at the lady he was calling upon at the Brunswick Hotel in Jermyn Street, London. She was young, certainly no more than twenty-one years of age, with a tall, supple figure, light hair, and bright grey-blue eyes. Features too irregular to be merely pretty suggested firmness, and even joyous recklessness. Graceful, self-assured, and exquisitely gowned according to the latest fashion, she was unmistakably a disturbingly attractive person.

Before he could speak, Belle Boyd moved swiftly toward the famous English journalist and writer and actually placed her life in his hands. In a low, musical voice she told the man who had reported the war in America for the *Daily Telegraph* that the manuscript she had just handed him was the story of her adventures as a Confederate agent. Funds sent her from home were being intercepted by the Federal Government, her husband had been imprisoned as a Southern spy, and she was now destitute. She assured him most persuasively that what she had to tell was well worth publishing and that the proceeds of the book would relieve her financial distress.

Later, alone in the dingy office where for thirty years he wrote his noted column, "Echoes of the Week," London's popular "G. A. S." found it absurdly difficult to shift his rebellious thoughts from the charming lady and her predicament to the merits of her story. But once again self-possessed and practical, he realized suddenly that at the age of twenty-one most lives are yet to be lived. With growing doubt he picked up the pages he had been given so dramatically, and examined them casually. As he read, his interest quickened, and soon he was completely absorbed in a thrilling narrative. And so, in May 1865, there was published in London *Belle Boyd in Camp and Prison,* with a highly enthusiastic introduction by George Augustus Sala, "a friend of the South."[1]*

This book is now out of print, and Belle Boyd died in 1900 in Wisconsin, borne to rest with military honors, not by Southern comrades but proudly and sadly by men and the sons of men who had fought for the Union. However, since her death hundreds of dramatic and controversial articles have been written about the remarkable career of the woman known to so many as "The Rebel Spy" and "The Siren of the Shenandoah." So she still lives on stirringly in the hearts of men and women fascinated and intrigued by these fragmentary recitals of her deeds.

To what was actually known of her, the fertile and often malicious gossip of time has inevitably added many strange legends. And today susceptible history is on the verge of recording falsely that Belle Boyd was not what she said she was, and even that she was someone she could not have been.

One reputable reference work brands her story as a "none too trustworthy account." Another, stating she married Cole Younger, partner of Jesse James and right-hand man of Quantrill, the guerilla leader, suggests cautiously that she was also Belle Starr, the "Female Jesse James" of outlaw days in the Indian Territory. A noted historian of her native Southern State discloses that, where she was born, "some say she was a myth and never existed at all."

Since her death there have been many to claim with vindictive relish and increasing confidence that her exploits were largely imaginary. Some have even sought to prove it by violent distortion of her own story. Further, in her native village, an influential critic recently dismissed her as "just a camp-follower," and in *Reveille in Washington* it is claimed that "controversies raged as to her chastity." Several of those who grudgingly admit some of her achievements charge that she was not loyal to the Confederacy. It has even been said that General "Stonewall" Jackson, to whom she carried vital intelligence at the battle of Front Royal, never heard of her.

Was Belle Boyd actually a heroine, or was she an impostor? Was she a "good woman" of excellent lineage and education, or was she an immoral, sordid and disloyal character of obscure origin and condition? Did "Stonewall" Jackson know of her activities on behalf of the South?

Carl Sandburg believes that on the evidence she could have been shot as a spy. Douglas Southall Freeman describes her as "one of the most

*Numbered notes at back of book give sources of information only.

active and most reliable of the many secret women agents of the Confederacy." And Joseph Hergesheimer, in a delightful and lyrical essay on her, declares "she was both a celebrated and important figure in the war she ornamented."

Her own narrative, written hurriedly as the war ended, is highly dramatic. But, though she needed money urgently, it was still so perilous a time that a strong sense of discretion wisely counselled reticence. There was much that could not yet be told. What she revealed was only what was not then dangerous to relate. With characteristic contempt for her Northern critics, she concerned herself solely with what had happened and forebore to mention her historic family background so utterly at variance with the ignoble status of prostitute and village courtesan imputed to her in the *New York Times,* the *Washington Evening Star,* and other hostile Federal papers.

In naming most of the officers involved in her experiences, she must have meant to provide unanswerable contemporaneous evidence of the truth of her story. Not one officer ever challenged her statements about him. But what she could not foresee was that her eventual detractors would await her death and that of her witnesses before claiming she lied.

In this book, her story is told again. But now it is amplified by the impressive testimony of others, by the official records, and by the papers and recollections of her descendants and connections. The officers she mentioned served at the places and in the capacities stated by her. And in these pages her witnesses testify eloquently that Belle Boyd was what she said she was, and did what she said she did.

These additions to Belle Boyd's tale do much more than supplement it. They substantiate it, and in so doing give it real historical significance. Her sponsors at the bar of history today are now too many, too definite, too convincing, and too reputable to be ignored or contradicted. Among the many Southerners are a Confederate Lieutenant-General whose father had been President of the United States, and a private who rose to Brigade Commander and subsequently became Adjutant General of Maryland and a Major-General, U. S. V. Among the equally numerous Northerners are found the war-time Provost Marshal of the District of Columbia, later a Brigadier-General, U. S. V.; and a Rear-Admiral, U. S. N., who, as a commander, had entered in the log of his ship his capture of the "famous rebel lady."

Records of the gallantry and the valor of the men of the South in the Civil War, or War Between the States, are today a priceless part of our historic national heritage. So is the story of the indomitable spiritual and physical courage of their women. Nowhere in the Confederacy did this feminine patriotic ardor flame higher than in the Virginian Valley where Belle Boyd was born. It was the irrepressible aggressive spirit of the women of this region that impelled General Shields to wire Secretary of War Stanton in the spring of 1862: "I can retake the Valley and rejoin General McDowell but you must send new men to keep it. The women will take it if we don't."

Belle Boyd loved the South passionately; so passionately, in fact, that when Secretary Stanton had her brought to Washington in the summer of 1862 and placed in close custody in the Old Capitol Prison, the *Washington Evening Star* complained bitterly that she was "insanely devoted to the rebel cause." It was this whole-hearted, unswerving devotion to the Cause that led her inevitably to further it constantly, heedless of consequences, with all the vitality and skill at her command.

Belle Boyd was quick-tempered, and feared no man. Had she lived to confront those who pretend that she was far more imaginative than truthful, or who say that she was Belle Starr, one more adventure could be related about her. Its precise nature is more than hinted in the graphic warning she sent a youthful aide of "Stonewall" Jackson in 1862, that if she ever caught that young man in Martinsburg she would cut off his ears.

Eighty years have elapsed since Belle Boyd gave Harry Douglas her "colors" to wear into battle, and the Lady and her Knight have long since passed on. Yet today it is still a high privilege to champion her blood-red colors ardently.

LOUIS A. SIGAUD.

Brooklyn, New York.
July, 1944.

CONTENTS

BELLE BOYD IN PHOTOGRAPHS

CHAPTER ONE

Childhood Years of Belle Boyd

N a pleasant day in 1855 the Boyds of Martinsburg, Virginia had been entertaining distinguished guests at dinner. Young and charming Mary Boyd was smiling happily at her husband Ben while their friends, about to leave, paid her gracious compliments as their hostess. Everything had indeed been perfect. But now, abruptly, hosts and guests were startled by odd rattling noises just outside. These increased alarmingly in volume. The door was thrust open violently and a white and brown spotted horse clattered into the room. He was brought to a halt by a slim tawny-haired girl about eleven years old who sat firmly in the saddle and eyed the company with evident indignation and defiance.

Ben Boyd moved forward quickly, but before he reached her, the child spoke.

"Well," she said with combative emphasis, "my horse is old enough, isn't he?"

For Mary and Ben, it was a most embarrassing moment. The mounted invader was Belle, their first born, who had been told earlier that day that she was still too young for social functions. Characteristically, she had ventured to dissent dramatically.

Her reception, at least on the part of her mortified parents, was ominous. For them, Belle had again gone too far, and parental exasperation threatened immediate and impressive retribution. But, as was to happen so often in later years, her spirited conduct completely conquered the most eminent among her victims. Greatly impressed by her reckless assurance and much diverted by her resolute defiance, the guest of honor, a high State official, interceded warmly for her and averted the Boyds' wrath.

"Surely," he declared, "so high a spirit should not be thoughtlessly quelled by severe punishment! Mary, won't you tell me more about your little rebel?"

Much of what he learned then about the youthful mischief with which Belle delighted to plague her family, her mammy, and her neighbors is still current gossip in Martinsburg. What she wished to do, and could see no good reason for not doing, she did. And so, a law unto herself, and frequently indulged by her affectionate parents, she challenged at an early age the strict conventions of her community and the even sterner code of her loving but inflexible and respectably prominent Presbyterian relatives.

In Gerrardstown it is still told how, as a six-year-old visiting her Campbell kin, Belle shocked her adult cousin Jimmie. Looking out of her window early one morning, she spied some unusually fine apples on a tree near the house. Impulsively, without waiting to dress properly or adequately, or to weigh the propriety of her act, she pattered out in bare-footed innocence to pluck the inviting fruit.

Among other relatives horrified by similar misbehavior were Maria and Eliza (née Reed), who were first cousins of Belle's paternal grandmother. Maria, with her husband Alex Cooper, had donated the land and much of the money for the erection of the Presbyterian Church in Martinsburg, and Alex was its ruling elder for forty-five years. Eliza had married Samuel Baker, also a church elder, and among her warm friends were the socially elect Pendletons, Faulkners, and Strothers, including the famous Strother known as "Porte Crayon." Eulogizing Maria Cooper after her death, Senator Faulkner of Virginia wrote that she was "a lady of great intelligence, brilliant conversational powers, and of great religious fervor and piety."[2*] What he omitted was that Maria Cooper was also a firm believer in stern discipline for children—a belief to which Belle certainly contributed extensively.

Born at Martinsburg on May 9, 1844, Belle was named Isabelle in honor of a great-aunt. Belle's godmother and her grandmother, Maria, were sisters who had married brothers: John and Samuel Boyd respectively. John and Isabella Boyd, after their marriage in 1803, had left Virginia and settled in Knoxville, Tennessee, but they kept in close touch with their Martinsburg kin, and were delighted when young Mary and Benjamin became parents.

Though Belle was born in Martinsburg, probably at the home of her grandmother, Mrs. Samuel Boyd, she was soon taken to Bunker Hill, a cross-roads hamlet some ten miles away. Here her parents had a pleasant two-storied house with walls completely hidden by roses and honeysuckle, the memory of which remained with Belle always. Around the house silver maples swayed their branches gently in breezes heavy with the scent of flowers in summer; and before it, at a short distance, Mill Creek flowed swiftly—a cheerfully talkative stream on an urgent, never-ending errand from the mountains to the sea.

*Numbered notes at back of book give sources of information only.

Sometime between 1849 and 1854 Benjamin Boyd, who had a general store at Bunker Hill, erected a stone building on Queen Street east of the railroad in Martinsburg, moved his store there and brought his family to live at 126 East Burke Street. At this time Benjamin was also directing a tobacco plantation. This must have been the one hundred and twenty-five acre farm adjoining "Glenn Burnie" in Jefferson County, inherited by Mary Boyd from her father, Captain James Glenn.

During her childhood Belle enjoyed the constant companionship of younger brothers and sisters, and probably saw much of her numerous young cousins. Outside her family, her particular playmates were her neighbors, Virginia and Betty Doll. What her favorite recreation was, is nowhere recorded. Yet her later experiences suggest it clearly. Long after her imprisonment in the Old Capitol, one of her jailers took pleasure in recalling the perfect figure of "a splendid specimen of feminine health and vigor." And in 1915 another had not yet forgotten that "open air and horseback exercise were in her case constitutional necessities." As a child she must have spent very many happy and energetic days afoot and on horseback exploring the lower and middle reaches of her beloved Valley. As for its past, legend and folk-lore had much to impart.

"I have discovered God's country!" exclaimed Governor Spotswood of Virginia, when in 1716 he and his roving Knights of the Golden Horseshoe passed through Swift Run Gap in the Blue Ridge Mountains and gazed with delight upon the fine land west of the Ridge. In the lovely Valley they came upon a limpid, murmurous stream, and to show that they had truly found a Garden of Eden they called it "Euphrates" in honor of that ancient river in Asia Minor fabled to have watered the first earthly abode of man. But the Indians had already given its crystal clear water an equally poetic origin and a more softly melodious name.

Since time primeval, the transparent current of the river has reflected the light of the stars brightly at night and mirrored the blueness of the sky faithfully by day. To the imaginative mind of the Redskin, the totem of its descent was no mystery. Born of the stars and of the sky, here was surely "Shenandoah"—Daughter of the Stars, Daughter of the Sky.

To the Indian, all that moves lives. The Shenandoah had its being in the Valley and drew its fluid life from that scenic land and its guardian mountains. In time the name of the river covered its whole dominion. But the stream retained its sovereignty, and the earth remained its tributary. The river alone is Daughter of the Stars. Where she dwells is her Valley—the Valley of the Shenandoah.

The daring white settlers who ventured over the Blue Ridge to this charming, fertile Eden prospered. Soon, beyond their hills was "Outside." Within, they carved out a rich spiritual and material heritage. Hardy, impulsive, courageous, they bred a Valley people with an ardent love for their native soil and a fierce pride.

It was to this historic Valley—the Valley of the Shenandoah—that Belle's ancestors, the Boyds, the Reeds, and the Stephensons, had gradually found their way.

When Belle reached the age of twelve, her parents decided that it was time for her to acquire a formal education outside the Valley. Accordingly, she was sent in 1856 to Baltimore to attend the Mount Washington Female College directed by the Reverend George Lewis Staley, D. D., of whom she always cherished a most grateful recollection.* She completed a four-year course at Mount Washington with emphasis on French, classical literature, music, and singing. Belle apparently took an active and happy part in the social life of her comrades, and it was here that she enjoyed the intimate companionship of her chum, Nina, which she was to commemorate in her selection of a stage name almost a quarter of a century later.

While Belle was in Baltimore, the Boyds in Martinsburg moved from East Burke Street to South Queen Street. Here, where the subsequently erected Gray Silver residence at No. 501 now stands, they occupied a substantial house which was to be their home throughout the war years. Directly across the street, at what is now No. 502, lived "Petey."

"Petey", the special friend of Belle and her very young brother, William, was a Mr. Peterman. He and his wife became greatly attached to their new neighbors and Belle, when home, was often across the road visiting. She was a great favorite of Mr. Peterman, whom she loved to tease, and he was proud of his nickname. It had fallen to his lot when tiny William had uttered it in a valiant attempt to say "Peterman."

Today† at No. 502, a pleasant, alert, active lady, who is more than eighty years old, tells of this friendship and shows a photograph of Belle Boyd in stage costume, a copy of *Belle Boyd in Camp and Prison,* and a small bowl bought in the Boyd store at Bunker Hill almost one hundred years ago. The lady is Miss Rebecca Peterman, and the picture and book were presented to her mother by Belle Boyd after the war. Though

*For data on school, see Item i, Sec. 1, Appendix A.
†November 1942.

in the region some may now venture to say Belle Boyd was only a myth, here in the old home of her friends there is still this much of a remembered and treasured yesterday to protest that not all has gone with the wind.

At sixteen, Belle made her entry into the social life of Washington. One of the homes in which she was often a guest was the residence of Secretary of War Floyd who was so soon to become a Confederate general. Belle's social status in the capital was hardly surprising, for the standing of her family and its connections was such as to open all doors to her.*

The Boyds claimed to stem from the Boyds of the County of Ayr in Scotland. In Ayr the proud record of the family goes back even beyond the Robert Boyd who died some time prior to 1240. For many centuries, the Boyds, a sept of the royal Stuart clan, and wearing the Stuart tartan, lived in Dean Castle, and the ruins of this fortress can still be found a mile from Kilmarnock in Ayr.[3]

Belle's grandmother Maria, who married Samuel Boyd in Berkeley County, Virginia in 1798, was a daughter of Private James Stephenson who served as a wagoner in the 15th Virginia Regiment and was at Valley Forge in 1778. Maria's grandfather, James Reed, was Lieutenant-Colonel of the First Battalion, Philadelphia militia, and his seven sons were also officers during the Revolution. Of these, Joseph, ensign in the Fifth Pennsylvania Line Regiment, died of wounds and exposure, Samuel, a lieutenant in the Fifth Pennsylvania, became a prominent lawyer in Martinsburg, and William, who served in several units, was later a member of the Pennsylvania Constitutional Convention, State Senator, Major General of militia, and State Adjutant General.[4]

Maria's brother, Major James Stephenson, was one of Martinsburg's most distinguished citizens. He held office as a local magistrate, was a County Delegate to the Virginia Assembly, and from 1803 to 1825 served three terms in Washington in the House of Representatives. He had led a company of riflemen under General St. Clair in 1791, and in the Fourth Sub-Legion one of his comrades-in-arms had been James Glenn, an officer with a distinguished military record in and after the Revolution.[5] No matter how intimate they became as officers, however, neither could foresee that Stephenson's nephew, Benjamin Boyd, would marry Glenn's daughter, Mary, almost fifty years later, and that one fruit of that happy union would be Belle Boyd.

In the winter of 1860-61, when Belle reached Washington, growing

*Full genealogical data in Appendix.

thunder clouds on the political horizon foretold plainly the rapid approach of inevitable conflict. For four years Belle had dreamed of pretty dresses, gay balls, official dinners, and attentive cavaliers. Now the dream faded before the impending storm of war and destruction. She was barely in time to take part in that last brief, feverish fling of entertainment in which, with forced animation, gayety, and amity, the sons and daughters of the North and of the South mingled before they became mortal enemies. In the divided nation's Capital there had already begun the underground struggle of deception and intrigue which was to influence military operations so greatly. In the armed services of the United States, officers from the South suffered bitter spiritual agony as they sought to decide honorably between two great but henceforth incompatible loyalties.

Though so eager to enjoy the happiness due her budding womanhood, the clear-thinking young girl, fresh from school at Baltimore, understood what was happening. Conscious of no need to make a decision as to her own allegiance, she engaged in no soul-searching. As she saw it, Lincoln's election had made the secession of Southern States certain. The North really intended more than the freedom of the Negro. It also meant to exclude the landed proprietors of the South from participation in national legislation. This she thought was particularly true of the New England merchants. To such an arrogant attempt to dominate, harness, and enslave the South, to such a threat to change its pleasant, leisurely, manorial way of life to a frenzied tempo of incessant trading for profit, the intensely partisan Southern girl saw but one answer. There remained, she believed firmly, but one effective way to make it.

South Carolina was first to secede. Other States followed her lead, and the cruel prospect of civil war became a far more dreadful reality. President Lincoln asked the States to furnish recruits for the service of the United States, and fixed a quota for each State. The Old Dominion supplied the men but, as Belle wrote proudly and still defiantly four years later, Virginia provided them for the Stars and Bars.

Her own place was no longer in Washington. Without delay, she left the Capital for her Valley.

In that magnificent land of incomparable beauty and bounteous plenty, the forces of the North and of the South were destined to fight back and forth savagely and incessantly. On the floor of the Valley, in its gently-rolling hills, and on its high, rugged mountains, its own knightly Ashby was to lead the cavaliers of his famed Laurel Brigade to great deeds; the Stonewall Brigade was to march and fight its way to renown; and the military genius of Jackson was to write its immortal saga with his mighty sword on the pages of history.

At the call to arms, from every farm, from every village, from every town, men swarmed in neighborly groups eager to uphold the cause of the South and to fight for the Valley. Their companies, their battalions, their regiments, were not military units only. They constituted embattled communities. The Fourth Company of the Second Virginia Infantry was not simply Company D. It was Martinsburg in arms. The Second Company of the same regiment was not just Company B. It was Shepherdstown in martial array. And so it was with other units. Their sum total was more formidable and indomitable than any army. It was the Valley incarnate.

Such was the stature of the men of the Valley. Its daughters came from a no less heroic mold. Scorning the conventional passive womanly role, they were eager to serve the Confederacy in every possible way with the same high courage as their men. They were ready to scout and spy for the Southern forces, run the Union land blockade, nurse the wounded and the sick, defy the occupying troops of the North, and, above all, by their heartening example and infectious devotion, to keep alight the flaming spirit that animated the Confederate forces to the very end. It was to the womanhood of the Valley that the habitually impassive Jackson paid eloquent homage when he told Henry Kyd Douglas impulsively that the ladies of Winchester were the "truest in the South."[6]

CHAPTER TWO

First Adventures

MONG the earliest to volunteer to fight for the South was Belle's father. Although forty-four years old, and not a man given to much physical activity, he decided someone else could run the store. His great-grandfather, Lieutenant-Colonel James Reed, had thought nothing of joining the American Revolutionary forces at the age of sixty-five, only five years short of his golden wedding anniversary. His grandfather, James Stephenson, had gladly served as a wagoner. So Ben Boyd considered it a privilege to become a private in Company D, Second Virginia Infantry, C. S. A.[7]

His choice was typical of men of his standing who could have sought and obtained military preferment. Recalling the spirit of those early days, Harry Douglas, himself then a private in Company B of the same regiment, wrote later in *I Rode With Stonewall* that "Society was plentiful for the ranks were filled with the best blood of Virginia; all its classes were there."[7]

Manhood of the lower Valley made up the regiment. But its arms and equipment came from the women, and Belle was prominent among those who raised funds for this purpose. Led at the outset by its organizer, Colonel J. A. Q. Nadenboush, the Second Virginia Infantry was soon ordered to Harper's Ferry. Dedicated by its Regimental Flag to "Our God, Our Country, and Our Women," it now proudly took its first martial step along the historic road that was to bring it immortal fame and honor as one of the five regiments of the Stonewall Brigade. By mid-June Mrs. J. W. McGuire confided to her diary (*Diary of a Southern Refugee*):

> "The Second Regiment, containing some of our dear boys, has been lately very actively engaged in the pursuit of these (Yankee) marauders, and we are kept constantly anxious about them."

It was at about this time that audacious Belle shocked the ladies of Martinsburg by openly waving to soldiers on the street. There could be no respectable reason, said convention, for such improper behavior. Yet historians relate that the ladies of the village descended *en masse* upon "Stonewall" Jackson a year later, cut off his coat buttons as souvenirs, and were about to snip off locks of hair when the embarrassed general contrived to escape. That these admirers knew him well enough to justify such familiarity is unthinkable. To suggest that their conduct was indiscreet would be unpardonable. Surely they were actuated by the same patriotic fervor and innocent affection that impelled Belle to wave to the soldiers and later inspired her on the battlefield of Front Royal to cap her fateful message to Harry Douglas with the stirring words: "Goodby. My love to all the dear boys."[8]

Such a message would arouse no feminine resentment today. But in our yet recent yesterday ladies were far more censorious. Typical of Belle's feminine critics was her Front Royal acquaintance Miss Lucy Buck. Lucy—frail, reserved, and fully two years older than Belle—did not think highly of the latter and said so frankly and often in her *Diary of Lucy Rebecca Buck.* The following comment by Lucy based on second-hand observation, hints gently, however, that she may have envied younger Belle her vitality, her popularity, and even her forthrightness.

> "In the late evening Belle Boyd, Alice Stewart and Mr. Jeffries came in. Belle told them all soon after she got here that she and Dr. Bogardus had traced up their relationship and found that they were cousins, and when he came in they were evidently very well acquainted from the way they conducted themselves. This I learned from Nellie—I was fortunately confined to my bed."[9]

With the departure of the regiment, the Boyd household became a desolate, lonely place. The habitually smiling face of Mrs. Boyd assumed gradually an anxious and careworn expression. She was a soldier's wife, but she was also a soldier's daughter, and her father's experiences offered no assurance that her husband would escape danger. In these difficult days Mrs. Boyd probably reviewed for her children the military background of their maternal grandfather.

Her father, James Glenn, had been born on the western slope of the Blue Ridge in Frederick County, Virginia. Restless, talkative, and aggressive, this grandfather of Belle Boyd ran away from home in 1777 at the age of fourteen and enlisted in Captain Blackwell's Company of the 10th Virginia Regiment. Four years later he was a scout and sharpshooter in the harried command of General Greene, racing in forced marches for the river Dan with the British in close pursuit. In October, 1781 he was among those at the taking of Yorktown—a triumph so momentous to him that Valley folklore relates he used it invariably as a historical landmark from which to reckon the occurrence of all other events.[10]

In 1791, when the Indians became dangerously active in the Northwest Territory, Glenn rode hurriedly from Shepherdstown to Winchester to join Captain Nicholas Hannah's Company in Major George Bedinger's Battalion. On September 29th he was made an ensign in the First Regiment, United States Levies, commanded by Lieutenant-Colonel Darke of the Valley. When shrieking Shawnees, Delawares, Wyandots, and Miamis struck and almost wiped out General St. Clair's entire force at daybreak on November 4th near the banks of the Wabash, Glenn led his company in place of its fallen commander. Later, seeing his friend, Raleigh Morgan, dangerously wounded, he placed Morgan on his own horse and, turning often to repel several Indians in close and persistent pursuit, led the animal to the comparative safety of the main body in retreat.[10]

Less than four months later, James Glenn was a lieutenant of infantry in the Regular Army, and assigned by General Anthony Wayne in September, 1792 to the Fourth Sub Legion. On the same day another officer, who had led a company of riflemen at St. Clair's defeat, joined the regiment. This was Captain James Stephenson, oldest child of Private James Stephenson and Colonel James Reed's daughter Mary.[10]

After taking part in the American return to the scene of St. Clair's disaster and the establishment of Fort Recovery at that spot, Lieutenant Glenn resigned from the Army in 1794, probably because of illness due to hard service and exposure. In September the restless soldier was again on duty as a captain of militia, and once more with James Stephenson. Reporting the peaceable quelling of disturbances in Maryland where Liberty Poles had been raised, Edward Carrington wrote the Lieutenant-Governor of Virginia, "I arrived at that place (Hagerstown) with Colonel Moses Hunter, Major Stephenson, and Captain Glen of Berkeley, who were kind enough to go over with me on the 17th inst." There is local evidence that as late as 1798 or 1799, when war with France threatened, James Glenn and his old comrade, Raleigh Morgan, were elected lieutenants in a company of men raised by Abraham Shepherd.[10]

In his early days as a soldier James Glenn had married Jane, youngest daughter of John and Margaret Duke. Surviving Jane and their three children, James Glenn married again. His second wife was Ruth Burns, a descendant of ancient families that pioneered in the Valley. To James and Ruth four children were born, one of whom, Margaret

Ann, died in infancy. The others were two daughters, *Mary Rebecca* and Frances Elizabeth, and a son, James William. To this son Captain Glenn, upon his death in 1832, left the home plantation near Charles Town known as "Glenn Burnie," and made ample provision for his widow and daughters from his extensive land holdings in Berkeley and Jefferson Counties.[10]

Mary Rebecca Glenn, mother of Belle Boyd, was born between 1825 and 1827. Some time between the beginning of 1841 and the middle of 1843 she married Benjamin Reed Boyd. Now, after about twenty years of marriage, she found her husband exposed to the same perils of war her father had courted most of his life.

Troubled Mary Boyd sought relief from her thoughts in her household duties. Her restless daughter Belle sought refuge in the companionship of books and the production of soldierly luxuries to send to her father. But these tame and monotonous employments palled quickly and became intolerable.

Some form of action became imperative. There must be something more women could do than to wait, and hope, and fear. Why not visit the Confederate camp at Harper's Ferry? With characteristic decision and energy, Belle gathered a group of neighbors who had friends and relatives among the Southern forces, and they were off.

Coming from the oppressively sad atmosphere of their homes, the visitors were amazed to find in camp the utmost animation and cheerfulness. Officers and men were as joyous and carefree as though they were not awaiting battle. And ladies, once more in the society of husbands, brothers, sons, and lovers, cast their sadness and worries to the winds, and lived only in the enjoyable present. It was a delightful picnic, and one that it seemed might last indefinitely. Said Henry Kyd Douglas: "Mothers and sisters and other dear girls came constantly to Harper's Ferry and there was little difficulty in seeing them. Nothing was serious yet; everything much like a joke."[11]

But the last of June brought an abrupt end to this fleeting happiness. The Federal Army under General Patterson was reported to be advancing, and so the ladies at the last moment and with the utmost reluctance, were sent home. Thereupon Colonel Thomas Jonathan Jackson, with some five thousand untried but eager men, marched out to reconnoiter and, if possible, check the enemy.

Before the approach of superior forces, the Confederates withdrew slowly from Falling Waters and deliberately engaged the Yankee advance guard in a heavy delaying skirmish. This was early on the morning of July 3rd, and in nearby Martinsburg the roar of artillery and the rattle of musketry was not only heard but also, growing in volume, indicated unmistakably the unfavorable outcome of the conflict. At about ten o'clock Jackson's men passed quickly through the town in full retreat but admirable array, their rear well covered by the protective screen of Turner Ashby's cavalry.

At a respectful distance behind the effective striking range of the horsemen of Ashby, came the Federal Army in triumphant procession. Fife and drum sounding, colors rippling in the breeze, and bayonets gleaming, twenty-five thousand Northerners marched into Martinsburg. Their gun-carriages rumbled through the streets, the gay plumes of their cavalrymen nodded and danced in victorious rhythm, and their infantry, flushed by their initial progress southward, cheered lustily. For the residents, it was an imposing but sad sight, and one destined to be repeated with tragic frequency in the years just ahead.

On this very first day of hostile occupation, Belle had her initial experience with the enemy. In itself a minor clash, it further inflamed her feelings against the North, and fanned her desire to take a more active part in driving the invader from her native soil.

With her Negro maid, Eliza, she had gone to the temporary hospital and, with several other ladies, was taking care of two Southern soldiers badly stricken with fever. All other patients had been evacuated by Jackson, but these men, because of their condition, he had been forced to leave behind.

As she stood by the bedside of one of them who raved in violent delirium, she was startled by the sound of heavy footsteps. Turning, she faced a captain of Federal infantry and two privates. The officer, holding a Federal flag in his hand, advanced to the beds, waved the flag over the sick men, and called them "—— rebels."

Astounded by such ungallant behavior, Belle said with cool scorn, "Sir, these men are as helpless as babies and have, as you may see, no power to reply to your insults."

"And pray," said he, "who may you be, Miss?"

To this inquiry, she made no reply. But her maid answered wrathfully, "A rebel lady."

The officer turned on his heel and, as he and his two companions withdrew, swore emphatically, "A —— independent one, at all events."

Much disquieted by this unpleasant incident, the ladies did not permit it to interfere with their duties. As it seemed desirable to remove the two patients to more comfortable and private quarters, they were placed on litters and a start made for the new location. But in the street Federal soldiers quickly crowded about them and began to threaten the defenseless Confederates. Their gestures and language grew so violent that Belle singled out an officer and appealed to him for aid. To her great relief, he quieted the turbulent men and made it possible for her party to proceed to a place of safety. But there remained with her one hateful thought: Might not her father also be the victim of such brutality? Under the goad of that fear, what had been a high resolve to serve the South effectively became a grim obsession.

The next day was July 4th. The eighty-fifth anniversary of the signing of the *Declaration of Independence*, it was the first not to be celebrated by a united nation. To make it even more sadly memorable for Belle, there occurred on that day one of the most tragic events of her life.

"Very much to the disappointment and possibly to the chagrin of the Secessionists," gloated the *American Union*[12], a paper printed by the Federal troops of occupation, the Fourth was fittingly observed in and about Martinsburg. Most of the regiments paraded, the military bands played national airs everywhere, and in the evening the surrounding hills were illuminated with fireworks. The rejoicing was enthusiastic and long, yet, said the paper, not the slightest disorder occurred, and the town provost-guard reported later that no arrests had been made.

But Belle found reality amazingly different. On that bright, sunny morning, to the harsh accompaniment of cheers, shouts, and imprecations, she heard the strains of "Yankee Doodle" resound early in every street. Whiskey began to flow freely. Quarrelsome soldiers defied officers who tried in vain to quell the budding tumult. Doors were crashed in, and houses forcibly entered. Intoxicated men destroyed private property wantonly. Shots were fired through windows. Chairs and tables were hurled into the streets. And when women begged that some cherished object be spared, they were rudely repulsed with a volley of blasphemous curses.

The home of the Boyds was not overlooked. A party of soldiers forced its way into the house and began to pillage. Having been told that Belle's room was decorated with "rebel" flags, they decided to seek these offensive emblems. However, her alert Negro maid, Eliza, rushed upstairs, tore down the Stars and Bars and managed to burn them before the soldiers could find them. The balked Federals then resolved to hoist a Federal flag over the house to mark the submission of the occupants to its authority.

The patience of Mrs. Boyd had gradually worn thin. At last she found it impossible to remain passive any longer. Moving toward the pillagers with a firm step, she said quietly, but with unmistakable determination: "Men, every member of my household will die before that flag shall be raised over us!"

In response, one of the soldiers thrust himself forward and addressed Mrs. Boyd and her daughter in the most offensive language. Sensing that violence would inevitably follow invective, and already inflamed herself by the alarming incidents of the past twenty-four hours, Belle reacted instinctively.

"I could stand it no longer. My indignation was aroused beyond control, my blood was literally boiling in my veins. I drew my pistol and shot him. He was carried away mortally wounded, and soon after expired."

Taking their wounded comrade with them, the soldiers left the house hurriedly. But once outside, some of them lingered to seek vengeance, for an agitated servant rushed in to announce that material was being piled against the sides of the building to set it afire. A messenger was immediately sent to Federal headquarters for aid. Fortunately, this arrived quickly, and the lurking offenders were arrested before they could accomplish their purpose.

At Federal headquarters, the report that a Southern woman had shot a Northern soldier caused much excitement and great indignation. The officer in charge and several members of his staff called speedily to investigate. Their inquiry was conducted with strict impartiality, and witnesses were put to detailed examination. The conclusion reached by the officer was that Belle Boyd "had done perfectly right." To avoid further trouble, he posted sentries around the house, and daily thereafter Northern officers visited the house as an additional precautionary measure. Otherwise the resentment of the Federal troops might have led to impromptu retaliation. Then, too, there was a civilian minority of Northern sympathizers, and some of them had just presented an American flag to the Twenty-first Pennsylvania Volunteers as a memorial of that unit's entry into the town.[13]

Probably because discretion was advisable while the war continued, Belle did not give the name and regiment of the man she shot. Writing in 1941, Mr. W. O. Stevens in *The Shenandoah and Its Byways*[14], states there is no Union record of the shooting, and implies it was imaginary.

Most of the Federal units at Martinsburg were "three month" volunteer regiments. There are therefore no comprehensive records regarding them except as to their muster rolls, engagements, and casualties. However, in the advance on Martinsburg, the Seventh Pennsylvania Volunteers captured at or near that town one hundred and fifty barrels of whiskey. Officially it appears that all the barrels were staved.[15] Unofficially, it is reasonable to surmise that some of the contents may nevertheless have been consumed rather than destroyed.

Coincidences alone may not fully account for the fact that Private Frederick Martin, Company K, Seventh Pennsylvania Volunteers, was buried in Martinsburg Cemetery on July 7th, and for the further fact that the official Pennsylvania records show his existence but not his death or burial[16]. War Department records confirm his death (cause unknown), but do not give the place of burial. That appears only in the newspaper of the Federal army of occupation with the report of his death.[17]

It does not follow that Frederick Martin was shot by Belle. But the absence of a State record of his death and the inadequacy of the War Department record suggest strongly that official records are hardly conclusive when they do not confirm privately reported incidents. It was surely not an imaginary event to which the *Daily Register* of Knoxville, Tennessee referred on February 14, 1863 when it spoke on its front page of Belle as "this fair and fearless Virginia heroine whose daring defense of her father's house * * * and whose invaluable services * * * have won for her from the Northern press the title of the most courageous and dangerous of rebel female spies."

When word reached the Confederate camp at Darkesville that Belle had shot a Union soldier, it was coupled with a false report that she had been thrown into jail. Immediately men clamored that she be rescued and volunteered to storm her prison. For their reaction they had valid sentimental reasons. She was the daughter of one of them, her grandfather James Glenn had served in the regiment commanded by the general for whom Darkesville was named, and General Darke had been an intimate friend of Ben Boyd's uncle, Major Stephenson.

In fact, the intimacy of General Darke and Belle's great-uncle had developed from an odd encounter between them on the field of honor where some grievance had brought them to cross swords. The one—tall, spare, and energetic—appeared armed with a tremendously long curved blade that suggested strongly to the startled onlookers a farmer's scythe rather than a cavalry weapon. The other duellist—short, rotund, and lethargic—had as his weapon a stubby blade not much longer than a dagger. The contrast was ludicrous, but no one saw it more quickly than Darke and Stephenson. Succumbing helplessly to uncontrollable laughter, they dropped their astonishing weapons, made peace, and became close friends for life.

Though it became unnecessary for the Confederates at Darkesville to attempt her rescue, Belle had learned with alarm of their foolhardy intentions. "It is with pride and gratitude that I record this proof of their esteem and respect for what I had done. It is with no less pleasure I reflect that their devotion was not put to the test and that no blood was shed on my account."

The leniency of the Federals in allowing the shooting of one of their men to go wholly unpunished seems incredible. But Washington was then practicing appeasement seriously. How seriously is best shown by the case of Mrs. Rose O'Neal Greenhow, aunt of Mrs. Stephen A. Douglas. Having transmitted from Washington to the Southern forces information which contributed materially to the Confederate victory in the first Bull Run (Manassas) battle, she was arrested. After a few months of genteel detention she was released and sent South in exchange for her promise to stay south of the Potomac. No Northerner was more shocked by this mild action than Allan Pinkerton. His detailed report on Mrs. Greenhow's activities is an interesting part of the official records.[18]

CHAPTER THREE

Courting the Death Penalty

THE daring seventeen-year-old Martinsburg girl soon found that exoneration did not mean freedom. The Federals realized she was potentially a highly dangerous foe and kept her under strict surveillance. Undiscouraged by their watchfulness, she began to take an active part in free-lance undercover activities. Far more enthusiastic than experienced, she was speedily in trouble again.

Belle's first step was to profit by her enforced acquaintance with the enemy. She was living within the Federal lines in a house guarded by Union soldiers, and visited frequently by their officers. Surely she should be able to learn something of what they knew.

Not every military man can refrain from speaking too freely to attractive and persuasive young women. Those most responsive to feminine charm often overlook the alert mind behind it and fail to fear that a pleasant lady may also be mercilessly hostile. Piecing together the careless remarks of her victims, Belle obtained much information as to the designs of the occupying troops. This was written down promptly and sent off by trusted Negro messengers to "Jeb" Stuart or other Confederate leaders.

Foremost among these messengers was Eliza. This young Negress, whose maiden name was Corsey, had married Samuel Hopewell, one of the Boyd slaves. Only a few years older than her mistress, Eliza was too young to have been her "Mammy" but she was Belle's body servant, or personal attendant. In this rôle, her life was always full of excitement. Before the war, Belle took great delight in horrifying the devoted young Negress by youthful pranks and misbehavior. During the war, she used the constantly terrified but thoroughly reliable Eliza as both messenger and accomplice in her activities on behalf of the South.

That the memories of those earlier days with her adventurous and irrepressible "Miss Belle" sweetened the old age of Eliza appears in many letters her grandchildren wrote for her. In some written as late as 1910, ancient Eliza, who died about ten years later, mourned the colorful past, thanked Belle's daughters for their gifts, and implored them to come back South to live. At the very end her mind mercifully erased the present and she lived again with her mistress in their great moments of the past.[19]

What soon brought Belle to grief was her lack of training in the art of transmitting military intelligence. Acting on her own initiative, and without instructions or guidance from the Confederate Secret Service, she wrote her messages in "clear" (not enciphered) and in her own hand. This violated the important rule that the nature of data transmitted and the identity of the sender must be concealed from the enemy in case of interception. When one of her messages fell into the hands of the Federals, her handwriting betrayed her.

Less than a week after the shooting on July 4th, the Third Assistant Provost-Marshal of the Federal army called for her and took her to headquarters. This provost officer was Captain James Gwyn of the Twenty-third Pennsylvania Infantry who later so distinguished himself that he was made a major-general.[20]

At headquarters Captain Gwyn ushered her into the office of an exceedingly irate colonel. This angry gentleman informed her that a letter of hers had been intercepted. He declared, with the utmost emphasis, that her offence was a very serious one. Mingled threats and reprimands followed, and finally an Article of War was read to Belle in a most solemn and significant manner:

> "Whosoever shall give food, ammunition, information to, or aid and abet the enemies of the United States Government in any manner whatever, shall suffer death, or whatever penalty the honorable members of the courtmartial shall see fit to inflict."

To the Federal officers, so youthful a prisoner must have seemed incapable of appreciating the gravity of her offence—an impression she doubtless did her utmost to foster. They warned her sternly, however, that if it were repeated the punishment prescribed would be carried out. Neither frightened nor abashed, Belle listened carefully. Then she arose, made a low bow, said with mock humility, "Thank you, gentlemen of the jury," and departed.

To sustain her during this ordeal, Belle must have drawn heavily upon the strength of character she had inherited from the stubborn, assertive, irrepressible Reeds. Merely the thought of James Randolph Reed, most spirited member of the Reed clan, would surely have steeled her to meet any calamity.

One of the seven sons of Lieutenant-Colonel James Reed, James

Randolph Reed was an intimate friend of General William Irvine. A lieutenant at Three Rivers and Ticonderoga in Anthony Wayne's Fourth Pennsylvania Battalion, James became a major in the "Congress' Own" Regiment, and ultimately a member of the Continetal Congress. Another friend of his was brilliant Thomas Lee Shippen, whose father, Dr. William Shippen, headed the Medical Department of the Continental Army. To Thomas, second cousin of "Lighthorse Harry" Lee (father of Robert E. Lee), Major Reed left by will his Eagle of the Society of the Cincinnati.[21]

Ever a thorn in the side of higher authority, Major Reed carried on a bitter feud with his immediate superior, Moses Hazen. On one occasion, a petition by Major Reed to which Colonel Hazen objected, by threatening to withdraw his men from the service, was approved by General Washington. On another occasion Major Reed brought charges against Hazen which were dismissed upon trial. When Hazen brought counter-charges against his subordinate, which were also dismissed after trial, Major Reed's tranquil answer to the charge of insubordination was that he had already been reprimanded for this by General Washington in person.[21]

Though Belle had seemed as calm as James Randolph Reed would have been in her place, she knew she had been in great danger. How great it really was, she probably never learned. Legend has it that on this occasion she was spared only because of intervention by President Lincoln. Considering the facts, the legend may thinly disguise the truth.

Belle's wording of the Article read to her is a remarkably accurate condensation of the actual provisions of Articles 56 and 57 in effect in 1861. These were new provisions, and it was then seriously doubted that American civilians could be tried by court-martial under them in place of civil trial. President Lincoln was greatly interested in these and other Articles giving military courts jurisdiction over civilians, and the Federal Government, anxious to have their validity affirmed, undoubtedly was unwilling to put them to the test except in a specially selected case under the most favorable circumstances.

No one could then foresee that the real test would come in the Lincoln assassination trial. In that case, which resulted in the hanging of a woman, the distinguished Reverdy Johnson of Maryland argued that Articles 56 and 57 could not apply to American civilians. (A more recent instance of unsuccessful objection to these provisions in their current form was the 1942 trial by military commission of the saboteurs landed on the shore of Long Island by a German submarine. Among those condemned and executed were American citizens.)

As the Federals began to suspect but could not prove, Belle had now extended her activities. "It is with unfeigned joy and true pride I confess that the suspicions of the enemy were far from being unfounded."

Among other things, she was engaged in systematic pilfering of Union sabers, pistols, ammunition and other supplies, and these were quickly smuggled into the Southern lines. The South was in sore need of such equipment, and the flow of small individual contributioins produced really substantial results. The extent of such traffic is best indicated by the experience of the Twenty-eighth Pennsylvania Infantry. In October, 1861 this alert unit found hidden in barns and outhouses and buried in the ground two hundred sabers, four hundred pistols, cavalry equipment for two hundred men, and some fourteen hundred muskets.[22] Most of these concealed items awaiting transfer Southward were doubtless of Northern origin.

Belle's decidedly unpleasant experience at Federal Army headquarters made an impression upon her. It was quite obvious it would not do to be caught again. To be sure, she could discontinue her activities. But that was unthinkable. So she continued fearlessly, but more cautiously, to do all she could for the Confederacy. It took the first battle of Bull Run (Manassas) to divert her momentarily to less dangerous channels.

CHAPTER FOUR

Confederate Courier and Agent

AT seventeen, a year older than the age at which her mother had married, Belle, physically and mentally, was a woman grown. Tall, slender, well-proportioned and graceful, her figure is the only point on which all her observers of both sexes have been unanimous. In their carefully considered judgment, it was nothing less than perfect.

Her face formed a long, shapely oval dominated by expressive grey-blue eyes that could be tenderly warm, brightly aflame, or as cold as ice. Light hair of a tawny shade, with a lurking hint of red that vanished as she grew older, was drawn back fully from a high forehead. A bold, aquiline nose, and a full-lipped mouth of generous width that parted to reveal even, white teeth above a firm but pleasantly rounded chin, completed features which have been described variously as homely, plain, or handsome. Too irregular to be merely pretty, they reflected habitually so pleasant and disarming an expression of youthful and artless animation that, coupled with other qualities, they made her a most attractive, if not a beautiful woman.

A voice low, musical, and vibrant, added much to her charm; and her laugh, like her disposition, was light-hearted and merry. She was intelligent, well-read, and an able and witty talker. She was also a most daring and accomplished equestrian, and a tireless dancer. But across her natural gayety rested heavily the shadow of a sadness born of the war, and a deep sense of responsibility demanding to be translated into action.

Vivacious in manner, in mood she could be gentle or furious, persuasive or commanding, beguiling or demanding, and she knew with unerring feminine discernment which would best serve her needs. Normally kind, indulgent, impulsive and forthright, when crossed, no matter by whom, she could be as severe, implacable, deliberate, and subtle as occasion required. And not the least of the qualities of this fearless and self-reliant young girl was an unfailing instinct to vitalize any appropriate occasion or event with dramatic utterance, action, or becoming attire.

Though martial in spirit, she had a thoroughly feminine urge for fastidious neatness of person and elegance in dress which she permitted no predicament to thwart. Hence Major Harry Gilmor carried forever with him the pleasant recollection that before a scouting expedition, "Down came Miss Belle, dressed in her neat-fitting habit, with a pretty little belt around her waist." A few months earlier at Culpeper Court House, an officer's wife met Belle and remarked forty years later: "What made her an object of special interest to every woman present was that she was exceedingly well dressed. It had been a long, long time since we had seen a new dress!" When released from the Old Capitol Prison for the second time Belle had with her two Saratoga trunks and a bonnet box crammed with many items she had contrived to have smuggled into her jail.

Late in July, 1861 when the first battle of Bull Run (Manassas) took place, Belle was at Front Royal, some forty miles south of Martinsburg, staying with relatives. This picturesque Virginian village at the western base of the Blue Ridge is located in a highly scenic setting which Belle loved, and often lamented was beyond her ability to describe. To her, one of its most attractive features was Happy Creek, a mountain torrent murmurous or turbulent according to season, and which, "stealing around obstacles to its course, sometimes bounding over them with headlong leap, at last finds its way to the valley and glides by the village in peace and beauty."

Belle's Front Royal relatives were the Stewarts. Frances Elizabeth Glenn, sister of Belle's mother, had married James Erskine Stewart of Martinsburg. He was a lawyer who had been in the Virginia Legislature, and for a time editor of the *Martinsburg Gazette*.[23] Having moved to Washington, the Stewarts, ardent Southern sympathizers, found their position there intolerable when war came, and fled to Front Royal.

As Confederate wounded came in from the battlefield of Manassas, an extensive hospital was organized in the village. Immediately, the niece of the Stewarts joined the staff as a matron. Despite this dignified title, Belle found her duties extremely laborious and heart-rending. Technically a "matron," her youth must have insured for her the unenvied performance of the myriad unpleasant tasks that are the normal lot of the lowest subordinate. What her surroundings were must be visualized in the light of the fact that modern military hospitalization was born of the lessons learned from the unspeakable horrors that made the hospitals of the Union and Confederate forces at least as deadly as their battlefields.

Yet Belle, wishing to do more, felt only that she was at least doing all a woman was usually permitted to do in her country's cause. In time the incessant strain of her hospital activities, and perhaps the resultant lack of outdoor exercise, affected her health severely. It became necessary for her to return home to recuperate.

Her mother welcomed her with understandable maternal pride and praise for the hospital work which she "in her fond affection styled heroic." Belle viewed her recent occupation more objectively. More than ever she wanted to play a man's rôle in the great conflict, and now she had a definite plan.

At the Front Royal hospital among the wounded she had overheard a conversation about army couriers. Why couldn't she be one? It was an idea certain to appeal to a venturesome girl, particularly one whose grandfather, James Glenn, had served as a scout and was said to have carried dispatches for St. Clair. She had also been greatly moved by the story of the exploit of "Miss D" whom she knew as "a lovely, fragile-looking girl, remarkable for the sweetness of her temper and the gentleness of her disposition."

All the South had been tremendously stirred by the great triumph of Manassas, and the exciting tale of its winning. But what the Southerners really took to their hearts was the simple account of the delivery of a message to the Southern command containing decisive information as to the impending movements of the Union troops before battle was joined.

A few days before Manassas, a cart stopped in front of General Bonham's tent. From it descended a girl in country garb who insisted upon seeing the general immediately. When he appeared, the young woman uncoiled her long, black hair, took from it a small, damp, crumpled note and handed it to the Confederate officer. It was a fateful dispatch brought through the lines by "Miss D" from Mrs. Rose O'Neal Greenhow, able agent of the South in Washington.

What the daring messenger, Betty Duval, had done, Belle must have felt certain she could do. She would become a courier. But how?

Further inactivity at home quickly produced unbearable restlessness. So in October Mrs. Boyd and her daughter set out for Manassas to visit the Confederate camp. At the camp, Belle and her mother lived in a large house occupied by wives and daughters of Southern soldiers. In these pleasant surroundings they passed several happy weeks made doubly cheerful by family reunions and the recent great victory. The relatives and connections they saw during this period must have included Mrs. Boyd's brother, James William Glenn.

Fifteen years earlier Belle's uncle had been a cadet at Virginia Military Institute for eighteen months. He was now a lieutenant in Company A, Twelfth Virginia Cavalry, and soon to be a captain. On October 15th a resident of Jefferson County had written Jefferson Davis that new recruits had taken the field under "Baylor, Glenn and Hess." Two days later Lieutenant-Colonel Turner Ashby reported to the Acting Secretary of War that at the skirmish at Bolivar Hill one hundred and eighty men "under command of Lieutenant Glynn" had been with him.

Young Glenn soon earned high praise from Ashby. On one occasion accompanied by only three men, he daringly captured a guarded enemy flag at night on the Potomac. When Ashby became a general he offered Glenn a majority. A record in Glenn's handwriting preserved at V. M. I. says tersely: "Declined promotion urged by Gen. Ashby. Ill-health, asthma."[24]

Like Belle, her uncle James W. Glenn was restless, daring, and popular. And like her he had also proved himself very much at home on a horse. In his case, the horse incident took place in Milldale, Virginia at "Mount Zion," one of the notable residences of Warren County. Erected in 1768, this fine mansion of spacious and harmonious design has been the home of the Earles, kinsmen of Belle Boyd, since 1840. One day Glenn and some friends were in the saddle before the house. A companion, knowing his adventurous temperament, said banteringly: "James, I dare you to ride your horse into the house!" Without the slightest hesitation, Glenn guided his mount up the steps and slowly traversed the fifty-foot long assembly hall. Such unexpected conduct may have disturbed the startled household momentarily but, like his impetuous niece in Martinsburg, James had someone close at hand to plead powerfully for him. This was his wife, Susan, a daughter of the Earles of "Mount Zion."

Who brought about at Manassas Belle's appointment as courier is not known. Perhaps Glenn mentioned his niece's name and ambition to Ashby, then commanding the Seventh Virginia Cavalry, and the latter, then in charge of scouting, took the necessary action. Or brave Harry Gilmor may have had a hand in it. Gilmor was, at the time, an officer in Company F of the same regiment in which Belle's uncle served. Years later in his stirring epic, *Four Years in the Saddle*, the daring cavalryman and scout praised the unflinching courage and boundless devotion to the Southern cause of the girl "whom I had known since the autumn of '61."[25]

Belle thereafter rode as courier between Generals Beauregard and

Jackson and their subordinates. On these occasions her favorite mount was "Fleeter." In an area where cavalry units of both sides raided and scouted deep into enemy lines, "Fleeter" was invaluable. Trained to kneel at command, his prompt obedience to such an order often enabled his rider to evade detection by Union patrols.

As a courier, Belle was now an official member of the Confederate intelligence service. Though not comprehensively organized at the outset of the war, this service was far more extensive than its Federal counterpart. This was natural for the Union troops were occupying hostile territory where resolute inhabitants were eager to collect military information and transmit it to the Southern forces. As early as August, the Twenty-eighth Pennsylvania Infantry learned how great this activity was in its sector. Innumerable agents, spies and sympathizers among the residents were busily engaged in signalling the Confederates. With Federal passes procured at Washington on plausible pretexts, men and women were constantly crossing from one side of the Potomac to the Southern forces on the other.[22]

At the end of 1861 the Confederate intelligence system was thoroughly organized. By then one of its most important phases was inland blockade running. The South had little manufacturing capacity and would soon be short of food. The North was seeking victory by cutting off supplies as well as by force of arms. If the South was to win, it had to break the land blockade.

At Jones' Ferry the Potomac is narrow, and Pope's Creek was an ideal place for small boats to land and hide. Here was the chief junction point on the route of agents from the North and couriers to the South. Tom Jones had a farm on the Maryland side and Ben Grimes one on the Virginia side. Both coöperated closely. But what made the Ferry really attractive, at least to male Confederate agents, was the pretty daughter of Major Watson. Hers was the exacting task of displaying guiding signals. To those who looked anxiously for them they were doubly welcome for it was well known that the person who often held their lives in her hands was a young and most charming rebel.[26]

The land blockade runners were specialists. They were also highly versatile for they had to function as necessity required as spies, letter-carriers, purchasing agents, and smugglers of contraband. Their activities, at first organized in the field, eventually came under the direction of the Confederate War Department through its Signal Corps. The full measure of their achievements, unfortunately, will never be known, for the records of the Confederate Signal and Secret Service were destroyed by fire.[27]

Nevertheless, some reliable information is available from a Southerner who, later editor of the *Mobile Register*, was an administrative official in the War and Navy Departments, C. S. A. throughout the war. His older brother, Edwin, a friend of President Davis, was Special Agent of the Confederate Government in France. Speaking in praise of the land blockade runners' exacting service, T. C. De Leon wrote in *Four Years in Rebel Capitals* that it required tact, fertility of resource, and cool courage.[28] He commented further that its most singular and romantic aspect was that many women engaged in running the border blockade.

These women, says De Leon, were almost all successful, and well nigh invaluable for the information they brought sewed in their riding habits or coiled in their hair. Nor were they coarse camp women or reckless adventurers.

"Belle Boyd's name became as historic as Moll Pitcher," declared De Leon. Others he recalled too. Among them were petted belles who cheerfully confronted danger to bring back news that women can best acquire, and who could—if they would—relate a quarter of a century later tales of adventure and night riding well calculated to raise the hair of the younger beaux about them.

But the name of Belle Boyd acquired even more than historic renown. In time, as the wonder of her exploits grew in the telling, it came to be legendary. To many of the younger generation she seemed an imaginary heroine akin to the other fabulous figures in the tales heard at their mother's knee. The poignant recollection of one of these children, going back more than a half-century in time, was revealed as recently as May 14, 1943 in a letter to the *Washington Evening Star* by "A. C. C." who said of Belle Boyd,

> "She was one of the 'story' subjects of the tales my mother told me. It was not so much as a Southern spy that my mother spoke of her, but as the bearer of much needed quinine for the malaria patients of Virginia."

In his *History of Berkeley County*, Willis Evans relates that Belle Boyd was a noted Confederate spy and scout who, donning male attire, rendered valuable service to the South.[29] But he adds conscientiously, "Some say that she was a myth and never existed at all."

Possibly "A. C. C." really thought her childhood heroine was an imaginary character. If she did, this belief did not endure, for, as told later*, her mother in the late '70s came to know the woman "who had been beloved of many malaria victims for the quinine she successfully had smuggled across the lines during the Civil War."

But Belle carried messages more often than quinine. And Martinsburg still remembers that the late Zephaniah Silver used to tell that as a sixteen-year-old boy in Jim Sencindiver's company he and a comrade took important dispatches to the Boyd home at night for Belle to "get across" to ranking Confederate leaders.

---

*(See p. 192.)

CHAPTER FIVE

The Night Ride to Ashby

HEN the weather grew cold at Manassas, the Boyds, mother and daughter, returned to Martinsburg. With the onset of winter, field activity was halted temporarily, and fears for the future were dissipated by the mirth and laughter of balls, sleigh-rides, and other seasonable festivities. In these the men of the Seventh Virginia Cavalry, commanded by Colonel Turner Ashby, took an outstanding part. They were very well acquainted in the region and their regiment had its headquarters in the village.

On December 14th, an important event occurred. In the hall in which the Masonic Order still holds meetings today, the Valley's beloved Turner Ashby was "entered an apprentice, raised and passed to the sublime degree of a Master-Mason in Equality Lodge, No. 136, Martinsburg." Among the Lodge Brothers he thus acquired was a middle-aged private of the Second Virginia Infantry. This soldier was B. R. Boyd—Belle's father.[30]

With the coming of milder weather early in 1862, Colonel Ashby and his men evacuated the town, and prepared for action. Like Jackson, Turner Ashby was an adopted son of the Valley. He came from just outside it in Fauquier County, Virginia, and was one of the most heroic and chivalrous figures the South has ever produced. A superb horseman, always well dressed, he seems to have first won Jackson's admiration and favor by a daring exploit during which his mount was a sorry looking plow-horse and he wore a farmer's suit of homespun.

On this occasion, in the spring of '61, the Knight of the Valley, his saddle-bags crammed with remedies for spavin and ring-bone, had impersonated a rustic horse-doctor and visited the Federal camp of General Patterson at Chambersburg. From this adventure he returned with a great amount of useful information. In time he became Jackson's main source of intelligence about the enemy, and Jackson upon Ashby's death paid him this remarkable tribute: "As a partisan officer, I never knew his superior. His daring was proverbial, his powers of endurance almost incredible, his tone of character heroic, and his sagacity almost intuitive in divining the purposes and movements of the enemy."[31]

But Ashby did not rely solely upon his sagacity and intuition to secure intelligence.

Jackson's strategy has rightly been termed Napoleonic in concept and execution. His "foot cavalry" was infantry that could march thirty miles a day. Accompanied by mounted men and some light artillery, it formed a compact, hard hitting, fast moving force. It appeared unexpectedly, struck savagely at larger enemy forces, slipped away between armies converging to annihilate it, and turned about occasionally to thrash some overconfident pursuer.

Yet, whatever credit may be due the principles of Napoleon and Jackson, the latter could never have won the Valley campaigns without vital military information from two sources: his cavalry, and the people of the Valley.

Both kept him thoroughly informed as to the location and movements of Union forces, and withheld knowledge of his whereabouts from the enemy. For the type of warfare he waged, this was essential to success. His information came not only from behind the Federal lines, beyond which his own scouts could not operate freely, but even on occasion from the very homes in which the staffs of Federal commanders were located and held their councils.

Jackson did more than accept this information gratefully. He demanded it constantly and earnestly. "The information I desire from beyond the lines," he instructed Ashby on April 7th, "is the position of the enemy's forces, their numbers and movements, what generals are in command, and their headquarters, and especially the headquarters of the commanding general."[32]

Some of this Ashby could secure through scouts and raids and patrols. But much had to be acquired from persons behind the enemy lines. Some of them were merely civilian sympathizers like the Winchester ladies who late in March had come out to Ashby with news that the Federals were evacuating the town and that a large column had moved to Berryville that morning. Others were actual Confederate agents. With both Ashby maintained contact and obtained all the data he could. By the end of May, Belle Boyd had risked her life at least twice to deliver information of the type Jackson demanded.

Before the Confederates had left Martinsburg, her father, home on sick leave, had given thought to his daughter's safety. As he prepared to rejoin his regiment, he decided that she would fare better deeper in Southern territory. The village was in constant danger of Union occupation and her past activities would hardly commend her favorably to the Northern troops. Accordingly, he sent her to her aunt at Front Royal.

Belle was warmly received by her aunt and uncle, and gleefully by Alice and Fannie, cousins of about her own age. But Miss Lucy Buck was not so pleased by Belle's reappearance at Front Royal. When she had first met Belle on New Year's Day, 1862, Lucy had jotted down in her diary that she was "not at all favorably impressed," and that the visitor from Martinsburg "seemed all surface, vain, and hollow." That same night, reviewing the events of the day, she added, "there was a consciousness of having compromised my dignity in mingling upon terms of equality and apparent friendship with persons whom in my heart I despise—persons I felt to be false and heartless. I never am brought into contact with such persons without feeling a conviction that if forced to confine myself to their society I shall become as frivolous apparently as they."[33]

Now in March, two months later, Miss Lucy still did not suffer Belle's presence gladly. On the 11th she went to the village from "Bel Air," the Buck estate, and later recorded under that date:

> "From Mrs. Boone's went to the hotel to see Miss Polly Haynie. Was seized on my way by Alice S.* and Belle Boyd who insisted on carrying us captive into the parlor. Made our escape but were re-captured in Miss Pollie's room and forced in self defense to comply with their request to sing and play. Our audience consisted of Dr. Dorsey, the young physician and some of the ladies. Made Dr. Blackford's acquaintance. Not at all favorably impressed."[33]

This musical soirée was probably not a social success. Whatever illusion of tranquility and enjoyment good manners may have been able to fashion, it could hardly prevail against the knowledge that the Northern forces would soon occupy Front Royal. The very next sentence Miss Buck wrote in her diary on March 11th was: "Fannie Stewart and her father leaving tomorrow for the South fleeing the enemy."[33]

When Mr. and Mrs. Stewart and their daughter, Fannie, left hastily for Richmond, Alice, Belle, and their grandmother, Mrs. Ruth Burns Glenn, remained behind to take care of the Strickler House and direct the staff. The Strickler House, now a weather-beaten, shabby structure still standing on East Main Street at the corner of High, was then a hotel, formerly known as Fishback's. Belle's aunt had taken it over when she and her husband had sought refuge in Front Royal.

*Belle's cousin, Alice Stewart.

After Kimball of Shields' division administered a setback to Jackson at Kernstown on March 23rd, the village of Front Royal was laid open to the Federal advance. Upon its occupation, the Confederates retreated far up the Valley. Daily Belle became increasingly alarmed for her mother's safety at home and finally decided to rejoin her. She had no trouble securing a pass from General Shields and, accompanied by faithful Eliza, reached Winchester without incident.

Here the local Federal Provost-Marshal interfered with her further progress, for someone had denounced Belle as a spy. The Provost, pending investigation, had determined to detain her.

Unaware of this dangerous development, Belle had entered a railway car to go on to Martinsburg. A Federal officer, who was taking some prisoners to Baltimore, noticed her and suspected her identity. Introducing himself as Captain Bannon, he asked: "Is this Miss Belle Boyd?"

Startled and perturbed, she answered curtly, "Yes."

Captain Bannon then said, "I am the Assistant Provost, and I regret to say orders have been issued for your detention, and it is my duty to inform you that you cannot proceed until your case has been investigated. So you will, if you please, get out, as the train is on the point of starting."

Belle was never one to obey an order docilely, no matter how elegantly expressed. Besides, she had a safe-conduct which even a Provost-Marshal could not safely disregard. "Sir," she replied coldly, as she settled herself more firmly in her seat, "here is a pass which I beg you will examine. You will find that it authorizes my maid and me to pass on any road to Martinsburg."

As she expected, the Assistant Provost was impressed and bewildered. If he held her, he flouted the general's orders. If he allowed her to proceed, he disobeyed his immediate superior. Meanwhile, the train was about to leave, and he had his prisoners to convoy. With typical Irish ingenuity Captain Bannon solved the dilemma. He wouldn't quite disobey either higher authority and he would pit one general against another. Sighing with relief, he told Belle: "Well, I scarcely know how to act in your case. Orders have been issued for your arrest, and yet you have a pass from the General allowing you to return home. However, I shall take the responsibility upon my shoulders, convey you with the other prisoners to Baltimore, and hand you over to General Dix."

Further discussion being useless, Belle submitted as gracefully as possible. At Baltimore, she was taken to the Eutaw House, given permission to see friends, and treated with all possible courtesy. In fact, she was handled as gently as Mrs. Greenhow ever was.

At the end of a week, the commandant, General John A. Dix, having learned nothing against her, released her and sent her home to Martinsburg. In this speedy disposition of her case, Belle was most fortunate. Other Federal generals would probably not have released her so readily for many considered denunciation without proof of guilt sufficient to warrant prolonged imprisonment. But she had fallen into the very gentle hands of a most particular Northerner. General Dix opposed arresting civilians solely on suspicion, and indicated his attitude by writing General Mansfield several months after Belle's release, "The exercise of this power of arrest is at the same time the most arbitrary and the most delicate which a state of war devolves upon a military commander. * * * I find that many of the persons imprisoned at Fort Wool were arrested by Colonel Dodge, and some of them on suspicion. This must not be repeated. * * * Imprisonment at Fort Wool is a most severe punishment at this season. * * * No citizen should be sent there for a light cause, and without pretty clear evidence of guilt."[34]

In Martinsburg Belle discovered that the Federals suspected her more than ever. She was immediately placed under very strict surveillance and forbidden to go beyond the village limits. These irksome restrictions quickly became intolerable. Mrs. Boyd appealed to the local Provost-Marshal, Major Charles Walker of the Tenth Maine Infantry.[35] This officer, probably as anxious to get rid of Belle as she was to get away, gave her mother a pass valid for both of them to proceed to Front Royal by way of Winchester. It was now about May 12th.

At Front Royal they hoped to get permission for Belle to continue on to Richmond to join relatives. What Belle probably also hoped was that the Federals would not happen to think that she might also want to report in Richmond what she had observed and learned in Martinsburg, Baltimore, Winchester, and Front Royal.

At Winchester Belle and her mother found that General Shields had forbidden travel between there and Front Royal. The local Provost-Marshal, Lieutenant Colonel James S. Fillebrown of the Tenth Maine Infantry[36], assured them that it distressed him to be unable to help them. But, as Belle suspected, he was a gallant and susceptible gentleman and soon, probably more to his surprise than hers, he had relented and the ladies were on their way.

When they reached the Strickler House, night had fallen and Mary and Belle Boyd, tired and hungry, were eager for food and rest. To their great surprise, they found the hotel brightly illuminated and the scene of much military hustle and bustle by the Northerners. Inquiring at the main building, they learned that it had been taken over by the Federals and was now occupied by General Shields and his staff.

But what had happened to Cousin Alice and Grandmother Glenn? Eventually Belle and her mother located them in a little house in the hotel court-yard to which they had been relegated by the Federals. Here, in what is locally known now as the "Belle Boyd cottage," Alice and her grandmother fervently welcomed Belle and her mother.

After dinner, Belle sent her card to General Shields and he called promptly to pay his respects. To her request for a pass to Richmond, he replied gayly that he did not dare entrust her to General Jackson's tender mercies. Courteous, well-mannered, and amply endowed with sparkling Irish wit, he teased her with carefree badinage. And he assured her that Jackson's army would be annihilated in a few days. Then she could freely wander whither she willed.

Though he spoke seemingly in jest, his unguarded words revealed that he expected immediate and complete success. What he said was definite and informative enough to be turned to good account.

Accompanying General Shields was his aide-de-camp, Captain Daniel J. Keily, a young Irishman, who later was made a brevet-brigadier-general for gallant and meritorious conduct.[37] The general presented his aide to Belle and thereafter, whenever he had the opportunity, Dan Keily besieged her with flowers and effusive messages. His nosegays and tender notes were unsentimentally discarded. But the military information he occasionally unwittingly disclosed, Belle gladly passed on to her receptive countrymen.

In her memoirs she discreetly refers to this young officer only as "Captain K." It is no fault of hers that he can be named now. As will be seen later*, the clue to his identity was furnished by a gentleman of Front Royal who described in 1914 a whirlwind visit Belle made to his home in June, 1862.

When, on the evening of May 14th or 15th, General Shields and "Captain K." left the little cottage, it was to attend a council of war

*See page 60.

held in the drawing-room of the Strickler House. Belle was right behind them. Whether she had learned from her visitors that the council was to be held is not clear. At any rate, she ventured in their wake to the main building, ready to profit by any opportunity that might present itself.

Immediately above the council room was a bedroom containing a small closet. In the floor of the closet someone had bored a hole. While Belle had never learned for what purpose it had been made, she recalled that it was there and realized that she could probably make good use of it. So she stole upstairs, put her ear to the opening, and found that she could hear distinctly the conversation going on below.

The conference lasted for several hours. When it ended at about one A. M., the concealed listener returned to her room in the cottage and enciphered hurriedly in a note all she had overheard that she considered important.* To rouse a servant to dispatch the message would cause enough disturbance to create suspicion. She must go herself She slipped out to the stables quietly, saddled a horse and headed for the mountains.

As a precaution, she took with her several passes she had received from paroled Confederate soldiers returning South. These proved invaluable, for twice she was challenged by Federal sentries who accepted her false credentials without question.

After a rapid ride of some fifteen miles through the darkness, she reached the home of Mr. M. Urging her mount up the steps, she knocked furiously upon the door, and at length a window was raised.

"Who is there?", a voice called out sharply.

"It is I," she answered.

"But who are you? What is your name?"

"Belle Boyd. I have important intelligence to communicate to Colonel Ashby. Is he here?"

"No; but wait a minute. I will come down."

As the window was lowered, she dismounted. Almost immediately, the door opened and Mr. M. drew her in quickly, exclaiming in astonishment, "My dear, where did you come from, and how on earth did you get here?"

"Oh, I forced the sentries," she replied, "and here I am; but I have no time to tell you the how, and the why, and the wherefore. I must

*For Confederate Army cipher Belle probably used, see Appendix B.

see Colonel Ashby without the loss of a minute. Tell me where he is to be found."

Mr. M. told her promptly that the Colonel's party was about a quarter of a mile farther up the wood. She turned to go, and as she was about to mount her horse, a door on the right of the threshold was thrown open and Ashby himself came out. Surprised by her presence, he cried "Good God! Miss Belle, is this you? Where did you come from? Have you dropped from the clouds, or am I dreaming?"

Tersely, she explained why she had come. She told him hurriedly the essence of what she had overheard, gave him the enciphered note, and for a brief moment relaxed to enjoy the satisfaction of a mission successfully completed. But she could not loiter. She must get back before her absence was noted. Without further delay, she took once more to her saddle and headed her horse for Front Royal.

Federal vigilance had weakened as the night waned. From the dark there came no sudden loud challenge as she rode along. At only one point did the rapid drumming of the hoofs of her horse rouse a sleeping sentinel to belated attention. As he came awake, she flashed by him and vanished from his sight and out of range around an abrupt turn in the road. Two hours after leaving Ashby, she was back in her room. Exhausted, as dawn broke she fell on her bed and slept.

With what news did Belle ride to Ashby? To what did it lead? Belle is exasperatingly silent on these points, but the official records strongly suggest the answers.[38]

In the East, McClellan was moving against Richmond. Northwest of the Southern Capital General McDowell was acting in support of McClellan's drive, and needed reinforcements. Banks in the Valley was instructed by the War Department that his operations there must be defensive only and confined to protection of the Northern Capital against attack by Jackson's greatly reinforced command. Accordingly, Banks fell back to Strasburg, about fifteen miles west of Front Royal. He was stripped of much of his force, for on May 2nd both Shields and Geary had been detached from his Valley command and placed under McDowell.

By May 15th, Geary's main force was already east of the Valley. But he had left a very small detachment at Front Royal under Major Hector Tyndale to protect the bridges. Shields, however, was still in the Valley, having moved eastward more slowly and much more reluctantly.

Shields was not primarily interested in taking Richmond. His consuming desire was to catch Jackson and destroy him. Hence, when detached from Banks with more than ten thousand men and ordered to join McDowell, preferably via Front Royal, Chester Gap, and Warrenton, he moved eastward unwillingly and constantly tried to have his route changed so he could trap Ewell and Jackson and wipe them out. McDowell was so well aware of Shields' obsession that he wired him Jackson was on his way east to Hanover Junction on the line toward Richmond, "so in coming east you will be following him."

At the council overheard by Belle, two important matters must have been discussed. These were: the exact route to be followed the next day and thereafter to join McDowell; and how to trap and destroy Jackson, who, according to McDowell, was somewhere along Shields' route and heading east toward Richmond.

Jackson, of course, was still in the Valley and actually southwest of Front Royal. He knew where Banks was, and that Geary and Shields were moving eastward, but he probably did not know how far they were going or that they had been officially detached from Banks and assigned to McDowell.

What he undoubtedly learned from Belle Boyd via Colonel Ashby was that Shields and probably Geary were joining McDowell and had therefore been taken away from Banks; that Shields and McDowell thought Jackson was moving east; that Shields meant to seek and trap Jackson's "demoralized" army eastward; that Banks' command was greatly reduced; and that most likely only a very small detachment would remain at Front Royal after Shields marched off.

To Jackson, certain possibilities must have been clear immediately. By cutting in at Front Royal, the Federal forces there could be destroyed, and the Confederate forces would then stand between Banks and the East. Banks could not move toward McDowell or toward Washington without being intercepted and, in view of his reduced strength, it might be possible to wipe him out completely. Shields and Geary might start back, but this would relieve McDowell's pressure on Richmond. Then, too, Fremont might race in from the west. But, if he struck hard and fast, they would all be too late. If Banks were completely destroyed, if McDowell were slow in sending Shields and Geary after him, if Fremont lagged, the road to Washington would be well ajar. . .

As Belle slept on, General Shields and his command left Front Royal. Before she rose, another Federal force had marched in. When she saw these new Northerners, it is likely that she believed Shields had left them behind. But he had not. They were a detachment of Banks' command which the War Department had ordered him to send to Front Royal to strengthen and maintain an impossible line of communications between Banks at Strasburg and McDowell far to the east. The new troops, totalling about one thousand men, were led by Colonel Kenly, and consisted of his First Maryland Infantry Regiment, some companies of the Fifth New York Cavalry, and a battery of field artillery.[39]

CHAPTER SIX

"Kindness of Lieutenant H——"

IT took a week for sudden and violent action to result from the various military developments in the Valley. During this period Belle remained in Front Royal. She had hoped to go farther South, but it seemed preferable to wait until she could travel more safely than roaming Federal columns then permitted. Once her decision to stay over with old Mrs. Glenn and young Alice was made, her mother returned to Martinsburg. Meanwhile Belle, unable as usual merely to sit and wait, found something exciting and dangerous to do.

On May 20th, Belle and Alice decided to visit Winchester, and asked the Provost-Marshal, Major Hector Tyndale of the Twenty-eighth Pennsylvania Infantry[40], for a pass. At first, he refused flatly, then reconsidered, and finally, probably remembering that he wouldn't be accessible, promised to issue one the following day. The next morning, May 21st, the two girls, accompanied by Eliza, prepared to leave by carriage. All they needed was the pass, but it hadn't arrived. They inquired, and learned to their dismay that the Provost-Marshal had left on a scouting expedition and would probably not be back until late that night.

Greatly perplexed by this untoward development, the two cousins wondered what to do. Had they known the nature of Major Tyndale's mission, Belle, at least, would have been even more greatly disturbed.

At midnight on the 20th, says Major Tyndale's official report[41], he set out with about one hundred and thirty men to scout southward. Over a mountain road "not on any map I have ever seen" he reached Browntown, eleven miles away. Here he learned that men of the Eighth Louisiana Regiment, previously reported as far off as Swift Run Gap, had been in Browntown the night before. He also learned that drums had been heard five miles southwest, that small bodies of enemy cavalry were on other roads, and that Confederate infantry and cavalry were expected to arrive in strength.

Back in Front Royal at noon on May 21st, Tyndale saw General Geary who was temporarily in the village. That afternoon the major wired General Banks about his scout and was thanked for his energy and enterprise. Possibly Tyndale, who later became a major-general, realized that his news indicated a probable attack in force on Front Royal very soon and perhaps over the Gooney Manor Road he had found on no map. But he said that this road could be defended against four-fold odds. And he stressed that Ewell's command must be in terrible condition, for a Confederate soldier, captured in civilian clothes, explained that Ewell had been unable to outfit him.

There is nothing to show whether Tyndale's wire to Banks on the 21st was as informative as his official report sent to Geary on the 22nd. If it was, surely Banks, who expected disaster to follow when left in the Valley with only a few thousand men, should have taken some action. Had he done so, the history of the next few days in the Valley and their effect upon vital operations elsewhere would undoubtedly have been materially different. But, as will be seen, Banks believed to the very last that Jackson's main attack would be at Strasburg from the south.

While Major Tyndale was making his way back over the Gooney Manor Road, Belle and Alice had found someone else who, with a little urging, might help them. This was Lieutenant H., an officer of the cavalry force stationed in the village. He was known to them and, noting that they seemed to be in some difficulty, he had stopped and asked politely what the trouble was. Belle outlined their predicament and, realizing that the Union pickets they would have to pass were from the lieutenant's own troop, said pleadingly: "Now, Lieutenant H., I know you have permission to go to Winchester, and you profess to be a great friend of mine. Prove it by assisting me out of this dilemma, and pass us through the pickets."

After some hesitation, the young Northerner consented. He mounted the carriage box, the ladies got inside, and they started off.

Meanwhile, at "Bel Air," Miss Lucy Buck had risen early to write a letter which Belle was to deliver for her. Miss Lucy, with two friends, Nellie and Kattie, walked over to the Strickler House to meet Belle. There, Miss Buck has recorded in her diary, she "found a carriage at the door in which was seated the young lady with a Yankee officer." She was quite willing to let Belle, whom she disliked so obviously, run the risk of delivering letters for her within the enemy's lines, and she must have understood that it was often necessary to have outwardly friendly relations with the enemy. She was nevertheless appalled by the discovery that Belle would consort so freely with the foe, no matter for what end. Upset beyond measure, she "concluded not to intrust my letter with one who appeared upon such familiar terms with those whom we most dreaded, so crossing the street we went on up to see Cousin Mary."[42]

Lieutenant H. did not accompany the ladies into Winchester. Shortly before they reached there, he left the carriage and continued on foot, having matters to attend to at the Federal camp on the outskirts. In town, possibly because of the delay in their departure, Belle and Alice found they could not return to Front Royal the same day. Accordingly, they remained overnight at the home of friends.

Early the following morning a gentleman of high social standing came to the house, and handed Belle two packages. His instructions regarding them were most explicit.

"Miss Boyd," he said, "will you take these letters and send them through the lines to the Confederate Army? This package is of great importance; the other is trifling in comparison." Then, handing her a little note, he continued: "This is also a very important paper. Try to send it carefully and safely to Jackson, or some other responsible Confederate officer. Do you understand?"

She replied earnestly, "I do, and will obey your orders promptly and implicitly."

Negroes were then conveniently considered by the Federals as non-suspect. Belle therefore concealed the more important package about the person of Eliza. The other she placed openly in a little basket and, without giving the matter much thought, wrote heedlessly on it, "Kindness of Lieutenant H——." She knew that this notation would get it by any casual inspection. What she did not stop to consider was that if real trouble arose these words might brand the indulgent cavalry officer as a willing accomplice.

The small note, by far the most significant paper given her, she decided to carry negligently in her hand and thereby convey the impression that it was of no consequence.

Her next problem was to obtain permission to leave Winchester. This promised to be most difficult for the Federals had pickets everywhere and their requirements as to passes had become more and more severe. Only recently, at the cottage in Front Royal, with a picket stationed between the farm-yard and the dairy, the dairy maid had perforce to go to the cows to milk them and to display to the picket a pass signed by the proper authority. The cows, having milk but no pass, were not permitted to come to her. In flippant protest against this nuisance, Belle had prepared a pass to which she somehow obtained the necessary official signature. This pass, pasted between the horns of the leader of the herd, read

> "These cows have permission to pass to and from the yard and dairy for the purpose of being milked twice a day, until further notice."

At Winchester, Belle knew the situation would have to be handled more seriously and subtly. Deciding that a bit of flattery might be helpful in the case of an officer who had been a little difficult on a previous occasion, she went to a florist and selected a handsome bouquet. This she sent to Lieutenant Colonel Fillebrown with her compliments and a demure request for a pass to return to Front Royal. The answer was not long delayed. The pleased Provost-Marshal wrote that he thanked the "dear lady for so sweet a compliment" and enclosed the pass.

Meanwhile Lieutenant H. had finished his business at the camp and had rejoined the ladies. The reunited party set out for Front Royal. But when they reached the picket lines outside Winchester, their further progress was rudely halted by two unpleasant looking men who later proved to be Federal Army detectives. They rode up, one on each side of the carriage, and, looking in at the window, one addressed Belle: "We have orders to arrest you."

"For what?" she inquired.

"Upon suspicion of having letters," came the ominous reply. He then peremptorily ordered the coachman to turn about and drive back to the headquarters of Colonel George L. Beal, commander of the Tenth Maine Infantry.[43] Upon arrival there, the alarmed passengers were curtly requested to alight and to enter the Colonel's office.

Alice Stewart was openly frightened and shook like a bird caught in a snare. Belle, equally upset by their unexpected arrest, realized that their only hope depended upon maintaining her presence of mind, and so she steeled herself for the inquiry. Outwardly she betrayed no symptoms of agitation other, perhaps, than the signs of irritation and annoyance natural in an innocent person wrongfully detained and accused.

The stern colonel asked her immediately whether she had any letters in her possession. She knew that if she answered that she had none, a thorough search would follow. Accordingly, she drew out of the hand-basket the less important package she had placed there, and handed it to her questioner.

He glanced at it and suddenly, in an angry tone, exclaimed "What! What is this? 'Kindness of Lieutenant H——'! What does this mean? Is this all you have?"

"Look for yourself," she replied coldly, and shook out the contents of her basket on the floor before him. "As to this scribbling on the letter," she continued, "it means nothing. It was a thoughtless act of mine. I assure you Lieutenant H. knew nothing about the letter, or that it was in my possession."

At this point, the young cavalry officer turned very pale. He had just recalled that he had in his pocket a small package which Miss Boyd had asked him to carry for her. He drew it out hastily and, without a word, tossed it on the table before the colonel. To his consternation and his superior's astonishment, this also had on it the fateful words: "Kindness of Lieutenant H——."

This undeniably made matters worse, and the situation was scarcely improved when the package was found to contain a copy of the decidedly rebellious journal, *The Maryland News-sheet.* From that moment on, Colonel Beal entertained no further doubt as to the Lieutenant's actual complicity and consequent guilt.

In vain Belle fought to exonerate him. She asserted his innocence, and pointed out repeatedly that the suspected officer could not have known that the packet contained so obnoxious a publication. It was obviously impossible, she insisted, that he could have been a willing accomplice.

Her efforts failed. The colonel's only response was to turn upon her and demand: "What is that you have in your hand?"

"What?—this little scrap of paper? You can have it if you wish; it is nothing. Here it is."

She stepped forward as though to give it to him. Actually, however, she meant to swallow it as a last desperate measure if its seizure appeared inevitable. Fortunately, the Federal colonel's concern with her and the small piece of paper she held negligently in her hand was only momentary. Thoroughly incensed by the behavior of Lieutenant H., his wrath was, in Belle's own words, "diverted from the guilty to the guiltless."

Colonel Beal not only seemed to ignore her presence thereafter and the precious note which she still held, but eventually ordered that she, her cousin, and Eliza be dismissed. However, as usual, she was to be kept under close surveillance.

Belle states that the investigation of Lieutenant H. continued, and that later upon the doubtful evidence of bare suspicion a court-martial dismissed him from the Federal service.

Subsequently she learned how their arrest had come about. A servant in the house at Winchester had seen the papers handed to her. He had informed the Union authorities there and they had wired Major Tyndale at Front Royal. The Major, already angered by her passage through the picket lines at that point without a pass, had communicated with Colonel Beal and arranged for the arrest. Belle adds: "Had it not been for the curious manner in which Lieutenant H. was involved in the affair, and in which that unoffending officer was so unjustly treated, very much to my regret, I should not have escaped so easily."

That Colonel Beal, later a distinguished major-general, conducted his investigation in so bungling a manner, completely ignored her rôle as the chief offender, and carelessly permitted her to return to Front Royal to carry out her mission, seems incredible. Yet on May 31st, "Correspondence of the Associated Press" in the *New York Times* and other newspapers throughout Federal territory, and a related article in the *Washington Evening Star*, contained the following significant item:

> "I have the following statement from an officer who participated in the battle of Front Royal: 'After you left Front Royal Belle Boyd made a trip to Winchester in company with a cavalry officer. While there she was arrested by the military authorities, but with her usual adroitness and assumed innocence she got clear of any charge of treachery, and returned to Front Royal again.'"

Who was Lieutenant H.? Belle considerately withheld the identity of her dupe. Nevertheless, there are several clues that point unmistakably to a specific individual.

Lieutenant H. was a cavalry officer and on May 21st he was stationed at Front Royal with a unit which was on duty in the village and charged with the maintenance of outlying pickets. This suggests that his regiment was the Fifth New York Cavalry of which two companies were a part of Colonel Kenly's command. However, he could have been an officer of the Third Indiana or the First West Virginia Cavalry, a company of one of these regiments having been left at Front Royal earlier in May by General Geary. Or his regiment could have been the First Michigan Cavalry, as Major Tyndale took men of that unit with his scout on May 21st.

But in all the cavalry regiments in the commands of Generals Banks and Geary, there was only one lieutenant whose name began with the letter H who was dismissed by court-martial. He was Lieutenant Abram H. Hasbrouck of the Fifth New York Cavalry, and adjutant of its Third Battalion.

Though this tends to show this officer was Belle's escort to Winchester, it is known that he was captured by the Confederates at Harrisonburg on May 8th. A history of the regiment states that his captors sent him to Richmond, but his official record indicates he was paroled and rejoined the regiment. While no date is given for his parole, if he was not sent to Richmond and was paroled in the field he could have been back with the regiment almost immediately and could have been at Front Royal on May 21st.[44]

Lieutenant Hasbrouck was not court-martialed until December 1863. If he was really Lieutenant H., Belle erred in stating he was dismissed from the service as the result of Colonel Beal's inquiry. She probably learned of his dismissal and assumed the inquiry had brought it about. But under General Orders, No. 106, Headquarters, Army of the Potomac, December 20, 1863, Hasbrouck, then a captain, was dismissed because a general court had found him guilty "on the charge of selling government horses."[45]

CHAPTER SEVEN

Belle's Famous Exploit

HE achievements of General Jackson in the Valley have been set forth fully by profound thinkers on strategy and tactics. But for classic simplicity there is nothing to equal the following terse description of his initial campaign.

> "Stonewall Jackson's men were few
> In the spring o' Sixty-two,
> But he kept the Bluecoats busy—
> Fact, he almost made 'em dizzy
> Stealin' marches, quickly cuttin'
> Round about the Massanutten."[46]

The Massanutten is a scenic mountain range completely within the Valley and divides it into two branches for a distance of fifty miles. Rising abruptly from the plain near Harrisonburg, it runs north and ends suddenly near Strasburg. Parallel with the Blue Ridge and of equal height, its sharper peaks have a bolder and more picturesque aspect. Its strategic value, pointed out by George Washington before the Revolution, was heightened by a good road crossing the mountain midway of its length and connecting Newmarket on the west with Luray on the east.

On May 15th, when Belle spied on Shields planning to trap Jackson southeast of the Valley, "Stonewall" was actually far southwest at Lebanon White Sulphur Springs. After a few days' rest, he moved to capture or disperse the Federal garrison at Front Royal and so get in the rear of Banks' greatly reduced force or compel him to abandon his fortifications at Strasburg. A message to Ewell brought the latter west into the Valley. Taylor's brigade left Ewell and marched west along the southern end of the Massanutten to join Jackson near Harrisonburg. The rest of Ewell's command turned north to go east of the Massanutten for a rendezvous with Jackson and Taylor near Luray, set for May 21st or 22nd.

On May 21st Taylor, whose father before becoming President of the United States had been "Old Rough and Ready" of Mexican War fame, led Jackson's advance north to Newmarket and then east across the Massanutten toward Luray. But Ashby's cavalry brigade had continued due north to maneuver impressively before Banks at Strasburg to create the impression that a frontal attack was intended there. Ashby, however, was under orders to rejoin Jackson in time for the assault on Front Royal and to leave behind small detachments to prevent or impede communication between Strasburg and Front Royal.

East of the Massanutten Ewell joined Jackson, and on May 22nd the latter's entire command moved north toward Kenly's force. That night the advanced elements of the Confederates bivouacked only ten miles from Front Royal and just west of the mountain road Major Tyndale had scouted the day before.

"Moving at dawn on Friday, the 23rd," reads Jackson's report, "and diverging to the right so as to fall into the Gooney Manor Road, we encountered no opposition until we came within one and a half miles of Front Royal when about two p. m. the enemy's pickets were driven in by our advance, which was ordered to follow rapidly."[47]

In the village a few moments earlier, Belle had been reading quietly to Mrs. Glenn and Alice when a servant rushed in and cried: "Oh, Miss Belle, I t'inks de revels am a'comin'!"

Springing up, she ran to the door of the cottage and looked into the street. It certainly seemed to be true. The Yankees, upset by some unexpected occurrence, were hurrying about in the greatest confusion.

Among those going by was an officer. She asked him what was happening. He replied that the Confederates were approaching in force under Generals Jackson and Ewell. They had surprised and captured the outer Federal pickets and had come within a mile of town without an attack being suspected.

"Now," he added, "we are endeavoring to get the ordnance and the quartermaster's stores out of their reach."

Instinctively, Belle wanted more details.

"But what will you do," she asked, "with the stores in the large depot?"

"Burn them, of course!", came the reply.

"But suppose the rebels come upon you too quickly?"

"Then we will fight so long as we can by any possibility show a front, and in the event of defeat make good our retreat upon Winchester, burning the bridges as soon as we cross them, and finally effect a junction with General Banks' force."

Turning over in her mind the information she had just received, and its relation to the facts already in her possession, she reëntered the house and started upstairs. At that moment, the sharp crack of a rifle came from outside, and immediately someone came rushing down the stairs and very nearly knocked her over. It was Mr. Clarke, Special Correspondent of the *New York Herald*, billeted in her aunt's home, and whose persistent attentions to her she had found very distasteful.

"Great Heavens! What is the matter?" he cried.

"Nothing to speak of," she said coldly. "Only the rebels are coming, and you had best prepare yourself for a visit to Libby Prison."

He turned about quickly and rushed back to his room without a word. She followed him upstairs, secured her field glasses and made for the balcony at the front of the house. As she passed Mr. Clarke's door, she noted that it was open, that the key was on the outside, and that he was inside packing his belongings. Such an opportunity could not be resisted. She drew the door shut quietly, and turned the key in the lock. Then she went out on the balcony. With her glasses she could see the Southern advance guard about three-quarters of a mile away marching on the town.

Seeing them approach, she felt conflicting emotions of hope and fear. At the heart of the latter was the knowledge that her father was with the oncoming Confederates. She knew that the Yankees had been planning to trap the Southern forces, but she felt that the information she had, if conveyed to Jackson, would secure victory. Without it, he was doomed, she thought, to defeat and disaster.

The intelligence she had was that Kenly had only a thousand men at Front Royal; that General Banks was northwest at Strasburg with four thousand men; that the small force north at Winchester could be readily reinforced by General White who was at Harper's Ferry; and that Generals Shields and Geary were a short distance southeast of Front Royal, while Fremont was west just beyond the Valley. To her, the real significance of these dispositions was that all of these separate units could unite to coöperate against Jackson.

Not all this information was personal knowledge. Some of it must have been contained in the little note given her in Winchester the day before and which she had probably read so as to be able to transmit the news verbally if necessary. What the complete picture undoubtedly meant to her was that the Confederates could strike a smashing blow at Front Royal and perhaps against other isolated Federal units provided they knew where all the Union forces were and could avoid being trapped if they converged.

But the note still had to be delivered, and with it the latest news as to the Federal force in the village, its strength, its disposition, its plan to burn the bridges, and its proposed line of retreat.

Animated by this realization, Belle hastened to the door. Standing about in voluble groups, she saw several men who had always loudly professed their attachment to the Southern cause. She told them hurriedly that she had valuable information to transmit to General Jackson. Would anyone there take it? With one accord, these oral patriots promptly refused the honor. Quickly they answered, "No! No! You go!"

No further time could be lost. Without hesitation and without conscious thought, she picked up a white bonnet and started at a run down the street, still crowded with scurrying Northerners. Soon out of the village, she continued on through the open fields without slackening her pace.

Meanwhile, after the Federal pickets had been driven in and their small body of supporting infantry had been routed, the Confederates came momentarily to a stop on a hill overlooking the town. Below them, the hurried movements of the enemy and the galloping of horsemen revealed the confusion created by the initial onset.

During the Confederate halt, says Henry Kyd Douglas, now a staff officer, General Jackson was taking in the situation before ordering an advance. He did not yet know that the Federals were so weak or "so unprepared by reinforcements for his approach."[48]

As "Stonewall" pondered, Douglas observed a woman in white glide out of town on the Confederate right. Heeding neither weeds nor fences, she ran rapidly up a ravine toward the Southerners and, waving a bonnet, seemed to be trying to keep the hill between herself and the village.

Douglas called General Jackson's attention to her just as she disappeared from sight and "Stonewall," at the suggestion of General Ewell, sent his young staff officer to meet her and learn her errand, a mission the latter confides "was just to my taste."

Racing on, and using the uneven terrain for shelter as much as possible, Belle hoped desperately that she would remain unobserved by the Yankees until she reached the advancing Confederates. But she knew that the dark-blue dress and the fancy white apron she wore over it made her far more conspicuous than was desirable, and she felt sure they made her visible at a great distance.

The Federals had placed their artillery on an eminence commanding the road by which the enemy was advancing. The Union infantry occupied the hospital buildings in force and both artillery and infantry kept up a constant fire on the Confederates.

Until now Belle had apparently escaped detection. But the Federal pickets, falling back, soon noticed her and immediately turned their fire in her direction. Many shots came dangerously near and some balls struck the ground so close to her as to throw dust in her eyes. The Yankees in the hospital, noting the new target of the pickets, also fired at her. Several balls pierced her clothing, but not one even grazed her skin. As she pressed on, she came under a cross-fire of artillery, and one Yankee shell struck the earth a scant twenty yards away. As it burst, she hurled herself to the ground, and shell fragments rained about her. Still uninjured, she rose and struggled on.

Fully aware now of the great peril into which her impetuous dash had carried her, fear and courage, the love of life and the steadfast determination to serve the cause of the South without faltering, fought their own battle within her. Recalling her sensations three years later, she marvelled at the ease with which she tore across the fields and "bounded over fences with the agility of a deer."

As she neared the Southern advance-guard, she waved her bonnet vigorously and significantly to indicate that it should press forward. A loud cheer from the First Maryland (Confederate) Regiment and Hay's Louisiana Brigade rang out in immediate reply and spontaneous tribute. Both units, without waiting for further orders, swept by her and dashed on toward the town at a rapid pace.

The main Confederate force was still hidden from her view by a slight elevation. As she realized that the advance-guard had charged on, the dreadful thought came suddenly to her that the Southerners might not be in sufficient force for a real assault and that the very men who had just cheered her would then be rushing to certain death. Overcome at last by fatigue, despair, and this frightful possibility, she faltered and sank to her knees. Instinctively, in that suppliant position, she prayed briefly and earnestly.

Strangely inspired and refreshed anew, all uncertainty forsook her. She rose again and went on. To her indescribable relief and joy, she caught sight of the Confederate main body within a short distance, and soon "an old friend and connection of mine, Major Harry Douglas, rode up, and recognizing me, cried out, while he seized my hand, 'Good God, Belle, you here! What is it?' "

"Oh, Harry," she gasped, "give me time to recover my breath."

For some seconds, she could say no more. But as soon as she could speak, she produced the little note given her in Winchester. Then she told Harry Douglas all the news she had, and urged that the cavalry be hurried on with orders to seize the bridges before the Federals could destroy them.

Belle relates that Douglas galloped off to report the matter to General Jackson. The General then rode forward and asked her whether she wished a horse and an escort for her return. She thanked him, refused his offer, and made her own way back to Front Royal.

Romantic young Douglas never forgot this encounter, and it is one of the high-lights in his memoirs, *I Rode With Stonewall*, published in 1940. When he rode out to meet the tall, graceful woman he had glimpsed, he was startled, momentarily, to hear her call out his name. "But I was not much astonished," he wrote, "when I saw that the visitor was the well known Belle Boyd whom I had known from her earliest girlhood. She was just the girl to dare to do this thing."

The young officer's story of what she told him is far more detailed and graphic than hers.

> "Nearly exhausted, and with her hand pressed against her heart, she said in gasps 'I knew it must be Stonewall, when I heard the first gun. Go back quick and tell him that the Yankee force is very small—one regiment of Maryland infantry, several pieces of artillery and several companies of cavalry. Tell him I know, for I went through the camps and got it out of an officer. Tell him to charge right down and he will catch them all. I must hurry back. Goodby. My love to all the dear boys—and remember if you meet me in town you haven't seen me today.' "[49]

As Belle gasped out her message to her friend Harry, numerous interested spectators of the stirring scene stored various details of it in their memories. Conspicuous among them were Dick Taylor, the soldierly son of "Old Rough and Ready," the fascinated adjutant of Ewell's command, and a private of the Fifty-second Virginia Infantry.

To General Taylor, commander of Jackson's advance units, the information that breathless Belle gave with the precision of a staff officer, was vital. He wrote later in *Destruction and Reconstruction* that Jackson knowing it earlier, had not mentioned it to him. And he revealed that it was he who, acting on it, launched the assault. "Convinced of the correctness of the woman's statements, I hurried forward at a 'double' hoping to surprise the enemy's idlers in the town, or swarm over the wagon bridge with them and secure it."[50]

In the case of Ewell's adjutant, it was the woman rather than her news which made the greater impression. In the manuscript records of his brigade he recorded that she "was to my eye pleasant and lady-like in appearance and certainly had neither 'freckled face, red hair, and large mouth' as the *New York Herald* said she had. She seemed embarrassed by the novelty of her position, and very anxious that we should push on."[51]

But it was probably the humble private of the Fifty-second Virginia Infantry who was most observant. Thirty-six years later, in a pathetic booklet he hawked about to make a living as a one-legged veteran, Ex-Private John Robson made two shrewd comments. He surmised that the news Belle brought was what "perhaps General Jackson may have been expecting." As to the statement by General Taylor that Stonewall had had the same information at least two days earlier, Robson, probably having in mind that the situation could have changed materially by the afternoon of the 23rd, added slyly that the old information Jackson had "only needed Belle Boyd to confirm it."[52]

According to Douglas, General Jackson and Belle Boyd did not meet on this occasion. He says that as he raised his cap and left her to carry her message to Jackson, she kissed her hand to him, and was gone. While he told "Stonewall" what she had said, and answered his commander's inquiries about her, he caught one last wave of her white bonnet as she regained the village and disappeared among the houses.

Soon, writes Douglas, the First Maryland Infantry and Wheat's Louisiana Battalion were rushing down into the town. It was then that General Jackson, who had never heard of Belle before, suggested, half smiling, that Douglas go on with the troops and see if he could get more information from "that young lady." No order was ever obeyed with more willingness and alacrity. And the distinguished author of *I Rode with Stonewall* relates:

> "I looked for Belle Boyd and found her standing on the pavement in front of a hotel, talking with some few Federal officers (prisoners) and some of her acquaintances in our army. Her cheeks were rosy with excitement and recent exercise, and her eyes all aflame. When I rode up to speak to her she received me with much surprised cordiality, and as I stooped from my saddle she pinned a crimson rose to my uniform, bidding me remember that it was *blood-red* and that it was her 'colors.' I left her to join the General."[53]

CHAPTER EIGHT

Consequences of Belle's Exploit

HEN Belle got back to Front Royal, she was utterly exhausted. However, a most potent and pleasant tonic quickly revived her. This was the enthusiastic acclaim of the Confederate soldiers now filing through the village and recognizing their heroine.

After young Harry Douglas, wearing her colors, left her to rejoin "Stonewall," Belle sought rest and quiet in the little cottage. Meanwhile, the news of her exploit spread from home to home, and soon came to the ears of Miss Lucy Buck.

The last time Miss Lucy had seen Belle, that young girl, two years her junior, had shocked her by being, seemingly, on familiar terms with the enemy. Alice Stewart was, of course, "a sweet girl" and she wished Alice would visit "Bel Air" more often, but Belle, she felt, was superficial, vain, and frivolous. Yet now she had to jot down in her notes:

> "Speaking of boldness reminds me of an exploit attributed to Miss Belle Boyd Wednesday. 'Tis said that she wished some information conveyed to the army about the time of the keenest firing and not being able to get anyone to go for her, she went herself to a most exposed point, where the bullets fell like hail stones about her riddling her dress."

Still doubtful, she added candidly:

> "I know not what truth there is in the rumor."[54]

In better-informed circles, it was more than a rumor. That night a courier rode to the Strickler House with a brief note for Belle written hurriedly at the home of Mr. Richards, just outside Front Royal. It read:

> "May 23, 1862
>
> Miss Belle Boyd,
>
> I thank you, for myself and for the Army, for the immense service that you have rendered your country today.
>
> Hastily, I am your friend
>
> T. J. Jackson, C. S. A."*

---

*See pp. 211-12, for discussion of this letter.

By now the tide of battle had rolled on beyond the village where the Federals had abandoned about $300,000 worth of stores that they had been too hard pressed for time to burn. The Confederate cavalry, having forded the Shenandoah, had cornered Kenly and compelled him to surrender. The infantry, headed by Taylor, had raced for the wagon bridge. It had gotten across, thanks solely to Belle, but it had been a very near thing indeed. The Federals had already set it afire and many Confederates burned their hands severely tossing flaming brands in the river. General Taylor's horse and clothing were badly scorched as he galloped over the bridge, stirrup to stirrup with an impatient Southerner he suddenly recognized as an aroused "Stonewall."

Had the bridge been destroyed before the Confederates could have crossed, it is unlikely that the great success achieved thereafter would have been possible. Once across, the roads west to Strasburg and north to Winchester were open, and Banks, his flank turned, could be trapped. He must fall back. But where? A knotty problem for Banks, it puzzled "Stonewall" as well.

If Jackson marked time at Front Royal or moved on Strasburg, Banks would head north for Winchester and get there first. If "Stonewall" marched headlong for Winchester to cut off that exit, Banks might slip east through Front Royal and add to the Union forces massing against Richmond.

The solution adopted by Jackson was to move diagonally northwest toward Banks' rear so that, whether the Federals chose to go north or east, the Confederates would be close enough to both routes to intercept them either way. At that, had Banks started immediately for Winchester he might still have escaped, for news of the attack at Front Royal reached him quickly.[55]

When Charley Greenleaf of the Fifth New York Cavalry rode to him with news of the attack on Kenly, the Federal general refused to consider the situation as serious. Still feeling Jackson intended a frontal assault on Strasburg, he sent only a regiment and two pieces of artillery to reinforce Kenly. But Greenleaf, returning toward Front Royal, turned back to tell Banks he had run into the Eighth Louisiana Regiment and learned that Jackson's forces against Kenly totalled twenty thousand.[55]

Banks, at last convinced, praised Greenleaf, and told him he had saved the Union army. In less than an hour, the Federals were moving toward Winchester. But it was then too late. Jackson struck Banks' column near Middletown, broke it in two, and pursued the forward part on through Winchester and Martinsburg to the Potomac, over which the Northerners hurled themselves to come to a halt at Williamsport, Maryland. But for inexcusable delay on the part of the Confederate cavalry under Ashby and Stuart, said Jackson, Banks might well have reached Winchester minus his entire army. "Never have I seen," he wrote, "an opportunity when it was in the power of the cavalry to reap a richer harvest of the fruits of victory."[56]

As it was, this Federal disaster was great enough to create in the highest military circles of the sensitive Northern Capital a panic almost hysterical in intensity. The Northern papers, possibly with public morale in mind, minimized the seriousness of the situation. Hence only the official records reveal fully the consequences that ensued when a young girl gasped out in General Taylor's hearing, on a hill above Front Royal on May 23rd, that the bridges must be seized before the Federals could destroy them.

Before May 23rd the Federal War Department had believed that Jackson, strongly reinforced, would erupt from the Valley in a drive for Washington. Yet it had stripped Banks of most of his strength to aid McDowell in the east and had then ordered Banks to hold off "Stonewall." When Kenly was overwhelmed, and Banks' flank was struck, the situation seemed so desperate that President Lincoln, the coolest and most resolute man in the Northern capital, found it necessary to take full control of remedial measures.[57]

On the morning of the 24th, the greatly flustered Geary had reported to Washington that he was reliably informed that Jackson with twenty thousand men was moving eastward from Ashby's Gap through Aldie toward Centreville, a town only twenty miles from the District of Columbia. The President disturbed, but not at all convinced, relayed the report to Saxton at Harper's Ferry, and asked pertinently, "What has become of the force which pursued Banks yesterday?"[57]

Meanwhile, on the same day, as it developed that Banks was being chased toward Martinsburg by Jackson, Lincoln ordered McDowell to lay aside the drive planned against Richmond and to set twenty thousand men in motion at once for the Valley. They were to capture Jackson and Ewell with or without the aid of Fremont. Banks was not to be counted upon for support. It was increasingly evident that he would have to be rescued.[57]

McDowell, acknowledging his instructions and sending Shields and Geary back toward the Valley, admitted the disaster was "a crushing blow." Also on the 24th, Fremont was urged eastward by Lincoln to relieve Banks by attacking Jackson. The presidential order left no doubt that the situation was most grave. It ended: "Much—perhaps all—depends upon the celerity with which you can execute it. Put the utmost speed into it. Do not lose a minute."[57]

Fremont, however, advanced slowly and with great reluctance, obviously impressed by reports that Jackson had between sixty and seventy thousand men. With the exception of Banks, already engaged, and the rash Shields, anxious to fight "Stonewall" anywhere, any time, the Federal field generals were alarmingly eager to steer clear of Jackson. Their excessive caution at length so exasperated the President that he wired sarcastically to McDowell on the 28th:

> "You say General Geary's scouts report that they find no enemy this side of the Blue Ridge. Neither do I. Have *they* been *to* the Blue Ridge looking for them?
>
> A. Lincoln."[57]

Probably Jackson could have reached Washington. But it would have served no useful purpose. He hadn't destroyed Banks, and the latter, with Geary, Shields, Fremont, and others, could now converge and overwhelm him. Moreover, his own men and supplies were exhausted. The best course for him was to withdraw quickly up the Valley to escape being trapped. And when his pursuers became bolder, he might turn on them, particularly if a Northern advance guard got too far ahead of its main body. Fremont was too cautious for that, but it was the sort of thing that might readily happen to a rash Irishman like Shields.

Pricked onward by Shields, Kimball, heading Shields' first brigade, reached the ridge east of Front Royal early on May 29th. The Twelfth Georgia Infantry, commanded by an officer with insufficient combat experience, held the village. He withdrew immediately, and the Federals entered so quickly that they were able to release some of the Northerners captured on the 23rd. In addition, they captured many Confederates. General Kimball noted later that there were "160 prisoners, including Miss Belle Boyd, a famous spy in the service of the Confederates." And General Sawyer records: "Among our prisoners was the celebrated Belle Boyd."[58]

Belle probably did not intend to remain behind. Her exploit was so well known that she could hardly hope it would remain a secret if the Federals returned. The sudden withdrawal of the Twelfth Georgia Infantry may have taken her by surprise. Or she may have felt that she could accomplish more behind the Federal lines and could talk her way out of any difficulties that might develop. She may even have decided to stay with the Confederate wounded. Already the dark blue dress she had worn in her dash across the battlefield had been cut up to make shirts for them.

It was a woman who betrayed her—a Northern woman Belle had impulsively befriended. Taken prisoner by the Southerners on the 23rd, the captive professed to be the wife of a soldier in the First Michigan Cavalry. Distressed by her forlorn condition, Belle provided her with clothing and saw in other ways to her comfort.

As soon as the Federals were back in Front Royal and had freed the prisoners held by the Confederates, Belle's protégé took great pains to reward her benefactress in a tangible but disconcerting manner. Hurrying to General Kimball, she denounced Belle as a most dangerous rebel and a malignant enemy. The general thereupon placed Belle under arrest, and sentries were stationed about the cottage. But when General Shields arrived, she was at once released. Thereafter she did not see "Annie Jones" again, or even learn her actual identity, until late in 1863 when, under far more distressing circumstances, both Belle and Annie were prisoners in the Old Capitol at Washington.*

By now the Northern press was acquainting its readers with Belle's activities as a Southern agent and her rôle in the battle of Front Royal. On May 31st the *New York Herald*, the *Philadelphia North American*, the *New York Times*, and other Federal papers contained an Associated Press item sent from Banks' headquarters at Williamsport, Maryland.

In this dispatch a war correspondent related that on the 18th at the hotel in Front Royal he had seen "an accomplished prostitute" who had figured largely in the rebel cause. Having seen her only recently at Martinsburg, he suspected that her presence at Front Royal meant mischief. He had pointed her out to the military authorities and recommended her arrest. Now it had become known that she had been carrying extensive correspondence through the opposing lines. And, speaking of the same woman, he quoted a Federal officer as saying:

> "'An hour previous to the attack on Kenly, Belle went out on a rise of ground south of the town, and was seen to wave her handkerchief toward the point from which the center of the attack was made.'"

This item was read widely in the South as well as in the North.

---

*See pp. 132 and 135.

That it came to the attention of Miss Lucy Buck and that she did not overlook the attack on Belle's character seems clear from her comment:

> "Had a paper announcing the evacuation of Corinth * * * It also took complimentary (?)* notice of Miss Belle Boyd's heroism on the 23rd."[59]

Belle always believed it was A. W. Clarke, correspondent of the *New York Herald*, who first defamed her in the Northern press. More than once he had intruded upon her and Alice so persistently that she had been compelled to bolt the door of their sitting room against him. She knew, too, that although he had escaped through a window when she locked him in his room he had later been captured by the Confederates. She had seen him being led away down the street with other prisoners, and he had called out to her vengefully: "I'll make you rue this. It's your doing that I am a prisoner here."

It was the vivid memory of these things that led Belle to write later: "It is to him that I am indebted for the first violent undisguised abuse with which my name was coupled in any Federal journal."

Yet Belle was wrong. Clarke could not have written the Associated Press item. After escaping from his room, he had cut the ferry line over the Shenandoah, and carried messages for Colonel Kenly who subsequently cited him for valuable service as a volunteer aide. Clarke, taken prisoner that day, was only released through the intervention of General Jackson on June 5th. Captured on the 23rd, he could not have written the dispatch sent from Williamsport, Maryland on the 28th.[60]

Whoever did write the abusive item was not entirely without qualms. At its very end he added a cautious hand-washing disclaimer that he had personal knowledge of anything other than undeniable proof of treason. His disavowal read: "Your correspondent cannot vouch for the strict accuracy of all the foregoing, but undeniable proof exists of her treason."

Where he secured some of his proof is clear. It must have been from the Fifth New York Cavalry, the regiment which maintained the picket lines which Belle slipped through. The history of this cavalry regiment states, regarding Banks' disaster:

> "Belle Boyd, the noted Rebel female spy, was undoubtedly instrumental in causing our defeat. It was afterwards ascertained that she was the bearer of an extensive correspondence between Rebels outside and inside our lines."[61]

**Sic!*

But the late Dr. Thomas A. Ashby, a distinguished citizen of Front Royal, tells a different story. According to his recollection of Jackson's Valley campaigns, written in 1914, Belle simply rode into the Confederate lines on May 22nd, gave "Stonewall" information that proved unreliable, and, "as far as I know, was never under arrest."[62]

His error as to the date may be dismissed as typographical. But when he asserts that Belle's information proved unreliable, he offers no proof and is flatly contradicted by General Taylor's statement that "it was true to the letter."

His claim that Belle was never under arrest is refuted by the written testimony of Generals Kimball and Sawyer that she was taken prisoner. Moreover, in May, 1862 Thomas Ashby was less than fourteen years old. At that age, his lack of knowledge of an event would hardly be conclusive proof that it did not occur. That he managed to remain in ignorance of it for more than half a century is even less impressive.

CHAPTER NINE

The War Department Arrests Belle Boyd

OTING that Northern papers published extravagant accounts of what they termed her "exploits" on May 23rd, the eighteen-year-old Virginian girl was no more favorably impressed by them than when they had called her a prostitute.

She mentioned disdainfully that one credited her with having directed the fire of the Confederate artillery throughout the engagement. A second, she pointed out, claimed that she had sustained the wavering counsels of the Southern generals by the force of her genius; and a third had described her, sword in hand, leading the attack on Front Royal. This arrant nonsense she dismissed with the scornful words: "As I believe that the veracity of the Yankee press is pretty well known and appreciated, I shall give no more extracts from their eloquent pages."

As all the surrounding area was again in Federal control, Belle thought once more of going farther South. General Banks, who had ventured back across the Potomac as Jackson withdrew up the Valley, was now at Front Royal, and his headquarters were at her aunt's. It was to him that, with probable misgivings, she applied for permission to leave.

"Where do you wish to go?" he asked.

"To Louisiana, where my aunt resides," she replied.

"But what will Virginia do without you?", he inquired teasingly.

"What do you mean, General?"

He smiled and said, "We always miss our bravest and most illustrious, and how can your native State do without you?"

Laughingly, she thanked him for his gallant compliment, and he then engaged her with the utmost good nature in conversation on the part she had played in his defeat. So considerate was his behavior under the circumstances that she thought him one of the most affable gentlemen she had ever met. Yet, as prudent as he was agreeable, he did not consent to her departure.

Meanwhile Shields had rushed westward and had been soundly thrashed at Port Republic on June 9th. Several of his officers had returned to Front Royal, and their story of the defeat dismayed the Federals stationed there.

One afternoon, about a week later, a boy of the village was startled as a young woman riding a spirited horse and accompanied by a Federal officer dashed up to his home. Springing from her saddle, she rushed into the house, asked a servant "where she could find the wounded officer," then hurried upstairs and entered the officer's room without ceremony. "This woman," says Dr. Ashby, "was the then celebrated Belle Boyd."

Belle does not mention this incident, and her reason for this visit can only be surmised. But young Tom Ashby, outraged by her abrupt invasion of his home, wrote more than fifty years later: "When she rode up to my home to see the wounded German officer she was playing the game of flirt and lowering the dignity of her sex."[63]

He added that there were two wounded officers in the Ashby home at the time. One was a Federal, attached to General Shields' staff, who had been shot in the face at Port Republic. The Ashbys had been told that this man was an officer in the German army, on leave of absence, who had joined the Union forces to learn about American warfare. A handsome, dashing fellow, quite popular with his comrades, he was the man Belle had come to see.

It is unfortunate that in the writing of his memoirs Dr. Ashby's recollections were so often inaccurate. The records show that only one member of General Shields' staff was wounded in the battle of Port Republic, and that he was not a German officer on leave from the German army. He was Captain Daniel J. Keily, an Irishman, aide-de-camp to General Shields. Cited for bravery and energy in the Port Republic engagement, he had received "a severe wound in the face while urging forward the men, and was carried off the field." Fortunately he recovered, and later was made brevet brigadier-general for gallant and meritorius conduct.[64]

In view of Tom Ashby's youth in 1862, it is likely that in later life he confused his recollection of Captain Keily with that of a German officer on a general's staff who was wounded in the throat in June of the *next* year. But this was the valiant Major Heros von Borcke, aide-de-camp and assistant adjutant-general of the Confederate cavalry leader, "Jeb" Stuart.[65]

When it is realized that Belle was calling on Dan Keily, her errand becomes less mysterious and in fact solves a mystery. For Captain Keily was surely the Captain K., aide-de-camp to General Shields, who had been writing Belle love-notes, sending her flowers, and giving her, unintentionally, valuable military information. That she called on him when he was severely wounded merely to flirt does not seem reasonable. Her visit was more likely a polite and purposeful call upon one with whom continuance of friendly relations might still yield military advantage. Or, in a period when courtesy toward a stricken enemy was often instinctive, it may have been simply an act of natural kindness.

Even to Thomas Ashby, Belle was a well-bred woman of some personal beauty, vivacious, attractive, and a skilled rider of spirited horses. He admitted that she did not lack energy, dash, and courage. "But," he asserted loftily, "she had none of the genius, inspiration and fervor of the true heroine." At the time of her visit to his home, she had, he wrote, already attracted considerable notice by her activities, but, in his opinion, neither the Federals nor the Confederates took her seriously. She played with both sides, he continued, a game that inspired no confidence in either, and was as far below the standards of the pure and noble womanhood of the South as a circus rider. "So much for Belle Boyd," he concluded. "Her heroism has long faded into the forgetfulness of her generation. She has found no decent place in history."

Tom Ashby, at least sixteen and a half years of age when the war ended, was older than many youthful Confederate volunteers. That he took no part in the conflict is stressed by his description of his book as the "reminiscences of a non-combatant." As for his parents, he relates that through the Federal General Duryee, billeted in their home, they purchased with Southern gold enough food and supplies in the North to last them throughout the war.[66]

His critical comments cannot be ignored. But as a child in 1862 he could have known little about Belle at first hand, and this little is shown to have become a highly confused and warped recollection. Many of his conclusions were undoubtedly hearsay derived from his parents and other elders. And no matter how estimable and patriotic they were, the Ashbys were not qualified by superior achievement to determine arrogantly Belle Boyd's place in history, or to complain that she lacked the spiritual qualities of true heroism.

Despite Dr. Ashby's prophecy, Belle Boyd has won an honorable place in Front Royal's history. In 1936 the County Centennial of Progress folder claimed proudly that "Belle Boyd, the famous Confederate spy, sometimes used Front Royal, as the base of her operations." During the Centennial celebration the Strickler House was a museum of which the most noted exhibit was the "historical Belle Boyd cottage." At the same time the local Warren Rifles Chapter, United Daughters of the Confederacy, sponsored a pamphlet entitled "Belle Boyd, Southern Spy of the Shenandoah." In it these ladies lauded Belle as "the pride of the Southern soldier, the admiration of Northern firesides, and the toast of the British Empire."[67]

Not long after Belle's visit to Dan Keily in the Ashby home, most of the Federals in and about Front Royal were withdrawn. Only the Third Delaware Infantry remained, commanded by Colonel Samuel H. Jenkins. A very large and stout man, Belle considered him coarse in both manners and appearance.[68]

Two other officers who remained behind produced a far more favorable impression. These were Major McEnnis, the provost-marshal, and his assistant, Lieutenant Preston, who were very courteous and kind.

It was on a day late in July that Belle noticed two men dressed as Confederate soldiers standing by a flag-tent pitched near the Stewart cottage. It was here that Federal passes to go South were issued. At her request, her grandmother sent for Major McEnnis, learned the men were paroled Confederates heading South, and secured permission to invite them to dinner.

Belle extended the invitation in person to one of the men. He accepted gladly. But he hoped they would dine soon for he had only two or three hours to get beyond the pickets. To his hostess, this promptly suggested an idea. Why not have him take news to the Southern lines? Impulsively she asked: "Won't you take a letter from me to General Jackson?"

He agreed readily, and she went off to write her message. But a hovering servant followed her, and asked: "Miss Belle! Who's dat man you's a-talkin' to?"

She answered, "I know no more about him than that he is a paroled rebel soldier going South."

The woman shook her head dolefully, and continued earnestly: "Miss Belle, dat man ain't no rebel. I seen him 'mong de Yankees in de street. If he has got secesh clothes on, he ain't no secesh. Can't fool Betsy dat way. Dat man's a spy! Dat man's a spy! Please God, he am."

Unconvinced, her mistress went to her room and wrote her letter. In it she detailed valuable information regarding the Yankee forces, their movements, and activities. Then she called the Confederate aside, gave him the letter, and said: "Will you promise faithfully, upon the honor of a soldier, to take the utmost care of this, and deliver it safe to General Jackson? They tell me you are a spy, but I do not believe it."

He denied the charge hotly, and left, swearing to act with fidelity and dispatch. Shortly after his departure, a Federal officer mentioned casually that the man was a Union spy headed for the Confederate lines.

Belle became really alarmed. She had given the man a paper which would enable him to move freely about Jackson's headquarters and command. Something had to be done promptly to remedy this. After much anxious thought, a possible solution occurred to her. Hastily she scribbled a few lines addressed to Captain Harry Gilmor of the Confederate cavalry. She described the man carefully, explained he was a spy, and admitted she had been duped into giving him a letter for General Jackson. Then she dispatched this message by "underground railway."

An old Negro was the locomotive, and an enormous silver watch with its works removed served as the mail car. Under forced pressure, the old man shuffled off to seek Gilmor in the hills, reminding himself to be sure to say, if asked for the hour, that his watch was broken and no longer kept time.

However, as Belle learned later, the Union spy did not go to the Confederate lines. Instead, he travelled north straight to General Franz Sigel who, since the end of June, was in command of a Union corps in the Valley. Placed in Sigel's hands, the letter was forwarded immediately to Secretary of War Stanton in Washington who lost no time taking action fraught with dire consequences for the writer of the message.

For the Yankee agent, the consequences were even worse. Belle, with characteristic interest in what happened to those who matched wits with her, records laconically that he was later caught on the Rappahannock and hanged. However, on this one point she seems to have been misinformed for he not only survived the War, but his own version of this adventure is now available to confirm her recital and to add some amazing details.

It was in July, 1862 that C. W. D. Smitley, chief of scouts of the Fifth West Virginia Cavalry, was sent from New Creek to Front Royal with orders to report to General R. C. Schenck. Upon arrival one of the General's aides informed him that Belle Boyd was in town on parole and was suspected of violating her parole. His assignment was to entrap her.

Presenting himself under an assumed name as a paroled Confederate officer, Smitley secured lodgings with a prominent resident of Southern sympathies. Discussing Belle Boyd with his host, and praising her valuable services, he learned, writes a comrade of Smitley, "that Miss Boyd was the sensation of the village, that the intensely loyal Confederates idolized her, and that she had a large following of Federal officers who were ready to do her homage."

That same afternoon his host's daughter invited Smitley to have tea with the fair Southern scout. Calling at the address given him, he was introduced to her in his assumed character, and found her "a lady of culture, a brilliant conversationalist, expert with the piano, and rather pretty." Other ladies called, squired by Federal officers, but Miss Boyd was the center of attraction. When she played and sang "The Bonnie Blue Flag," the Federal scout stepped forward boldly in his Confederate rôle and defiantly added his powerful bass voice to hers.

This audacious conduct, he claimed, gained him Belle's complete confidence. Soon she told him how she was violating her parole and urged him not to consider binding his own parole to the hated Yankees. A few days later at an evening party she favored the masquerading Smitley with marked attention. Incensed by this and the contrasting coldness with which Miss Boyd treated him, the aide of General Schenck, who had assigned Smitley to his task, taunted Belle Boyd with the revelation that her favorite was a Yankee scout.

Scornfully resentful, the Southern girl refused to believe this treacherous disclosure. But, relates Smitley's comrade, the following morning she called on Scout Smitley for an explanation, greatly agitated and crying like a child.[69]

So ends abruptly the Northern version of the story, leaving much untold. Both narratives agree fundamentally, yet vary significantly. And of the two principals, it is certainly Belle Boyd who is more discreetly reticent.

After this incident, the Federals in Front Royal knew what Belle's activities were, either through the message she had given their agent or through her revelations to Smitley. They were certain to do something about it, and Belle's immediate problem was to figure what their course would be.

For two months she had been trying to get permission to go farther South. But the Yankees did not want her to leave for they felt she would take information to the Confederates. Detaining her, however, meant that she might gather information within their lines, and would only have to worry about transmitting it. Now that the Northerners had proof that she was actually sending out intelligence they had to decide immediately whether it was wiser to send her South or to imprison her.

Belle knew or suspected what their local decision would be. On Saturday, July 26th, she appeared in Warrenton, said the *New York Tribune*, in the company of a wounded captain of the rebel Black Horse Cavalry who had been paroled. Here Belle openly offered to take letters to Richmond for three dollars each.

On the 29th, three days later, what she apparently desired happened. A Federal officer called upon her in Front Royal, speaking plainly of her activities and saying that further misconduct would produce decidedly unpleasant results. He stressed that the Yankees, once thoroughly aroused, would not hesitate to inflict the severest punishment.

He urged her to leave Front Royal immediately. It was no longer a matter of granting her earlier requests for permission to leave. She was being asked to go willingly, or suffer the consequences. Belle admitted she would not mind going to Richmond, and the relieved officer promised to secure a pass for her. It was agreed that she would leave on Thursday, the 31st.

A most unpleasant situation had produced remarkably helpful developments. She was going to Richmond and would have a Yankee safe-conduct. But the private letters she had accepted were merely incidental to her main purpose. What she undoubtedly planned was to report to the Confederate War Department the information she had been able to collect within the enemy lines and had already tried to send to Jackson.

The intelligence she possessed must have been along lines similar to the news in the report sent from Charlottesville to the Southern Secretary of War on July 28th by a Confederate courier. This agent stated that General Pope's forces, in the very region Belle had visited on the 26th, totalled about thirty-five thousand men. Located mainly around Sperryville and Washington, they were on the move, headed, perhaps, for Swift Run Gap and the Valley. This dispatch was signed "S. D. Boyd, Courier, War Department."[70] And it was addressed to George W. Randolph, Secretary of War, who was, as Appendix A shows, a cousin of the widow of Belle Boyd's cousin, Dr. William S. Bell, former mayor of Chattanooga.

That Stephen D. Boyd and Belle Boyd collaborated closely in their Confederate intelligence work is likely. Stephen Boyd's son, now Commissioner of Revenue, Warren County, Virginia, recalls that Belle and his father were very close friends. She visited Stephen Boyd often after the War at his home in Browntown and claimed the Browntown Boyds as kinsmen. Among the possessions of S. D. Boyd's descendants is an autographed photograph of "Belle Boyd of Virginia" which she presented to him many years after the War.

But Belle did not get to Richmond. The Federals in the village were willing to let her go to be rid of her. Higher authority, however, had other plans. She must leave Front Royal, but for a destination other than Richmond. Orders were issued, and in Washington and the Valley men moved to obey them.

On Tuesday, July 29th, in the late afternoon, Belle, her cousin Alice, and Lieutenant Preston were on the cottage balcony. Watching the setting sun sink slowly behind the serene hills, their conversation turned to nostalgic memories of the peaceful past. They recalled its happiness and joys, deplored the divided and unhappy state of "our country," and agreed sadly that the future promised but a continuance and even an increase of calamities. For the moment, they were not enemies, but heart-sick Americans conscious only of national disaster.

As twilight deepened into gloom, and their forebodings grew darker, the sound of horses' hoofs drew their attention, and they saw a large body of cavalry approaching the house. Belle, aroused from her sad thoughts, took it to be a Federal scouting party on its way to the mountains to surprise Harry Gilmor's cavalry. Again a rebel, and her mind once more attuned to purposeful activity, she hurried to her room and wrote Gilmor a brief note of warning. As soon as this was off by the reliable "underground railway," she retired, and slept soundly, her sleep undisturbed by her unhappy reflections at twilight or by any premonition of impending disaster.

She rose early the next morning. After breakfast she stood at the cottage door observing idly the movements and activities of those at headquarters. Her attention was soon drawn to several Yankees engaged in dragging out a carriage and preparing to harness horses. A strange feeling came over her, and she found herself ruled by a single insistent thought. She must know for whom the carriage was intended.

Going up to the balcony, she had a better view. The street before the house was filled with cavalrymen. They were dismounted, and lounged about, but their horses were at hand and they were evidently waiting for the order to mount. As she sought to interpret the meaning of this scene, a servant came and said: "Miss Belle, de Provo' wishes to see you in de drawin' room and dere's two oder men wid him."

She descended immediately. Awaiting her, she found Major Mc-

Ennis, the Provost-Marshal, whose face betrayed nervousness and excitement, and two other men. One, a tall, fine-looking officer, was Major Francis T. Sherman of the Twelfth Illinois Cavalry, later a brigadier-general, whose regiment had been stationed at Martinsburg since late June.[71] The other man, a coarse-looking civilian with an unkempt, grizzly beard, was short, and had a mean, vile expression. He glanced about constantly with small, restless eyes incessantly watchful and suspicious. His features were, Belle thought, extremely repellent, and depicted ferocity, cunning, and cowardice. She was not surprised when he proved to be one of Secretary Stanton's hirelings—a detective of the United States Secret Service.

Without further preamble, Major McEnnis said briefly: "Miss Boyd, Major Sherman has come to arrest you."

"Impossible!' she cried. And then, angrily, demanded, "For what?"

Before the Provost-Marshal could answer, Major Sherman spoke. He assured her in a very kind but firm tone that although the duty he had to perform was painful to his feelings he must nevertheless execute the orders of the Secretary of War without question. As he finished speaking, the detective produced a document and proceeded to read it. As far as Belle could recall later, it ran as follows:

"War Department

Sir:

You will proceed immediately to Front Royal, Virginia, and arrest, if found there, Miss Belle Boyd, and bring her at once to Washington.

I am, respectfully,

E. M. Stanton."

CHAPTER TEN

In Close Custody to Washington

STUNNED by this order signed by the dread Secretary of War, and instantly aware of its implications, Belle made no further protest.

But the detective then announced that he must examine her belongings. Thinking of the evidence he would find if not hindered in some way, she begged a few moments of grace to enable her servant to prepare her room for his visit, and asked leave to withdraw. Taking his consent for granted, she started upstairs and stopped short in amazement as the Secret Service man promptly followed. Again she asked him to wait. Saying gruffly that he knew she had papers she wanted to hide, he pushed violently past her and entered her room.

First, her clothes were turned inside out in a thorough search, and cast upon the floor. Then the detective noticed her desk and portfolio and made ready to examine their contents. Eliza forestalled him, however. Snatching up as many papers as she could hold, she rushed headlong to the kitchen. There she thrust them into the fire. But among the documents not destroyed were several in Belle's handwriting. These Mr. Stanton's agent confiscated, as well as a handsome pistol which a Federal staff officer had given her the year before in token of his admiration of her spirit in protecting her mother.

The detective also broke open a private writing-table and took from it personal papers of Mr. Stewart. He then turned to Belle and in a rude tone and most offensive language ordered her to be ready to leave in thirty minutes. Her request that Eliza be permitted to accompany her was denied, and the one trunk she was allowed as luggage was soon strapped to the back of the waiting carriage.

Bracing herself for the ordeal ahead of her, Belle walked into the drawing room and announced in steady, unbroken accents that she was ready. Her composure remained unshaken as her grandmother and Alice wept bitterly, and Eliza, clasping her about the knees, begged leave to attend her. The servant's hold was broken, and Belle was hurried out the door and into the carriage.

News of her arrest had spread quickly, and many citizens had joined the soldiers in the street. Head high, she met the gaze of her neighbors proudly. In most eyes she saw the comforting tribute of unmistakable sorrow and sympathy. But there were others, too, which reflected with equal clarity both satisfaction and exultation. Finding herself so closely watched by friend and foe, she resolved to be neither an object of pity to the one nor a subject for derision to the other. Though her heart throbbed violently, her eyes remained dry and not a muscle of her face quivered. Not a single outward sign betrayed the inner turmoil and emotion in the heart of the eighteen-year-old girl at the prospect of prolonged captivity or worse.

If Belle caught the eye of Miss Lucy Buck on this occasion, what she saw there was certainly neither sympathy nor sorrow. Miss Lucy's journal contains this unfeeling comment:

> "Belle Boyd was taken prisoner and sent off in a carriage with an escort of fifty cavalrymen today. I hope she has succeeded in making herself proficiently* notorious now. They say they are going to put her within our lines and keep her there."[72]

Of course, Thomas Ashby maintained Belle was never arrested—as far as he knew. Why he did not know of this particular instance is best suggested by the fact that he had typhoid fever that summer.[73]

As Belle's carriage moved off, the Federal cavalry formed about it. She estimated that her escort numbered about four hundred and fifty men, and their formation was that of cavalry proceeding through enemy territory. The usual advance and rear guards preceded and followed the carriage, and upon each flank fifty scouts were detached in skirmish order to guard against lateral attack.

In this fashion they went on until a hill was reached commanding a clear view for several miles in all directions. Here the cavalcade halted, field-glasses and signal whistles were put to considerable use, and other unusual activity was engaged in. To the youthful prisoner, still suffering severely from shock and apprehension, the behavior of her escort was most disturbing.

She noted with dismay that the carriage had been stopped under a large maple tree. From its sturdy trunk there extended significantly across her line of vision a long, heavy limb from which her imagination immediately suggested an inert human figure might soon dangle. Could it be that she was about to be dragged out and hanged?

In silent, solitary agony she awaited fearfully the brusque announce-

---

*Sufficiently?

ment that here was her journey's end. Instead, to her immeasurable relief, the now welcome command "Forward!" rang out suddenly, and they went on again, her carriage at a walking pace.

Later she learned that the great precautions taken for her removal, including the halt upon the hill, had been due to fear that Ashby's cavalry would attempt to rescue her. Ashby had been killed in June, but his brigade was as active as ever, and such men as Belle's uncle, Captain Glenn, and his comrade Harry Gilmor, were quite capable of following her captors well into Federal territory in a mad effort to free her.

Upon the outskirts of Winchester, another unit of the regiment joined them. As the carriage rolled solemnly through the town, guarded closely by the impressive force of some five hundred brave sabers, residents rushed to their windows and doors to watch the unusual procession. What they thought was happening, Belle did not know. Her senses of humor and perspective restored, she suspected that they could only believe that the vehicle containing her small person was a funeral car bearing some noble and heroic Federal warrior fittingly to his eternal resting place.

At six o'clock on Wednesday evening the carriage came to a stop before the headquarters of General Julius White, a quarter of a mile beyond Winchester. She was ordered to alight, and was ushered into the presence of the general. He received her with a graceful bow and bade her welcome with marked courtesy. She returned his salutation with as much ease as she could muster, and asked what he meant to do with her.

"Tomorrow," he answered, "I shall send you on to the commanding officer at Martinsburg. He can best inform you what is to be done with you. You will rest here after your journey for the night."

General White's reply was clearly a polite evasion. He had earlier that day wired Mr. Wolcott, Assistant Secretary of War:

> "Mr. Cridge is here with Miss Boyd as prisoner. What shall be done with her?"[74]

From Washington, Mr. Wolcott had telegraphed the Secretary of War's orders:

> "Direct Cridge to come immediately to Washington and bring with him Belle Boyd in close custody, committing her on arrival to the Old Capitol Prison. Furnish him such aid as he may need to get her safely here."[74]

With her normal assurance almost completely regained, Belle

promptly asked leave to spend the night with friends in Winchester. The Federal commander refused this request fretfully. He added that it would take a whole cavalry regiment to guard her, and that though the rebel cavalry might not enter the town to attempt a rescue, he had no doubt the citizens themselves would try it.

Undismayed, the artful girl made another attempt to escape, at least temporarily, from the intimate vigilance of her captors. "But, surely," she pleaded, "you do not mean that I am to stop here, defenseless and alone in a tent, at the mercy of your brigade? I never yet slept in a tent when I was present with our army, and," she queried audaciously, "how can I endure such a penance in the camp of my enemies?"

"My own tent," replied the general, with a low bow, "has been properly prepared for the reception of a lady. Whenever you wish to retire you can follow your inclinations; and you may rest assured you shall sleep in perfect security."

Further protest was clearly useless. Supper was brought in and placed on a table arranged with a dazzling display of rich silver plate. The thought that the real owners of this fine tableware were probably at the moment miserable outcasts in want of food effectually destroyed any appetite her sufferings had left her. She ate sparingly and silently, then rose from her camp-stool, and begged leave to retire.

The General rang a small bell, and ordered the Negro who answered it to show her to his tent. There she listened to the steady tramp of sentries pacing to and fro outside, and sought in vain to distract her thoughts from her plight. Body and spirit again overwhelmed by the heavy burden of her grief, she sat restlessly upon her camp-stool, feverish hands pressed hard against her aching head. Yet in time, exhaustion triumphed, and she fell asleep. But while she slept in security, as the general had promised, her sleep did not remain long undisturbed.

At about three-thirty in the morning she was awakened suddenly by the sound of several muskets fired in rapid succession. Then followed the ominous beating of the long roll on the drums. Just outside her tent she heard several officers stumble out to their horses and gallop off to the outposts. Her heart beat high with hope. Did this night alarm mean her deliverance? Lighting a candle, she sat down and anxiously awaited developments. The first came in a roar from the darkness. "Put out that light! It is some signal to the rebels. Do you hear me?"

She blew out the light, and a few minutes later the drums signalled the end of the disturbance and of her hope of rescue. What had caused the commotion, as an upset sentry explained to his incredulous superiors, was an obstinate cow which had strayed from a nearby field and had disregarded an order to halt, although twice repeated. The soldier, knowing something was moving in front of him, and unable to distinguish it clearly, fired when his command was ignored. His nervous comrades on adjoining posts had immediately done likewise. The offended cow had promptly betaken herself back to her field, and the equally annoyed Yankees, once they grasped the Confederates were not really upon them, retired again to their tents.

Roused at dawn, Belle was ordered to make ready to leave at once for Martinsburg. As her carriage set out, she noted her cavalry escort had been reduced to about two hundred troopers. Their destination was reached at about one o'clock in the afternoon. Major Sherman, observing that the prisoner was exhausted by fatigue and renewed anxiety as to her fate, had his wife accompany her to the Federal camp just north of the village.

Here in the tent of the commanding officer she learned she was to be taken to Washington at two o'clock on the morning of the next day. Her head bursting with pain, she begged the Union commander to permit her to spend the intervening period at her home on the outskirts of the village. But for Mr. Cridge, this request might have been granted. He pointed out to the colonel that Secretary Stanton would probably take exception to an indulgence which would enable her to communicate with enemies of the United States. Then, having prevented her transfer to the Boyd home, he went there and looked for any letters she might have sent her mother.

Meanwhile a carriage arrived at the camp from which a lady stepped dressed in deep mourning and wearing a heavy veil. Despite this attire, Belle recognized her mother immediately and rushed into her arms.

Mrs. Boyd renewed her daughter's plea to await her departure at home. Again the colonel refused to grant it. However, he permitted her removal to Raemer's Hotel next to the railroad station. As soon as the prisoner, her mother, and Mrs. Sherman reached the hotel, a cordon of twenty-seven sentries was placed about it, three guards were posted in the passage leading to the captive's room, and one stationed outside her door. Only then were the other members of her family allowed access to her.

For the trip by rail to Washington, it had been arranged that Mr. Cridge should be the prisoner's only escort. The idea of his company was so offensive to her, however, that she sent for Colonel Holt[75] and implored him to substitute an officer in his place. Under the War Department's orders, this was impossible. But the colonel relented to the extent of detailing First Lieutenant William J. Steele, Company C, Twelfth Illinois Cavalry, to "escort duty."[76]

As the time to leave approached and Belle realized that she was indeed beyond hope of rescue, her self-control gave way to a passionate outburst of grief. After this long repressed emotional disturbance had subsided, she passed into a stupor which nothing penetrated but the sudden ominous whistle of the locomotive of the waiting train. Pulling herself together by a tremendous effort, she rose to meet the demands of the next few moments and soon found herself seated in a railway carriage.

How she reached the station remained a blank in her memory. She only recalled that Lieutenant Steele was constantly beside her and that she felt grateful for his presence. Once more fully conscious of her surroundings, she thought for a moment that Mr. Cridge had remained behind. Looking about, she found, however, that Mr. Stanton's agent had taken the seat on her left.

Lieutenant Steele, not knowing that she was to be taken to the Old Capitol Prison, suggested that upon arrival in Washington she should go to Willard's Hotel, enjoy a short rest and then go to the Secretary of War's office. But Mr. Cridge's instructions were otherwise, and he used sharp words to tell the young cavalry officer so.

The train reached the capital at nine in the morning. News of Belle Boyd's arrest having preceded her arrival, many persons had gathered at the station to see the "wonderful rebel." As she stepped to the platform, the chief of detectives, Lafayette C. Baker, who had been wired by Cridge, seized her roughly by the arm and shouted gruffly: "Come on! I'll attend to you."

He pushed her through the crowd, but Lieutenant Steele came forward and protested vehemently against such ill usage. The only reply he received was a torrent of profane abuse. The prisoner was thrust into a carriage, and the driver given the order: "Drive to the Old Capitol." But before he could drive off, the persistent lieutenant rejoined them and asked to accompany her to the prison. Though this was bluntly refused, he insisted and warned the detectives that he meant to stay with her until she was out of their hands.

The ride was short, and the jail soon came into view. A vast brick building, somber, chilling, and repellent, its dull, damp walls were pierced by narrow windows darkened by heavy iron staunchions. At this first sight of her new home, Belle reflected bitterly that those who were casting her into prison without preliminary accusation and trial were the tender-hearted emancipators who shuddered so at the mere thought of the wrongs done the blacks.

Her lament was not without justice. Hundreds of persons were now being subjected to military arrest and detention without formal accusation or trial. It was an easy, though illegal, way to render them harmless, and whenever further detention became useless, military commissions released them informally without establishing their innocence or their guilt. That their constitutional civil rights were violated was officially neither of concern nor consequence.

As the prison doors closed with seeming finality upon Belle, the conscientious historian Frank Moore jotted down in his notes for his great work:

> "A woman named Belle Boyd, who had been acting as a rebel spy and mail carrier to Richmond from points within the lines of the Union Army of the Potomac, was captured near Warrenton, Va. and sent to the Old Capitol Prison at Washington."[77]

At about the same time more piquant details were being retailed by the Northern press. Notable among the articles was an item from Martinsburg by a correspondent of the *Philadelphia Inquirer* which appeared later in *Leslie's Illustrated Newspaper*, was printed in part in the *Washington Star*, probably appeared in many other papers, and may have played a part in Belle's arrest.[78]

It related that Belle, leader of the rebel female spies in the Valley, was sharp-featured, black-eyed, and twenty-five years old—in appearance, at least. Enjoying all the advantages that society, position, and education could confer, she had a subtle mind suited to the days of Charles II or Louis XIV and which Mazarin and Richelieu would have delighted to employ.

She had, wrote the correspondent, a certain dash—"a smart pertness, a quickness of retort, and utter abandon of manner and bearing which were attractive from their very romantic unwontedness." And for pathos, he provided her with a "pious, good old mother" who greatly deplored her daughter's activities. But he neglected to explain how the attractive, fun-loving Mrs. Boyd could be, at the age of thirty-seven, a pathetically venerable figure afflicted with a vexatious daughter twenty-five years old.

The *Inquirer's* man complained that Belle was exercising her wiles upon young and inexperienced lieutenants and captains to whom she was presented as "Miss Anderson" or "Miss Faulkner." Paternally and patriotically he had warned many of her victims. But, nevertheless, he had to admit that, aided by a trained band of youthful feminine assistants, she continued to identify Federal regiments and learn their strength by pumping new arrivals.

Moreover, within a mile of Martinsburg, Mrs. Charles J. Faulkner and her two accomplished daughters were also extracting intelligence from Federal officers. This Virginian lady, whose husband had until lately been United States Minister to France, was, the correspondent added, "the wiliest and most experienced diplomat in the Valley of Virginia. She is more dangerous than Belle Boyd because she is more adroit and has a large social influence and greater means of accomplishing her purposes."

One immediate consequence of this article and similar ones was a belief, persistent to this day, that Belle and the Faulkners were intimately related. Within a few days it was being stated that the two ladies were sisters. Perturbed friends of the ex-minister's wife wanted no Federal interest either in the Faulkners' well-known activities for the South or in their alleged connection with a recently arrested rebel spy. On August 8th the *Washington Star* printed two indignant letters about both subjects. One, signed by "A Unionist," denied Mrs. Faulkner was a secessionist and called the item about her cruel and unjust. The other asked that the false statement that Belle Boyd was a sister of Mrs. Faulkner be contradicted, "for this young lady is not connected in any way with Mrs. Faulkner."

Mrs. Faulkner, a daughter of General Elisha Boyd, was Miss Mary W. Boyd prior to her marriage. It was therefore easy for Yankees in the Valley to confuse her with the Mary Boyd who was Belle's mother, or to assume that the two Boyd families were closely related. Moreover, the Faulkners lived in Martinsburg at Boydville, an estate inherited by Mrs. Faulkner from her father, and Belle Boyd and her parents lived on South Queen Street within a stone's throw of Boydville.

No American record is found of any blood tie between the Boyds of Boydville and Belle Boyd's family. However, both lines seem to descend from the Boyds of Kilmarnock, Scotland, and in that case are branches of the same parent stock.

CHAPTER ELEVEN

The First Day in the Old Capitol Prison

WITHIN the famous prison, Belle was ushered into a small office. A clerk looked up casually and said her business would be attended to immediately. As he finished speaking, Mr. Wood, the Superintendent, entered. A potent personage in official Washington, he was a powerfully built man of medium height, with brown hair, a fair complexion, and keen bluish-grey eyes.

His greeting to her was: "And so this is the celebrated rebel spy. I am very glad to see you, and will endeavor to make you as comfortable as possible. So whatever you wish for, ask for it and you shall have it. I am glad I have so distinguished a personage for my guest. Come, let me show you to your room."

They crossed the hall, ascended a flight of stairs and came to a narrow passage with several doors opening upon it and a sentry pacing its length. Mr. Wood led her to Room No. 6 and informed her it was hers.

Repeating that she should ask for anything she wished, and promising to send her a servant, he added cryptically that she would not be locked in her room as long as she "behaved," and then withdrew. His meaning became clear when she read a copy of regulations sent her a few minutes later. This warned that communication with other prisoners would be punished by locking her door.

A casual, half-hearted inspection of her quarters did not take long. The scant furnishings consisted of a wash-stand, a looking glass, an iron bed-stead, a table, and some chairs. Two very large windows took up almost all of one side of the room, and from them she could see Pennsylvania Avenue and, in the distance, the former residence of General Floyd, ex-Secretary of War, where she had passed many happy hours. This memory reminded her forcefully that her present situation was deplorably different and plunged her into a sad reverie from which she sought to rouse herself by asking for a rocking chair and a fire. Though the weather was hot, and the room very warm, she imagined that the sight of a bright blaze would make her immediate surroundings seem more cheerful.

But nothing could erase the bitter realization that she was a prisoner of state in the famous Old Capitol.

A large brick building on A and First Streets, it had acquired its name by housing Congress temporarily after the actual Capitol was burned by the British in 1814. When Congress moved to permanent quarters, it became a very fashionable boarding house much patronized by members of the Senate and House. Within its walls the inaugural ceremonies for President Monroe were held in 1817, and John C. Calhoun died here in 1850. From its portals Commodore Stephen Decatur walked forth to the duel in which he lost his life. In 1933 an article in the Presidential Inauguration Program pointed out that where the Supreme Court Building now stood the Old Capitol had held prisoner, "Belle Boyd, the celebrated Confederate spy."

In 1861 it was already a dilapidated structure, but still capable of housing many guests, provided they were forcibly detained. Putting it to such use, the Government increased its accommodations greatly by connecting the facilities of "Duff Green's Row," an adjoining building also known as the Carroll Prison. Most of the rooms in the combined buildings were less than thirty feet square, but eighteen to twenty-five prisoners were placed in each. On November 9, 1863 the *Washington Star* recorded that the arrival of more than two thousand prisoners jammed every corner thoroughly, including the yard where "they stand packed as closely as apples in a barrel."

The rooms and bedding were filthy and alive with vermin. The food, according to one finicky captive, was generally musty rice and pork or beef in a state of semi-putrefaction served in heaps on the mess-room tables without knives, forks, or plates; and, says another fastidious patron, it had an odor strongly suggesting an ancient garbage heap. The halls were constantly patrolled by sentries, the guard was changed very noisily every two hours, and the stench from the very primitive and inadequate sanitary arrangements was nauseating and noxious. The only relief from these conditions was a half-hour outdoors daily which some prisoners, including Belle, were not allowed to enjoy.[79]

One wing had rooms devoted to prisoners kept in solitary confinement, and cut off from all conversation or privilege of recreation. In a room on the second floor of this section, says John Marshall, "the well-known Belle Boyd was confined." Here the list of names of occupants scribbled on the walls vied in length and respectability with the registers of the largest and best hotels. Though the Old Capitol housed thousands of no particular prominence, it was also the repository for all notable prisoners of war and of state. Among newly arriving "Fresh Fish!" so greeted by the inmates, were such dignitaries as Governors Vance, Letcher, and Brown.[80]

When Belle requested a fire and a rocking-chair, her needs were promptly supplied. Her trunk, having been most carefully searched, was brought in shortly after this. An intelligent Negress was then assigned to attend her, and this woman soon became extremely useful in ways her jailers had not intended. To secure her services, the prisoner first had to ask the sentry at her door to summon the corporal of the guard, and the latter would call her attendant. But as the Federals believed all Negroes loyal to the Union cause the woman was never searched. So, although sentinels were posted within sight and call of each other upon every floor, Belle experienced no difficulty in maintaining communication with friends in the city and elsewhere.

As the rocking-chair and the fire failed to comfort her, Belle began listlessly to unpack her trunk. At that moment her dinner arrived. It hardly promised to be satisfactory or adequate, and, moreover, she had understood that Secretary Stanton had ordered her placed on a bread-and-water diet. However, to her surprise, she was offered then and throughout her imprisonment her choice of such items as soup, chicken, steak, Irish stew, boiled corn, potatoes, tomatoes, cantelopes, peaches, pears, and grapes.

As this was not the revolting fare about which the inmates complained loudly and long, and which they suspected consisted of army provisions condemned as unfit for human consumption, plainly someone had worked a miracle. The meals probably came from the Old Capitol sutler from whom prisoners in funds could buy supplies. But Belle, though she had money, did not pay for them. As early as August 4th, the *Washington Star* reported that a leading secessionist had visited her in jail two days earlier and provided her with luxuries. He may have arranged for her food, but she thought it was furnished by her jailers in defiance of Stanton's orders. In the light of subsequent developments, she was possibly right.

Close upon the heels of the armed guard who removed the tray after her first meal, came two official visitors. These were Superintendent Wood and Mr. Baker, chief of detectives. The latter announced formally that he desired an interview on behalf of the Secretary of War. In him and his companion, Mr. Stanton had selected to deal with his eighteen-year-old captive his two most dangerous and unscrupulous aides. Both men were skilled in the examination of enemy agents, and, although they did not ordinarily get along well together, they formed the Federal Government's most successful and merciless pair of inquisitors.

Baker was a special agent of the War Department and for the past six months had headed the National Detective Police. Later, in recognition of his important services, he was made colonel of the First District of Columbia Cavalry Regiment, and eventually a brigadier-general. It was he who, when President Lincoln was assassinated, hunted down John Wilkes Booth.[81]

Wood was understood to have served with Walker's guerillas, had long been acquainted with Secretary of War Stanton, and was believed to exercise great power over that high official. This belief was held so widely that it was commonly said in Washington that Stanton was at the head of the War Office and Wood at the head of Stanton. Strong-minded, thoroughly self-possessed, and incessantly aggressive, Wood respected no authority, military or civil, and was rarely bested in any controversy. His lack of political finesse proved no appreciable disadvantage. By 1865 he had become head of the Secret Service Division of the Treasury Department.[82]

Belle's two callers were redoubtable enough to anticipate little difficulty in her case. They probably expected a routine performance ending with an admission of guilt and satisfactory expressions of repentance and abjuration.

Seating himself at her request, Mr. Baker promptly launched into an impressive but evidently habitual exhortation. He felt sure, he said, that she was already tired of prison life, mentioned casually that he had come to secure a confession regarding her offences against the Union cause, and suggested that, as the Federal authorities had plenty of proof, she might as well admit her guilt at once.

"Sir," she replied, with a knowledge of her rights, to be expected of a lawyer's niece, "I do not understand you; and, furthermore, I have nothing to say. When you have informed me on what grounds I have been arrested, and given me a copy of the charges preferred against me, I will make my statement; but I shall not now commit myself."

Unabashed by this first rebuff, Mr. Baker continued the usual procedure. He read aloud to her the oath of allegiance prisoners were customarily invited to take, waxed eloquent about the enormity of her offence, professed that the cause of the South was hopeless, and asked her to take the oath. Had she done so, she would, of course, have been released instantly. But then she would have been scorned and shunned by the South as a renegade, and forever distrusted by a Federal Government ready to charge her with treason if she ever again served the Confederacy.

As Belle struggled to find words sufficiently vigorous and yet ladylike to answer him, Mr. Baker again pressed the oath upon her. Unwisely he reminded her that the dread Secretary of War, Mr. Stanton, who had sent him, would receive a faithful report of the interview. In a tone certain to be heard well beyond the door her inquisitors had carelessly left open, she retorted boldly: "Tell Mr. Stanton from me, I hope that when I commence the oath of allegiance to the United States Government, my tongue may cleave to the roof of my mouth, and that if I ever sign one line that will show to the world that I owe the United States Government the slightest allegiance, I hope my arm may fall paralyzed by my side."

Mr. Baker patiently recorded this outburst in a notebook, and then, realizing that he had failed to subdue this young rebel, declared angrily: "Well, if this is your resolution, you'll have to lay here and die; and serve you right."

But the thoroughly aroused Belle was now past all fear of restraint and punishment. Warming to her theme, and in a raised voice addressed more to the world at large than to her harassed tormentor, she cried out: "If it is a crime to love the South, its cause, and its President, then I am a criminal. I am in your power; do with me as you please. But I fear you not. I would rather lie down in this prison and die, than leave it owing allegiance to such a government as yours. Now leave the room, for so thoroughly am I disgusted with your conduct towards me that I cannot endure your presence longer."

To her great surprise, she was answered by loud calls of "Bravo! Bravo!" But these hearty explosions of approval were not uttered by the stunned Mr. Baker and Mr. Wood. They came from outside the open door, where delighted Confederate officers and English prisoners crowded about their own doors and hailed her outspoken denunciation of the Federal Government and its overtures with an enthusiastically responsive outburst.

At this point, Superintendent Wood, who at the moment seemed to hold Mr. Baker in less esteem than usual, decided to intervene. Turning to his frustrated companion, he said curtly: "Come, we had better go. The lady is tired." And he prevailed upon him to leave.

What did the flouted Baker now think of the prisoner? His report to Stanton is not available, but he mentions her significantly in his history of the Secret Service. Here, in his description of the Lincoln assassination conspiracy, he assessed the qualities of Mrs. Surratt, who was hanged, by quoting a distinguished correspondent of a New York paper:

> "Treason never found a better agent than Mrs. Surratt. She was a large, masculine, self-possessed female, mistress of her house, and as lithe a rebel as Belle Boyd or Mrs. Greenbrough.* She had not the flippancy and menace of the first, nor the social power of the second, but the rebellion has found no fitter agent."[83]

As to Wood, he was clearly delighted by Belle's performance. "She was," he said, "a good talker, very persuasive, and the most persistent and enthusiastic rebel who ever came under my charge." He noted that while she received large sums of money from her father she spent these freely for the comfort of her fellow-prisoners. And he did not overlook that "her figure was perfect" and that the flippant and dangerous rebel was "a splendid specimen of feminine health and vigor."[84]

As a matter of fact, the tough-fibered Superintendent was as much Belle's captive as he was her jailer. Though Stanton headed the War Department and Wood was said to govern Stanton, the "rebel Joan of Arc," as the *Philadelphia North American* termed her, was never very firmly under the thumb of either.

Wood, contradictory and yet likeable, was a Virginian, pledged to the North, with a weakness for Southerners. Among the more turbulent of his charges, he quickly recognized kindred spirits. In protecting them against ill-treatment by higher authority, he keenly enjoyed the added satisfaction of ignoring the express orders of his superiors and particularly of Secretary of War Stanton.

Among the women prisoners in the Old Capitol, he had a particular liking for Belle Boyd and Mrs. Greenhow. Mrs. Greenhow clashed with him often in tilts that both greatly enjoyed, and in her memoirs gave him in oblique words a respect utterly at variance with her usual disdain for all men. The more forthright Belle wrote of him that he was prone to be proud of his plebeian extraction, and added, with understandable assurance: "I can safely aver that beneath his rough exterior there beats a warm and generous heart."

She had many reasons to think and say so, and one may well have been that her jailer was perversely defying Stanton's orders regarding

*Greenhow.

her food. The record is certainly clear that he defied Stanton as to solitary confinement and other matters, and the only question is how much he was actuated by regard for the lady and how much by contempt for his chief.

The extent of Belle's subjugation of Mr. Wood is probably best indicated by a delightful bit of gossip in the reminiscences of General W. E. Doster who, as a youthful major, was Provost-Marshal of the District of Columbia in 1862. He relates that when Belle was released from the Old Capitol and sent South, Secretary Stanton refused to allow her to buy a wedding trousseau in Washington. But the lady and Mr. Wood again proved a match for the Secretary of War. Doster continues: "After she arrived at Richmond, however, she sent a schedule of the articles she wanted to Mr. Wood, the superintendent, who, I understood, forwarded them to her under flag of truce."[85]

Naturally the prisoners in the Old Capitol did not allow their jailers precedence in honoring Belle. Scarcely had Wood and Baker withdrawn from the inhospitable atmosphere of Room No. 6 when an impetuous fellow, enthused by the sentiments and courage of the newest inmate, hastened to pay tribute. A low, significant cough drew her attention, and as she turned toward the door something small and white fell at her feet. Picking it up, she found it was a minute nutshell basket upon which were painted miniature Confederate flags. Round about it was wrapped a small piece of paper bearing a few eloquent words of sympathy. Greatly comforted by this gift, she wrote a hasty reply to the Englishman who had sent it, and at the first opportunity tossed it to him through the open door of his room across the passage.

That night Belle found it impossible to sleep. The spontaneous expressions of sympathy she had received were greatly cherished, but her situation was too dangerous to permit lasting consolation. As the need for defiant action receded, reaction set in, and fatigue gained ground. Yet her mind dwelt tirelessly upon her predicament. Rising from her bed, she walked to the window and looked out over the quiet city. Its slumber seemed agitated and unnatural. Both her mind and body ached for the healing touch of the clear, fresh air of the cool fields beyond it.

Throughout the night she remained by the window—watching, thinking, and praying. Her room had formerly been a committee-chamber of Congress, and during her seemingly endless vigil she imagined that she heard Clay, Webster, Calhoun, and other legislative giants declaim again against the abuses and errors of their time and give powerful aid to the cause of liberty. As the first faint light of day touched her windows, exhaustion finally triumphed, and the feverish images vanished. Throwing herself upon her bed, she surrendered gratefully to deep and dreamless slumber.

CHAPTER TWELVE

Incidents of Prison Life

HEN Belle rose the next morning, she was somewhat refreshed. But again she had to face the realities of her situation. What was to happen to her? How long must she wait to know? To brood over these questions was to invite a mental collapse. Desperately she sought to occupy her mind with other things.

Shortly after nine o'clock, her attendant appeared with breakfast. A few moments later the guard outside her door was relieved. Listening attentively, she heard the new sentry receive his instructions. He was not to permit the lady to come outside her door or to talk with the men in the opposite room. If she requested anything, the corporal of the guard must be summoned. Then came the emphatic parting injunction: "Now don't let these d—n rebels scare you."

After breakfast, she turned to the local papers for distraction and found accounts of her capture and distorted summaries of her career. These publications being Federal, their references to her character, motives, and exploits were far from complimentary.

Probably the most significant item about her in the local press appeared on August 4th in the *Washington Star.* This paper, edited by a close relative of the mayor of Washington, had unusual facilities for the gathering of inside information, and the article on Belle Boyd was so revealing as to cause an investigation by the War Department.

The deeply interested ladies of the Northern Capital learned from the *Star's* reporter that when seen at the Old Capitol, two days earlier, Belle was wearing a plain frock, low in the neck, and her arms were bare. Though "romancers" had described "this notorious female spy" as beautiful and educated, it now seemed, said the paper, that she was merely a brusque, talkative woman, perhaps twenty-five years of age, with keen, courageous grey eyes. Her teeth were prominent, too, and she was disappointingly meager in person.

Washington also read that in Martinsburg Belle had been steadily disliked by "the proper people," had been groaned at there the week before, and was considered in her native village to be, if not a village courtesan, at least something not far removed from that low station.

"Being insanely devoted to the rebel cause," this unsavory person had decided to become a spy. She went riding with young officers, was said to have been "oddly associated" with a Union general, about whose head she boasted she had once wrapped a rebel flag, and in various ways had acquired a regular budget of intelligence of Federal plans for the Southern forces.

The *Star* asserted that she had admitted in prison that she had informed Jackson of the Union situation at Front Royal, and it claimed that her admissions would convict her as a spy. It added that a leading secessionist of Washington had already visited her in jail and given her luxuries. In fact, several gentlemen had waited upon her. She had talked with them freely, saying she intended to be paroled. Jackson, it appeared, was her special idol, and she expressed romantic desires to occupy his tent and share his dangers.

Having shown clearly that Belle was sordid, unprepossessing, and none too bright, the *Star's* writer allowed patriotic exasperation and exaggeration to be tempered suddenly by instinctive admiration. He concluded lamely: "She takes her arrest as a matter of course; and is smart, plucky and absurd as ever."

The War Department's reaction to this article was violent. The prisoner had been ordered kept in solitary confinement. Who had dared to violate that order, and why? The Department fretted and fumed over these questions for a day or two, and then proceeded to get them answered.

Meanwhile Belle was becoming more closely acquainted with her fellow-prisoners. On their way to their half hour of recreation outdoors, most of them passed by her door. Soon her identity became generally known and she recognized several old friends and acquaintances formerly in the Confederate Army in Virginia. Late one evening, two new arrivals were placed in the adjoining room and, learning that their friend, Belle Boyd, was their neighbor, lost no time in communicating with her.

At about eleven o'clock, as she sat reading her Bible, a sharp knock on the wall to her right brought her attention back to earthly matters. There followed the rasping sound of a busy knife scooping out plaster. When the point of a long blade pierced the wall, she sprang up and went to work with a will on her side to enlarge the hole. Soon it was big enough to afford passage to tightly rolled notes no bigger around than a man's fore-finger. The clandestine correspondence begun in this way proved to be a source of much pleasure to both sides and helped while away many a tedious hour.

In the room just above hers, where the aggressive Mrs. Greenhow had been lodged, were some gentlemen of Fredericksburg. Loosening a plank in the floor, they also entered into correspondence with her. As to the rooms across the hall, there were no vulnerable walls to pierce. But small notes wrapped securely around marbles were rolled deftly from one room to another behind the backs of sentries. This particular pastime had the added merit of reducing the guards to a highly nervous condition of constantly whirling and unsuccessful watchfulness.

On August 6th the War Department was upset further by another indication of continued public interest in its prisoner. On that day a monster war meeting had been held in front of the Capitol at which President Lincoln and other high officials had spoken. At the height of the ceremonies, a woman had been arrested, the *Star* reported on the 7th, for speaking and acting in a manner annoying to loyal persons. Questioned by the authorities, the woman admitted she had been born in Richmond and that her people were there. Interrogated about Belle Boyd, she said she was anxious to see her. Her husband had already seen Belle and wondered why she hadn't been arrested earlier. She herself had passed frequently by the prison, but she denied that she had ever waved her handkerchief. However, on one occasion when ordered to move on she had replied that if they did arrest her she would not care. She had friends in the prison and would then have a chance to see them.

On the day the *Star* published this intriguing item, the War Department began its investigation. In a letter authorized by Secretary Stanton, Assistant Secretary of War Watson wrote the District Military Commandant, General Wadsworth, that the *Star's* article on the 4th, if true, showed that the Secretary of War's order to keep "the rebel prisoner and spy, Belle Boyd" in close custody had been violated. Mr. Watson then set forth that a demand had been made on the editor for the names of those alleged to have had access to her and the authority giving them permission to see her. No answer had been received, however, because, "as this Department is just informed, the editor is absent from the city."

Wisely deciding that the editor would be in no hurry to return to reply to these pointed questions, the Assistant Secretary of War gave the Military Commandant the following order:

> "You are directed immediately to cause a strict investigation to be made on the following points, viz:
>
> 1. Whether the order committing Belle Boyd to close custody has been violated?
>
> 2. When and by whom and under what authority every such violation was committed?
>
> You will report to this Department the result of the investigation."[86]

With promptness that stressed the seriousness of the matter, General Wadsworth made a detailed report the same day. He informed Mr. Watson that his aide, Major Meneely, had visited the prison on the 2nd with Mr. Van Buskirk of the Post Office Department. Both men saw and conversed with Belle Boyd. The order to commit her to close custody had not been communicated to General Wadsworth. Mr. Wood had received it though and he did not object to the gentlemen seeing Miss Boyd. In fact, Major Meneely had understood Mr. Wood to say that a Dr. Hale had also seen the prisoner. General Wadsworth ended his report by stating he would try to learn whether Mr. Van Buskirk had given the *Star* its information.[86]

General Wadsworth's report reveals War Department inefficiency in failing to communicate to the Military Commandant its order to keep the prisoner in close custody. Further, it suggests that the Washington secessionist who visited Belle in the Old Capitol may have been Dr. Hale. It also shows Mr. Wood disregarding an important order of the Secretary of War, known to him. And it emphasizes how much Belle Boyd withheld in writing her book. She made no indiscreet reference to Dr. Hale or other visitors on this occasion, no statement that Mr. Wood allowed her to see them, and no revelation that the Superintendent later sent her a wedding trousseau by flag of truce. Instead, she wrote warily: "I can safely aver * * * there beats a warm and generous heart."

Soon after this Major Doster, the youthful Provost-Marshal of Washington, became interested in this disturbing prisoner. Writing about her more than half century later, the sedate and distinguished general's pulse quickened again pleasantly as he reminisced.

The first time he called upon Belle, the prisoner was reading *Harper's* and eating peaches. She was plainly a lively, spirited young lady, full of caprices, and a genuine Rebel. Her dashing manner and air of recklessness made her interesting, but her features he thought too irregular to be pretty. She had become noted because of the information she had given Jackson and the influence she had acquired through coquetry over Union officers under General Banks.

Major Doster never saw the charges against the prisoner. Significantly he explains that this was because she was arrested by order of the Secretary of War. However, Mr. Cridge, the detective who had arrested her, told him she had been a Confederate scout riding between the Northern and the Southern lines, and equally intimate at headquarters on each side.

The only woman prisoner then in Washington, she was the center of much attention, and evidently enjoyed it. Flippantly, she remarked to Major Doster that she could afford to stay in prison if Stanton could afford to keep her. There was so much company and so little to do, she said, and, besides, she could brush up on literature and get her wedding outfit ready. But the outdoors and horseback riding were constitutional necessities for her, and as time went on her cheerful defiance waned. She languished for want of physical activity and begged leave to walk outdoors accompanied by an officer. This request, Doster says, was referred to Secretary Stanton and denied. The impudent Mr. Wood, however, promptly overruled the Secretary.

Though she became gradually more subdued, the Provost Marshal relates that she was never ill-humored. Courageously enduring her tedious and companionless imprisonment, she jested with the prison surgeon and asked him often when he intended to give her the pleasant medicine he had wittily prescribed for her, and which was—freedom. She openly admitted being a rebel to the backbone, and constantly expressed her willingness to help the Southern cause to the limit of her ability.

Yet, when about to be sent to Richmond, she was, perversely, not quite ready to go. Her fiancé, a Confederate officer, was also a prisoner in the Old Capitol and, like her, scheduled for return South. So, with the possibility of an early wedding in the offing, Belle expressed a desire to buy her trousseau in the Northern Capital before leaving. It was then, states Major Doster, that the unromantic Secretary of War refused her plea, and that the gallant Mr. Wood once more rushed to her assistance.[87]

At the beginning of her imprisonment, sitting at her open door to observe the varied activities going on beyond was Belle's main occupation. But it was a privilege she soon forfeited. About the fourth morning after her arrival, as the prisoners filed downstairs to breakfast, a little Frenchman managed to hand her, unobserved, a half length picture of Jefferson Davis. It was not in her nature to conceal this symbol of her allegiance. Jubilantly she hung it over her mantelpiece with the provocative inscription: "Three cheers for Jeff Davis and the Southern Confederacy!"

Lieutenant Holmes, a prison official better known as "Bullhead," caught sight of the picture, and rushed into her room like a madman. Tearing the picture down to the accompaniment of violent oaths, he declared: "For this, you shall be locked in." Thereupon he closed the door, turned the key in the lock, and departed.

This severe punishment was enforced for several weeks. In the sultry summer heat, the air in her room became so oppressive and noxious that she grew ill and believed she might die. At last, Mr. Wood paid her a visit. Noting her conditiion, he ordered her door to be kept open again. Soon after, ignoring Mr. Stanton's refusal of permission, he granted her the indulgence of a half-hour walk daily in the prison yard.

For part of the period she was locked in, Belle was nevertheless in touch with all the inmates. She had established contact with the room on her left, and as it joined with many others it became a channel through which intelligence was freely transmitted to all parts of the prison. Much of this information was more recent and reliable than the rumors circulating in Washington, for Belle's two neighbors on the left were a Major Morse of General Ewell's staff and Major Norman R. Fitzhugh, adjutant-general of Jeb Stuart.[88] Major Fitzhugh, with important Confederate plans in his possession, had been captured on August 17th near Louisa Court House by the First Michigan Cavalry.

CHAPTER THIRTEEN

Friendship, Tumult, Romance

S Belle's strength gradually left her, she found it increasingly difficult to stand the hardships of prison life. Though she was the only woman held in the Old Capitol, there was one prisoner in a worse situation. Her sensitive heart overflowed with sorrow and pity for him as she watched from her doorway the "old gentleman almost bent double with age. His long, white hair hung down to his shoulders, whilst his beard, gray with the touch of old Father Time's fingers, reached nearly to his waist."

Who was this enfeebled ancient, and what awful crime was laid to his account? In answer to her circulated query the answer came whispered back through the prison walls that he was a Mr. Mahony, editor of a paper in Dubuque, Iowa, and that his offence was upholding the Constitution.

However, D. A. Mahony was far more vigorous, in spirit, at least, than his sympathetic feminine observer suspected. In his paper, the *Dubuque Herald*, he had fearlessly denounced certain Federal policies. The not unexpected result had been his seizure at home without observance of due process of law and without consideration for his age or welfare. Hurried away like the victim of kidnappers fearing pursuit and apprehension by aroused neighbors, he had been removed to Washington and flung into the Old Capitol. His arrival there on August 21st was announced the next day by the omniscient *Star* with the comment that he was "charged with discouraging enlistments and aiding the rebels." Undeterred by his fate, his numerous and militant supporters at home continued his campaign. Shortly they notified him in the Old Capitol that he had been nominated for Congress in the Third Congressional District of Iowa.

Today, outside of the modern *Telegraph-Herald* building in Dubuque, the name and career of this courageous spirit are barely remembered. But in significant literature he has left an imperishable memorial. This is the scathing indictment of the War Department's crusade against civilians in his book *The Prisoner of State* which he had the temerity to publish in mid-war in 1863, and the distribution of which is said to have been forbidden by express order of Secretary of War Stanton.[89] In this volume the grateful author laid aside his political sword of vengeance long enough to devote many eloquently respectful pages to the young girl from whose heart when she first saw him in the Old Capitol welled up the cry, "Poor old man! What an unfit place for you!"

It was on the night of the 21st, his first in the jail, that Mahony, haunted by thoughts of home, was startled to hear a woman's voice singing, "Maryland, My Maryland!" What was a woman doing in the Old Capitol? Was she a prisoner? It was the first time he had heard this Southern song. Its words, so stirring to Southern hearts, were so warmly expressed by the singer that even the sensibilities of those not in sympathy with the cause of the South could not fail to be profoundly touched. No one indeed could listen unmoved to this lady putting her whole soul into sentiments of devotion to the South and defiance to the North. The pathos of her voice, her forlorn condition, and her melancholy manner when singing, affected all hearers with compassion, and on this and other occasions, wrote Mahony, aroused an interest which came near "bringing about a conflict between the prisoners and the guards."

Despite a natural concern with their own troubles, the Dubuque editor and some of his roommates immediately manifested a lively interest in the lady. On inquiry, they learned she was Belle Boyd. Several had never heard of her, and all wished to know more. "Who was she, where was she from, and what did she do?"

The variety of available information was bewildering for legend was already in the making, and nowhere more industriously than in the Old Capitol. The most generally acceptable story included a weird and distorted mixture of the items *Leslie's Illustrated Newspaper* had just printed about the three redoubtable "feminine desperados" of the South—Belle Boyd, Mrs. Faulkner, and Belle Jamieson.

The inquirers were told by Confederate prisoners, who proudly professed to know her family, that Belle Boyd was the daughter of a respectable Presbyterian clergyman of Martinsburg, and the sister of Mrs. Faulkner whose husband was the late Minister to France.

When General Banks was in the Valley, the tale continued, Belle had invited him and other Union officers to a ball. She then rode at night some sixty miles to "Stonewall" Jackson, informed him of her action, and gave him details of the strength and disposition of the Federal forces. She rode back immediately and, having no equal, man or woman, as an equestrian, completed one hundred and twenty miles in twenty-four hours.

On the night of the ball—according to the story—Bell contrived so successfully to divert General Banks' attention from military affairs that he even permitted her to drape the folds of a large and elegant secesh flag over him. Meanwhile, "Stonewall" had marched up and, knowing from Belle the weak points of the Federals, attacked Banks' forces so boldly that panic ensued and resulted in an overwhelming defeat which left the Valley in the hands of the Southerners.

After this great exploit, the description of which is a fantastically embroidered but still recognizable blending of Belle's night ride to Ashby and her great service to Jackson at Front Royal, she, according to the inspired informants of Mr. Mahony, went to Washington. Here, with entrée to the best society, she did not spend her time uselessly. She decided to sketch the Federal fortifications across the Potomac, procured a pass to cross the long bridge and, unfortunately, being less cautious than zealous, was detected making a sketch of a fort, and was arrested. Following this incident, which obviously credits Belle Boyd with some of the activities of Belle Jamieson in Florida, Belle was promptly sent to the Old Capitol.

Mr. Mahony and his comrades did not rely for long on others for information about the young woman whose voice had charmed and uplifted them. Their room, No. 10, was directly over hers, and Mr. Mahony and a Mr. Sheward, rummaging in a closet, quickly uncovered the opening in the floor their predecessors had used, and saw Belle's light below. Soon they were exchanging mail regularly with her by means of lowered strings, and the Iowan journalist wrote later that this prison correspondence would make a most interesting chapter of Old Capitol history. "But," he added, "the time for this is not yet."

It is also Mr. Mahony who reveals that the young girl an Associated Press correspondent termed an accomplished prostitute and the *Washington Star* called a village courtesan impressed her fellow-prisoners very differently indeed. Whenever Belle appeared in the prison yard the Confederate prisoners paid her every mark of respect their miserable situation permitted. Most of them doffed their caps as she neared them, and she, with natural grace and dignity a queen would have envied, extended her hand to them as she passed along. When she left, prisoners and jailers alike felt deeply that they were parting from someone for whom they had high personal regard. So great and impelling was this sentiment that every inmate sought to secure some token of remembrance from her, and nearly every one bestowed upon her in return such mark of esteem or affection as his means allowed. All rejoiced whole-heartedly when she was released. "There was not a gentleman in the Old Capitol whose emotions did not overcome him as he saw her leave the place for home."[89]

According to Miss Leech in *Reveille in Washington*,[90] Belle was fond of shouting insults at passing Federal soldiers. But the Dubuque editor in pointing out that she was the target for coarse jests and foul talk by such soldiers makes it clear that there was nothing vulgar in the effective taunts and rejoinders with which she defied them. For instance, after the decisive Northern defeat at the second battle of Manassas, she called out gleefully to the foot-sore soldiers coming back to the Capital, "How long did it take you to come from Bull Run?" When the infuriated men shouted back: "Hush up, you d—n b—h, or I'll shoot you!" she cried back scornfully: "Shoot me? Go meet men, you cowards!" Whenever answering comments provoked or outraged her too much, she stuck her secesh flag through the bars and, leaving it there, retired from the window and closed her ears to further imprecations.

That one very sensitive individual might react strongly to the presence of any woman in so fearful a place as the Old Capitol is understandable. Mr. Mahony's sincere tribute to Belle Boyd might therefore be minimized as simply the graceful and facile exaggeration of a particularly impressionable newspaperman. Fortunately, there is available surprising confirmation of the homage paid her in the even more emotional testimony of another prisoner.

It was, says James J. Williamson, some time in February, 1863, more than five months after Belle had been released, that he and several other prisoners were singing "Maryland, My Maryland!" As they finished, another prisoner, Gus Williams, walked over to them and said approvingly: "You boys sing that well, but I've heard 'My Maryland!' sung here in the Old Building in a way that would make you feel like jumping out of the window and swimming across the Potomac."

Who had sung like that, they asked him. The answer made by rustic Gus in artless phrases that echoed emphatically Mr. Mahony's more polished words has been preserved in the recollections of prison life in the Old Capitol which James Williamson wrote almost fifty years later:[91]

> " 'When Belle Boyd was here,' said Gus, 'I was on the same floor. She would sing that song as if her very soul was in every word she uttered. It used to bring a lump up in my throat every

time I heard it. It seemed like my heart was ready to jump out—as if I could put my finger down and touch it. I've seen men, when she was singing, walk off to one side and pull out their handkerchiefs and wipe their eyes for fear someone would see them doing the baby act.

" 'She left soon after I came in. I was glad to know that she was released, but we all missed her. Even some of the Yankees, although they would not show it while she was here; but when she was sent away they missed her sweet singing—Rebel songs though they were. One of them told me it made him feel sad to hear her sing.' "

To Gus and his comrades, Belle was no accomplished prostitute—no village courtesan. Nor was she just a pleasant, brave and patriotic girl of the Southland. By the grace of her womanhood and her warm-hearted affection for them, she was to these ragged, filthy, poorly-nourished, sickly, vermin-infested countrymen of hers all of the beloved women they had left at home. In her smile, her glance, and her voice, in the touch of her hand, in her comradeship, they sought in the agony of their captivity and found miraculously the cherished qualities of every remembered daughter, sweetheart, mother, and wife. For unless Gus Williams lied, this is all he meant when he said:

" 'And on Sundays, when there was preaching down in the yard, she would be allowed to come down and sit near the preacher. If you could only have seen how the fellows would try to get near her as she passed. And if she gave them a look or a smile, it did them more good than the preaching. You wouldn't hear a cuss word from any of them for a week, even if one of the guards would swear at them or threaten them.' "

But not all the esteem and affection surrounding her could protect Belle fully from many consequences of captivity. On one unhappy occasion, an involuntary breach of the rule prohibiting communication between prisoners brought punishment upon a relative. This happened when, walking up and down the seven-by-nine-feet area available to her outdoors, she suddenly recognized among the men nearby her cousin, John Stephenson, a young officer who served with Mosby, and probably in the First Virginia Cavalry. Impulsively, she rushed to him to exchange a few words of greeting. But the quickly advanced bayonet of a guard came between them. She was sent back to her room immediately, and her cousin John was at once removed to the guard-house.

A more serious occurrence took place shortly after this. Having a loaf of sugar she wished to present to officers across the passage, she asked the sentry's permission to pass it over. As he said gruffly, "I have no objection," she thought this sufficient. But as she placed the sugar in an officer's hand, the sentry, without warning, struck her left hand so violently with the butt-end of his musket that her thumb was broken. The attack was so unexpected and the pain so great that she burst into tears.

When her feelings were again under control, she demanded that the sentry summon the corporal of the guard. He refused, and she courageously stepped forward to exercise this right personally. The enraged sentry thereupon lowered his musket and presented his bayonet at her menacingly. She, says Mr. Mahony in his flowery style, was brave and unterrified, and dared the craven-hearted fellow to carry out his threat. As she advanced, the guard's bayonet blade pinned her to the wall by her dress and inflicted a flesh wound on her arm.

Fortunately, before the maddened soldier could do her more serious injury, the corporal of the guard, attracted by the commotion, came rushing upstairs to learn its cause. The sentry was immediately taken off post. What punishment, if any, was given him Belle never learned. She suspected it was no more than brief confinement in the guard-house. It is Mr. Mahony who reveals what might easily have occurred. The temper of the Confederate prisoners witnessing this scene was such that had the guard hurt Belle badly, "he would have been torn in pieces before it could be known to the prison authorities what had happened."

As Gus Williams said, the prison guards may have missed Belle's sweet singing when she left, but one part of her performance, which Mr. Mahony records, it is unlikely they ever became unduly enthusiastic about, and it may be that the guard who attacked her may have found it particularly offensive. Often, when singing "Maryland, My Maryland!" she would stress the words, "Huzza! she spurns the Northern scum!" Invariably, the guard before her door, knowing himself to be the only Northerner in view, would take personal offence and harshly tell her to hush. Flaring up, she would reply defiantly, "I shan't do it!" Then, repeating the objectionable words: she would act them out by seizing a broom and vigorously sweeping the floor behind the walking guard. The sheer bravado of this dramatic gesture never failed to reinvigorate and inspire even the most dejected Confederate prisoner.[89]

Secret service work taught Belle to be close-mouthed about official matters. As her reticence often extended to her private affairs, it is not surprising that she wrote nothing about her prison romance.

Who was the Confederate officer to whom she became affianced in the Old Capitol? Neither General Doster nor Superintendent Wood gives his name. But Editor Mahony was well informed. The old gentleman from Dubuque confides that Belle's fiancé was Lieutenant McVay, a handsome, dashing, and gentlemanly individual in the room across the passage from her, and that many envied him his good fortune.

It was said of McVay that he had been left for dead on a field of battle, was subsequently revived, and taken prisoner to the Old Capitol. That he was highly enterprising is evident from his successful courtship of a young woman confined alone in her room, locked in during most of her stay, and forbidden to communicate with other prisoners. There was romance in his courting, but it was far from private or intimate. It was pathetic love-making restricted exclusively to ardent notes persistently rolled to and fro on marbles under the eyes of their comrades and behind the backs of their guards.

When Robert W. Chambers' stirring story of a Union woman spy, *Special Messenger*, first appeared as a magazine serial about thirty-five years ago there were so many who professed to believe that it was a record of Belle Boyd's career that the famous author made their obsession the subject of a special preface when the tale appeared in book form. He wrote, not too cryptically: "In the personality and exploits of the 'Special Messenger,' the author has been assured that a celebrated historical character is recognizable—Miss Boyd, the famous Confederate scout and spy. It is not uncommon that the readers of a book know more about that book than the author. R. W. C."[92]

Why any of Mr. Chambers' readers should have confused his heroine, a Union spy, with Belle Boyd, a Confederate agent, is not readily apparent. To be sure, one episode takes place in the mountains of West Virginia and the heroine is reported to have been educated in an exclusive Southern school. But these two items are hardly adequate justification.

However, there is in Mr. Chambers' story a soldier left for dead on a field of battle, who is subsequently revived, and is loved by the woman spy. So, despite Mr. Chambers' preface and the fact that nothing else in the book even remotely resembles Belle Boyd's adventures, it is still being said that the *Special Messenger* is a book of stories about Belle Boyd. Meanwhile, with equal obstinacy, it is being overlooked that a quarter of a century later, Mr. Chambers made Belle a fascinating and authentic character under her own name in his great success, *Secret Service Operator 13*.[93]

While Belle actually got her trousseau, she did not marry Lieutenant McVay, and there is nothing to indicate what happened to him and their romance. However, Mrs. John Burns Earle of "Mount Zion" at Milldale, Virginia, recalls having seen a letter written in 1862 by Susan Glenn, Belle's aunt by marriage, stating that Belle was about to marry a Confederate soldier.

CHAPTER FOURTEEN

Over the Lines by Flag of Truce

LATE in the evening of August 28th, the Old Capitol became a bedlam. The cause of the uproar was an announcement by Mr. Wood. Belle, reading by her open door, first heard it when the excited superintendent reached her floor. Neither she nor the other prisoners could believe their ears when he roared out: "All you rebels get ready! You are going to Dixie tomorrow, and Miss Belle is going with you." There was a moment of incredulous silence, and then all the prisoners gave three hearty cheers, while Belle cried out with joy. Thereafter pandemonium prevailed throughout the night.

At last the Federal and Confederate Governments had completed arrangements for the formal exchange of prisoners, and this step at the Old Capitol was the first result. The next day General Wadsworth, commandant of the district, wrote General Dix at Fort Monroe that he had been directed to forward to him all prisoners of war at the Old Capitol. He added:

> "I forward likewise Miss Belle Boyd, a young lady arrested on suspicion of having communicated with the enemy. I have agreed that she shall be placed over the lines by the first flag of truce, which is in accordance with her wishes. No specific charge or information have been lodged against her."[94]

On the same day Special Orders, No. 175, of the District, provided that the prisoners were to be taken forthwith via the transport *Juniata* to Fortress Monroe by a detail of one officer and twenty men. It also directed that "Miss Belle Boyd" was to be turned over to General Dix to be sent through the lines to the South.[94]

In accordance with this order, the prisoners, to the number of about two hundred, were lined up in the Old Capitol courtyard, taken into the street, and formed into line. A carriage was furnished for Belle and she stepped into it with Major Fitzhugh who had been detailed to stay with her. There was a dense throng outside the prison, and as the carriage drove off the Confederate prisoners cheered and the street resounded with applause, the crowd joining in joyfully.

On August 30th the *Washington Star* published some exceedingly shrewish comments on the turbulent scenes that had occurred at the prison gates when the prisoners left. It revealed that "a few" persons had gathered there, and that most of them, unblushingly and without disguise, made a full display of Secesh sympathies. It described many very carefully and warned them to take a hint from the fact that they had been observed.

These Secesh sympathizers included, "a female arrayed in black silk, the one arrayed in spotted delaine, * * * the one arrayed in light colored bombazine, and also the gentleman carrying the baskets." The latter, the paper remarked with malicious significance, was young and seemed quite healthy enough to stand a draft. It mentioned also an elderly lady with auburn curls whose hifaluting expressions of sympathy were absolutely sickening, a brazen woman with a child in her arms who appeared to enjoy kissing her hand to the rebels, and a rather pretty young woman, wearing a white straw bonnet with green ribbon, who drove by in a carriage to which a "gray" horse had been treasonably hitched.

The outraged *Star* further recorded bitterly that it could relate numerous other evidences of Secesh sympathy, that a small Confederate flag hung from the bars of a window drew numerous nods and smiles, and that "a man dressed like a gentleman rode by in a carriage, and deliberately waved his hat, and gave a slight cheer."

Why the Federals freed Belle is no clearer than their release of Mrs. Greenhow after she sent Beauregard information enabling him to win the first battle of Manassas. They may have felt it desirable to get rid of Belle to break her ties with Confederate sympathizers in Washington, or because she improved the morale of her fellow-prisoners too greatly. And they may have reasoned that if she were sent South she would not dare to enter the Union lines again and would therefore be harmless.

But it is unlikely that they released her without securing adequate compensating advantage. In the case of soldiers, exchanges were usually made on a basis of numerical equality. As to officers, they were often exchanged man for man on a basis of equal rank, or on terms of several of lower rank for one of higher standing. With respect to Belle, in a special class as a spy, it is possible that she was exchanged for some Union secret service agent held in the South. But the legend that on this occasion she was traded for Colonel Michael Corcoran of New York is without foundation. As the records and General Corcoran's memoirs show, he was exchanged for Colonel Hanson of Kentucky.

Belle was no ordinary prisoner. The War Department's intense interest in her makes this obvious. It began with her arrest by special agent Cridge, sent from Washington. It continued with efforts to keep her incommunicado, and the reference of her slightest requests to the Secretary of War for decision. At the time of her release, the Department's interest was still great enough to cause special provisions to be inserted about her in the orders for a general exchange.

The War Department had ample evidence on which to convict her if she had been tried. There was the letter she wrote to General Jackson which fell into the hands of General Sigel. There were the incriminating papers Cridge found in her room. There were the revelations she made to Union scout Smitley. And there was her conduct at the battle of Front Royal, not only openly admitted by her in jail but also a matter of common knowledge in the Northern Capital and in the Old Capitol, and freely discussed in the Federal press.

General Wadsworth's statement that Belle Boyd was arrested on suspicion did not mean that she was merely suspected. It meant only that she was arrested without a formal accusation having been made against her. This had made it possible, in line with the arbitrary procedure then practised by the Federal Government, to keep her in jail indefinitely without trial and without offering evidence.

As General Wadsworth also wrote, no specific charge or information had been lodged against Belle. In other words, no accusation against her had taken the form of charges under the Articles of War triable by a military court or commission, or the form of an "information" (formal accusation) presented to a non-military court and alleging commission of a criminal offence. Why General Wadsworth wrote this to General Dix was probably to provide legal clearance for her release. No prisoner could be released or exchanged against whom formal military or civil charges were pending.

Before Belle's capture, the enemy press resorted to fantastic exaggeration of her ability, achievements, and charm. When she was arrested and therefore no longer to be feared, it gave a gusty sigh of relief, and turned vengefully to equally immoderate disparagement of the allure it no longer dreaded. When, in the summer of 1862, *Leslie's Weekly* reported the glad tidings that, "Belle Boyd, the Secesh Cleopatra, is caged at last," it could not resist adding: "It appears that she has red hair and large teeth and a loud, coarse laugh." And when the *New York Herald* sent a tough-minded reporter to gaze upon her he found, as Mr. W. O. Stevens puts it, that her glamour was not working, and that she had "a freckled face, red hair, and a large mouth."[95]

General Ewell's young adjutant is not the only one who has taken exception to the minimizing of Belle's activities by stripping her imaginatively of her great personal charm. In his magnificent biographical work on Abraham Lincoln, the historian Carl Sandburg brushes such journalistic trivia aside impatiently with the explanation: "This was mere propaganda, for Belle Boyd had moderate-sized teeth and could laugh pleasantly when she chose."[96]

Mr. Sandburg was, of course, far more concerned with her achievements than with her personal appearance. How they impressed him he indicates, after outlining her career up to this point, by stating: "On the evidence she could have been legally convicted as a spy, shot at sunrise, and heard of no more, but she became one of two hundred prisoners exchanged and sent to Richmond."

Strange as was the treatment of Belle Boyd from arrest to release, her case was not unique. There is a remarkable parallel in the Federal proceedings against the noted Antonia F. later in the same year.

In his history of the Federal Secret Service, General Baker relates that Miss F. at Fairfax Court House was suspected of enemy activity. Accordingly, he sent a female detective there to investigate. This woman soon wormed herself into the confidence of the suspect and obtained confidential disclosures. The Southern girl was then arrested and taken to Washington, and on her person were found private letters from men in the rebel service together with her commission as an honorary aide-de-camp, issued by General J. E. B. Stuart in October, 1861.

Baker's report to Secretary Stanton charged that Miss F. had performed active service under her commission, had come within the Union lines as a spy, had secretly and perfidiously obtained information and treasonably communicated it to the Confederate forces. The report concluded: "I have ordered Miss F. to be placed in confinement in the Old Capitol Prison."[97]

Miss F., later identified as Miss Antonia Ford, was released several months later. Like Belle Boyd she was severely affected by her imprisonment in the Old Capitol. In his campaign memoirs, Colonel John Esten Cooke of General Stuart's staff relates that "when she was released and sent South to Richmond, where I saw her, she was as thin and white as a ghost—the mere shadow of her former self."[98]

It is possible therefore that the Federal Government, with unwarranted optimism, thought constant recollection of their sufferings in prison would deter Belle Boyd and Antonia Ford from further objectionable activity.

CHAPTER FIFTEEN

Suspect or Aide-de-Camp?

T dawn on the 30th the *Juniata* cast off and went down the Potomac. Late in the day, it dropped anchor at the mouth of the river and here the night was passed. At four o'clock the following morning, it continued on its way and arrived at Fortress Monroe that evening, where it was boarded by Lieutenant Darling of General Dix's staff.

On each side lay General McClellan's transports laden with soldiers preparing for a drive on Richmond. Inspired instead of dismayed by this sight, the happy home-farers reacted patriotically by singing Southern songs interspersed with loud cheers for "Jeff Davis." The *Juniata* got under way again and steamed up the muddy waters of the James. Later, as it rounded a bend in the stream, the house of Mr. Aikens came in view, and from a window waved the Stars and Bars. Only then, at the sight of that banner flying over Confederate soil, did Belle realize that she had been freed, and was really going home.

The ship was met at the wharf by Colonel Robert Ould, the Confederate Commissioner for exchange of prisoners, and his assistant, Mr. Watson. Both supervised the landing of the passengers. That evening Belle enjoyed the society of the Aikens' family and spent the night under their hospitable roof. The next morning, September 2nd, a Colonel Allen sent his carriage and horses from Richmond to convey her to that city.

That Robert Ould permitted Belle to enter the Southern lines is significant. It indicates that this strict Confederate Commissioner did not share the views of the biased *Associated Press* and the *Washington Star* as to her moral character.

Recently, in *Reveille in Washington*, Miss Leech has asserted, without giving a single supporting detail, that "controversies raged about her chastity."[99] The only apparent "controversies" were of a singularly odd nature. Some Northern papers smeared Belle's name as gleefully as some Southern papers characterized "Abe" Lincoln as "Ape,"—and with as little justification. Later, when Belle Boyd was in the North and was interviewed, more reputable Union publications, particularly in New England, were surprised to find her a lady in appearance and conduct and were honorable enough to say so. As the Southern press never viewed her otherwise, it engaged in no "controversies" about her.

Had Belle been even the most repentant of all errant Magdalens, Commissioner Ould would nevertheless have refused to admit her. In a letter of reproach to his Federal confrère regarding two immoral women sent through by the Federals in 1863, his words, "Sir: I send back to you two strumpets." are but the beginning of a classic of outraged morality. Continuing nobly, the Commissioner wrote of "holy feelings," stressed "the sanctity of a pure woman's character," and mourned the dishonor cast upon "the purity of a flag of truce." So irate did the high-minded Mr. Ould wax that he seems to have taken the affair as a possible reflection upon his own honor, for he said sternly, "If I did not believe you were imposed upon, I would be justified in taking this matter as a personal affront."[100]

Mr. Ould and Southerners in general undoubtedly knew how vilely the Northern press had assailed Belle's character, for the Federal newspapers were read widely in the South. But if they paid any heed to these attacks, it must have been solely to honor her for having suffered such abuse in the service of the Confederacy. The warmth of her home-coming reception permits no other inference.

Her first welcome occurred on the road to Richmond. Riding now as an honored guest, and no longer a captive, the young woman was surprised to note, as they passed close by the encampment of the Richmond Light Infantry Blues, that the famous Confederate unit was drawn up in review order. Her heart swelled with understandable pride and pleasure when the Blues presented arms as her carriage went by.

In town, she proceeded to the Ballard House where she had been told rooms were in readiness for her. That evening she was serenaded by the city band, and received such flattering greetings from everyone that the bitter recollections of her captivity began to seem unreal.

On September 3rd the local press mentioned her arrival. In reporting that on the 2nd about two hundred Confederate exchange prisoners had reached the city, the *Richmond Daily Dispatch* named but two of this great number. "Among the officers," it said, "was Maj. Norman R. Fitzhugh, A. A. Gen. of Stuart's Cavalry Division, a brave officer, who was captured a short time since." Then it added: "Miss Belle Boyd, of Winchester, who has become celebrated from the fear in which the Yankees held her, was also among those who arrived."

After about ten days at the Ballard House, she moved to Mrs. W.'s boarding house on Grace Street, where she enjoyed the company of many old and warm friends. Among celebrities then at Mrs. W.'s were General and Mrs. Joseph Johnston, General Wigfall, members of the latter's family, and many others. Here one evening, while she was engaged in desultory conversation, an officer who had been a fellow captive at the Old Capitol came up to her, bowed, and silently placed in her hands a note and a small box.

The box contained a gold watch and chatelaine, both handsomely enamelled and richly set with diamonds. Mystified by such costly gifts and doubting that they were actually intended for her, she read the accompanying note and learned that they were presented "in token of the affection and esteem" of her fellow-prisoners in the Old Capitol. For more than a month the young girl had withstood bravely and calmly all that had happened to her, but now she could not master the emotion that overwhelmed her when suddenly confronted by this unmistakable evidence of the cordial sentiments entertained for her by those whose hardships she had shared and made more endurable. So, as the varied scenes of her existence in the Old Capitol flashed through her mind, many moments passed before she could find words to express her appreciation to her comrades' spokesman and trust herself to speak them with some pretence of self-possession.

After this, Belle remained in Richmond but a short time, for her father came to take her home. Martinsburg was now held by the Southern forces, and she was most eager to be there.

Soon after the battle of Antietam on September 16th, Belle rode out to the Confederate encampment, accompanied by a friend of the family, to pay a visit to General Jackson. According to her description of this incident, the General came out as she dismounted at his tent, placed his hands gently on her head, and assured her of his pleasure at seeing her well and free once more. Then he warned her that if his forces were obliged to retire it would be necessary for her to leave Martinsburg to avoid being found within the Northern lines and imprisoned again. He added that he would give her timely notice, and that she should be prepared to act accordingly. As she left, he said fervently: "God bless you, my child." This parting phrase, the last words she was to hear from the General's lips, she treasured forever in her memory.

An aide-de-camp of "Stonewall" Jackson has also left a record of a call made on the General by Belle at about this time. This officer, later the Reverend James Power Smith, was originally a corporal of artillery, became a lieutenant and subsequently a captain. His interesting historical contribution, relating to a date shortly after September 20th, 1862, reads:

> "One day at Bunker Hill, the notable female scout, Belle Boyd, made her appearance on horseback, with the escort of a young Confederate cavalryman. She was well mounted, and quite a soldierly figure, and asked to see General Jackson. But the General was averse, and more than once refused to see the young woman, of whose loyalty he was not altogether assured. She was much disappointed and went away quite angry with the aide who had denied her admission to the general's tent. Some days after this she sent a message that if she ever caught that young man in Martinsburg she would cut his ears off."[101]

Captain Smith's factual and not unfriendly recital requires full acceptance. But it presents several problems. Were Belle and he referring to the same occasion? If so, why does her story differ so greatly? And, above all, why was "Stonewall" Jackson less than absolutely certain as to Belle Boyd's loyalty?

In view of Belle's remarkable accuracy regarding all other matters, it may be that she went to Bunker Hill twice. Why she remained silent regarding so painful an incident on one of these visits can be readily understood. After her imprisonment in the Old Capitol, she would have expected, quite naturally, a far more agreeable attitude on the part of the General. And her temperament was such that while her militant message to "Stonewall" Jackson's aide was in character, it also represented a remarkable exhibition of restraint, under the circumstances. Subsequently, when any temporary misunderstanding was cleared up, it is possible Belle decided not to mention so distressing a matter as much out of consideration for the General as for her own pride, and to set forth only the details of her satisfactory call.

That the misunderstanding was temporary is reasonably clear. To begin with, had the General possessed definite evidence that she was disloyal he would not merely have refused to see her when she, with an angry perseverence hardly suggestive of guilt, insisted on seeing him. He would have taken decisive measures to make her harmless. What Captain Smith wrote was not that the General had real cause to doubt her loyalty but only that he was not altogether assured regarding it. Had these suspicions been subsequently confirmed or even never dissipated, Belle's after career would inevitably have been greatly different. She would not have been permitted to serve the South again, and she would certainly not have become a bearer of official dispatches to England. Harry Gilmor, one of Jackson's most daring cavalry scouts, would have been among the first to know Jackson's doubts. Had they been justified in the least, Major Gilmor would not thereafter have praised Belle for her boundless devotion to the Southern cause.

What made General Jackson a little uncertain about her? She had just been released by the Federal authorities, had spent about two weeks in Richmond, and had visited the General right after coming back to her home which was then within the Southern lines. Consequently, she seems to have had no opportunity to do anything after her release which could have seemed questionable. Being held captive by the Federals for a full month was hardly an indication of anything else than unlimited devotion to the South. True, the North had been strangely lenient, and she quotes "Stonewall" as writing her a little later that if she were taken prisoner once more she "possibly might not be released so soon again." Had he then feared for a time that her inexplicable release by those who had actual proof of her services to him was a trap? Did he believe for a moment that she had secured her freedom by promising to serve the enemy and betraying him? Had he heard, too, and been made uneasy by earlier irresponsible gossip to the effect that her associations with Federal officers were not solely on behalf of the Confederacy?

Whatever General Jackson did think, Captain Smith's words convey unmistakably that the young girl he referred to deliberately as a noted scout was eager to confront the general, and that "Stonewall" was equally anxious not to see her. Their respective attitudes were surely inconsistent in that they actually reversed the usual conduct of suspected scout and mistrustful general. Moreover, there is a magnificent assurance in Belle's aggressive and irate behavior which reveals all of the fierce anger of outraged innocence and loyalty and nothing of the apprehension of one conscious of wrong-doing.

By now it had become necessary for General Jackson's command to leave the Valley in line with Confederate plans for military action to the east. His first move was to Winchester, and, as arranged, he sent word in advance to Belle and placed an army ambulance at her service for transportation.

Acting upon his advice, she went to Winchester, and while there indicates she was commissioned a captain and made an honorary aide-de-camp—honors more in accord with her services than the doubts disclosed by Captain Smith. Two months later her relatives in Tennessee were admiring the evidence of this distinction. "When she came to us she showed us a handsome 'Riding Habit'—new; made of the grey Confederate cloth and trimmed in black braid, with the rank of 'Capt.' on the collar." Proudly she confided to her kinsfolk that this uniform had been presented to her by the Confederate Army in appreciation of her heroism and loyalty.[102]

Her new rank carried with it various privileges. One was that she be accorded the respect and courtesies due officers. Another was that she might assist at reviews of troops. Subsequently, when Confederate forces were reviewed in the presence of Lord Hartingdon and Colonel Leslie, and again when General Wilcox's division was inspected by Generals Lee and Longstreet, she attended these ceremonies on horseback with the staff officers of the various commanders. But while her new status pleased her, it did not change her.

It was only a matter of weeks before stories began to accumulate about her informal conduct in her new station. A typical one, told at Culpeper Court House, has it that "Once, when riding out to review some troops near Winchester, she met a soldier, a mere boy, trudging along painfully on his bare feet." General Jackson's new aide-de-camp immediately dismounted, took off her own shoes—fine cloth gaiters laced at the side and trimmed with patent leather—and made him put them on. A companion remonstrated with her, and suggested that such shoes would not last the boy long enough to justify her sacrifice. With true maternal instinct and understanding, the young woman not yet nineteen years of age, replied gently: "Oh, if it rests his poor feet only a little while, I am repaid. He is not old enough to be away from his mother."[103]

Then Belle rode on serenely, unshod, and unconcerned by the fact that at the review her lack of footgear would attract attention and invite comment. With characteristic indifference as to what was thought of her, she left it entirely to others to remember and relate this and many similar instances of her kindness of heart.

CHAPTER SIXTEEN

To Tennessee at "Stonewall" Jackson's Suggestion

HILE the main Confederate force in the Valley remained near Winchester, Martinsburg changed hands often. When it was held by General Wade Hampton, Belle paid many visits to her home and on one occasion was almost captured. A large party had accompanied her, and upon arrival a dance had been improvised. The dancers were soon warned that the Yankees were coming, but paid no heed as similar alarms had proved groundless in the past. But in this case the cry of "Wolf!" was justified. The party broke up hurriedly and its members barely got away under cover of a heavy skirmish. It was on this fleeting visit that Belle saw her mother for the last time in almost a year.

Meanwhile the Yankees were advancing in strength by way of Culpeper Court House, and the Confederates left the Valley to take part in General Lee's counter-move. Belle, in company with the wives of officers, was well in advance of General Jackson's main body, but the servants and luggage of the ladies were somewhat to the rear in divisional ordnance wagons. The ladies themselves passed through Flint Hill and went on to Charlottesville. En route Belle stopped off at Culpeper Court House, where General Lee was assembling his forces, and spent a night at the home of Mrs. Rixey, a favorite starting point for runners of the Federal blockade.

As General Burnside had just replaced McClellan in command of the Northern forces, this was about November 10th. Snow had fallen the first week of the month and the Confederates were already suffering keenly from the early wintry weather. Insufficiently clothed and shod, they particularly lacked overcoats and many were wearing blankets wrapped around them like shawls.

When Belle reached Mrs. Rixey's in search of food and shelter, snow was falling heavily and a strong, icy wind was piling it into drifts. But inside the house all available rooms were taken, and the tired traveler knew no other place to go. She would accept anything. Was there no accommodation at all in weather like this for an unexpected but not unknown guest? Not even a spare cot in another lady's room?

A few moments later Mrs. Rixey was asking the wife of the regimental adjutant of the Thirteenth Virginia Cavalry whether she would share her room with a lady who had just arrived. Mrs. Grey—to give her the name used to conceal her identity in her reminiscences, *A Virginia Girl in the Civil War*[104]—consented immediately. Not more than twenty years old and recently married to a gentleman of Petersburg, Virginia, she herself was embarking on a strange adventure for a young woman gently reared. Within a day or two she was to run the Federal blockade for personal reasons. She had determined to see her mother in Baltimore and to smuggle through on her way back a fine Confederate uniform and accessories for her husband.

After agreeing to share her room with a stranger, Nellie Grey descended to the parlor and found it crowded with a merry party of Confederates. Many, including several high-ranking officers, belonged to the nearby army. Others, like herself, were waiting for a favorable opportunity to run the blockade.

Mrs. Rixey brought over and introduced the lady who had just come, but Nellie did not catch her name. She seemed to be nineteen, or, perhaps, twenty—rather young, Nellie thought, to be traveling alone unless one were married. And how exceedingly well dressed! Naturally, it made her the immediate center of interest to women who had gone so long without seeing, much less wearing, a new gown.

Soon everyone in the room had been attracted for the men discovered also that the fascinating newcomer was a brilliant talker with much to tell and seemed to prefer to converse with them. Her monopoly of masculine attention piqued the other ladies momentarily, but when they learned how devoted she was to the Cause they were willing to forgive her anything.

She told her listeners that she had recently returned from Washington where she had been a Federal prisoner. And she showed them a watch presented to her by her fellow-captives. She then spoke of her prison life and adventures. In later years Mrs. Grey was to regret that she could not recall the details of this narrative. But on that evening as she listened, her attention was gradually distracted by insistent thoughts of her own family.

Deserting the circle about the speaker, Nellie Grey slipped out of the room, went upstairs to bed and fell asleep before her roommate came up. It was only the following morning when they woke up face to face in the same bed that, said Nellie, "she told me she was Belle Boyd; and I knew for the first time that my bedfellow was the South's famous female spy."

If Nellie had any doubt that her companion was a Confederate agent, what happened next dissipated it effectively. Belle, preparing to bathe, produced a large bottle of cologne and casually emptied its contents into a basin. Such luxuries were then available to very few women in the South and foremost among them, naturally, were the daring ones whose task it was to run the blockade, and who alone could look forward with any confidence to renewing their supply. The youthful bride was tremendously impressed. Forty years later she revealed: "It was the first cologne I had seen for more than a year, and it was the last I saw until I ran the blockade." But it was later that day at dinner that the wife of the adjutant of the Thirteenth Virginia Cavalry really came to know and love Belle Boyd.

As Mrs. Rixey's guests dined, a servant informed Mrs. Grey that a soldier wished to see her. In the hall, she found Dick, her brother-in-law, once a noted dandy and now, arrayed in miserable and filthy misfit rags and tatters, a most abject and pitiable-looking creature.

Nellie begged Dick to dine with her but, embarrassed by his frightful appearance, he refused to enter the dining room or the parlor and tried to screen himself behind a hatrack. As they spoke, the dining room door opened and the ladies, including Belle Boyd, came out. Retreat was out of the question for Dick, and with what grace he could muster under the circumstances, he went through the introductions that followed.

The understanding women who surrounded him took in the situation at a glance and went into action. One purloined a shirt of her husband, another fetched a pair of socks, and a third contributed homespun drawers. As they rushed about to gather these sorely needed contributions, their only hesitancy was a fear of offending him and they discussed how to make him accept their offerings.

But Mrs. Grey's brother-in-law was far beyond any concern with punctilious ceremony. He was radiantly grateful for any assistance, and his strength and courage had greatly revived, thanks to the thoughtfulness of two ladies. According to Nellie: "While we held council he had been in Mrs. Rixey's and Miss Boyd's hands, and had had a good dinner."

But Belle knew, too, that he needed something more warming than just a good dinner. As Dick prepared to leave, she came running downstairs with a large, new, blanket shawl. "You must let me wrap you up, Lieutenant," she said quietly, and, putting it around his shoulders, pinned it together snugly.

He blushed, and mindful of his manners sought half-heartedly to refuse. Such a shawl was too fine, too costly for him. He could not take it. But the determined young lady paid no heed. Firmly, yet gently, she replied: "I can't let you go back to camp in this thin jacket while I have this shawl. It is serving our country, Lieutenant, while it protects her soldier from the cold." As he ventured a last protest that she might have use for it, she continued: "I may need it? No, no. I can get others where this one came from."

In the face of such pleasant and insistent feminine solicitude, Dick yielded gladly. As he started off, after taking leave of the ladies, Nell Grey rejoiced to see that his warm reception had brought some of the old care-free humor back to his eyes again. But even as the ladies watched him go, they saw him stop, take off his shoes, and carry them. The army had given him the shoes that very morning but they did not fit, and his bruised feet could no longer endure them. As he went on, those who still watched were grieved to see that his blood etched his foot-prints on the snow.

It must have been then that Mrs. Rixey or someone else told Mrs. Grey that Belle on her way to attend a review near Winchester had removed her shoes and given them to a bare-foot Confederate lad. Surely it was then too that Nellie Grey was informed of the many similar incidents that caused her to say at the turn of the century: "I have heard of many generous deeds like this done by Belle Boyd." Of course, according to the arrogant and inaccurate Dr. Ashby's verdict on Belle: "her own sex in the South repudiated her." But it may well be, in the discerning eyes of history, that Nell Grey and the other ladies at Mrs. Rixey's repudiate and even indict Tom Ashby.

That same day, Belle left Culpeper Court House. Mrs. Grey says thoughtfully: "She seemed to feel that she had the weight of the Confederacy on her shoulders, and took the afternoon train for Richmond." Possibly Belle did go to Richmond before proceeding to Charlottesville. But as trains ran to both towns from Culpeper Court House, Mrs. Grey may have erred as to her immediate destination.

Did the young traveler actually feel that she carried the weight of the Confederacy on her shoulders? Perhaps. But her gravity may have had another and more personal cause. The night before she had worn a new gown. If this dress was part of the trousseau bought and forwarded so gallantly by Mr. Wood, was she not still thinking of Lieutenant McVay? Had he been killed, or was he missing in action, and again abandoned for dead on some battlefield? Or had their romance ended because of a lovers' quarrel? Whatever the reason, there must have been a hidden sorrow in her heart regarding her engagement. And had they known its nature, the envy the ladies had felt the night before at the sight of her new dress might well have been surpassed by silent but understanding sympathy.

After a few days in Charlottesville, Belle became restless away from home and longed to rejoin her mother. She knew, of course, that the village was held by the Federals but she apparently cherished an unreasonable but understandable hope that the Union forces would overlook or not detect her return. Even the fact that her uncle, Captain James W. Glenn, had been taken prisoner recently did not seem to daunt her.

In his service with the Twelfth Virginia Cavalry, Captain Glenn had had several narrow escapes. In Warren County, Virginia, the following story of one of these adventures is still often told. Glenn and several of his friends, some of whom are said to have been Mosby rangers, were heartily enjoying a substantial dinner in the old Earle home at Milldale when someone ran in and warned, "The Yanks are coming!" By the time the enemy entered the house, not a Confederate was in sight. They had been hidden in a recess under the front stairway behind a secret panel, children in the house had been hurriedly seated at their vacated places, and the apologetic Federals found that they had intruded upon a large Southern family at dinner.

But Captain Glenn was not always so fortunate and, like his niece, eventually spent many unhappy days in a Federal prison. All that is known of his capture is this laconic statement in his own handwriting in the records of the Virginia Military Institute: "*Prisoner.* Four months in Fort Delaware, late in fall of sixty two—inside Federal lines."[105]

The last three words suggest that he was captured after entering the Federal lines on a scouting expedition or raid. In that case, his fate was well calculated to make his niece realize her return home might well end even more disastrously. Her uncle, being presumably in Confederate uniform when captured, was at least safe from the severe penalties applicable to spies which might well be invoked against her.

Eventually Belle's unrest grew so great that she wrote General Jackson and asked his opinion as to the advisability of her return home.

She indicated that she was quite prepared to run the risk of capture, but would abide by his decision. The General promptly sent the following reply:

"Headquarters, Army of Virginia.
Near Culpepper Court House.

My dear Child:

I received your letter asking my advice regarding your returning to your home, which is now in the Federal lines. I think that it is not safe; and therefore do not attempt it until it is, for you know the consequences. You would doubtless be imprisoned, and possibly might not be released so soon again. You had better go to your relatives in Tennessee, and there remain until you can go with safety. God bless you.

Truly your friend

T. J. Jackson"*

In Belle's memoirs the date of this letter is given incorrectly as January 29, 1862. As it was written after she left the Valley late in September and after she stopped off at Culpeper Court House in November, Joseph Hergesheimer, in *Swords and Roses*, is quite right in saying of the January date, "that is impossible, it must have been later." But how much later?

In an article on Belle Boyd by R. Q. Nicholson in the *Northern Virginia Daily,* Mrs. E. R. Richardson suggests that the date intended was January 29, 1863. She then points out that Jackson was not near Culpeper Court House that month.[106] But Belle arrived in Tennessee before the end of 1862 which shows that the correct date for the letter is between November 10th and the end of December. The original letter not being available, only one clue remains. When did Jackson reach Culpeper Court House?

In General Longstreet's account of the battle of Fredericksburg, he states that on November 5th Lee's headquarters were at Culpeper Court House. Lee's Army of Northern Virginia consisted of two corps: the First Corps, under Longstreet, at the Court House, and the Second Corps, commanded by Jackson, still at Winchester. General Longstreet adds that in the latter part of November General Jackson was ordered down to Fredericksburg.[107] And the route "Stonewall" followed is carefully given by one of his staff officers.

Major Harry Douglas writes that Jackson left Winchester the last

*See pp. 211-12, for discussion of this letter.

week in November and made long and rapid marches via Strasburg and Woodstock to New Market, then went east over the Massanutten Mountain and the Shenandoah River to Luray Valley. His forces next crossed the Blue Ridge at Fisher's Gap, and continued by way of Madison Court House and Orange Court House, arriving in the vicinity of Guinea Station and Fredericksburg not only in time for the battle which occurred on December 13th, but with some days to spare.[108]

What is significant is that at Madison Court House General Jackson was no more than fifteen miles from Culpeper Court House and was therefore, as the heading of his letter reads, "near Culpepper Court House." That Jackson got even much closer is quite likely. His letter to Belle Boyd was not addressed from his headquarters but from Army headquarters, and Lee, the Army commander, had headquarters at Culpeper Court House while Stuart was located nearby. Presumably Jackson, while proceeding to his station east of Lee's center, went to report to his superior or to see General Stuart. Whether he did or merely went through Madison Court House, the letter was evidently written at the end of November 1862 and probably on the 29th.

When Belle did get the letter, she spent no more time thinking of returning to Martinsburg. She headed South, and though she doubtless did so reluctantly she learned in a few months that she had received sound advice. This happened when the General's prophecy that imprisonment was certain to follow her discovery within Federal lines came to pass.

CHAPTER SEVENTEEN

Belle's Reception by the South

ELLE reached Tennessee about the end of December, 1862. Here she was warmly welcomed by numerous hospitable descendants and connections of her great uncle and great aunt, John and Isabella Boyd, who had moved to Tennessee from Virginia more than half a century earlier. And in Knoxville lived Belle's first cousin, Samuel B. Boyd, who had left Martinsburg when Belle was seven years old and had married one of their Tennessee cousins, Isabella Reed Boyd. It was in Samuel's Knoxville home that his and Belle's grandmother, Maria Stephenson Boyd, had died only four years earlier while on a visit from Martinsburg.

So for six weeks or more Belle visited numerous kinsfolk with whom her family had maintained intimate contact through travel and correspondence. But as there were no young persons of her age among them, she became restless and even discontented and wanted to be "on the go" once more. It was then that the widow of her relative, Judge Samuel B. Boyd, a former mayor of Knoxville[109], prevailed upon Belle to spend the winter and spring in her home. Mrs. Boyd had a lively family of boys and girls, and they lived in the old Blount Mansion, one of the showplaces of the town and the former residence of Governor William Blount.[110]

It was on February 12th, 1863, that Belle's stay at the Blount Mansion began. News that "the rebel spy" was with her cousins spread through Knoxville quickly and on the following evening a large and enthusiastic assemblage gathered before the Boyd home to see and serenade her. After several airs had been played, the crowd clamored for her to come out on the balcony. Reluctant to make a public appearance, Belle asked General "J." to thank the gathering for her. But they insisted on seeing her, so she stepped out, said a few words, and was vastly relieved when this ordeal was over.

This is merely Belle's account of what happened. But the article that appeared the next day on the front page of the *Daily Register* makes it possible to determine beyond question whether Belle recorded events factually or imaginatively.

> "This fair and fearless Virginia heroine, whose daring defense of her father's house, when Charlestown,* Va. was first invaded by the Yankees, and whose invaluable services in conveying information to our lines in spite of the espionage of the craven foe, have won for her from the Northern press the title of the most courageous and dangerous of rebel female spies, is now sojourning in this city at the residence of her cousin, Samuel B. Boyd, Esq. She was serenaded last night by the Florida Brass Band, and on being loudly called for by the crowd appeared at the window and made the following laconic and graceful response:
>
> 'Gentlemen, like General Johnston, I can fight, but cannot make speeches. You have my heartfelt thanks for your compliment.' "

In her memoirs, the officer who attempted to speak in her place to the citizens of Knoxville is referred to only as "General J." But the *Register's* quotation of her remarks suggests strongly that he was General Joseph E. Johnston and that her comment on him related to his lack of success in addressing the crowd in her stead. This possibility is strengthened by the fact that this distinguished Confederate soldier was then ranking commander of the Southern forces in Tennessee and was in the State at the time by order of the War Department to investigate the military fitness of General Bragg. He had probably met the Virginia heroine before as she records he was at Mrs. W.'s boarding house in Richmond when she stopped there five months earlier after her release from the Old Capitol Prison.

"Aunt Susan" Boyd and her four children knew and loved Cousins Ben and Mary of Martinsburg, and so exerted themselves wholeheartedly to make Belle's stay with them delightful. As party succeeded party in the Blount Mansion and other Knoxville homes, one of these young Tennessee cousins, much like her in temperament and her own age, became particularly attached to Belle. This pleasant, vivacious comrade was Sue Boyd, a lively, fine-looking girl who lived to reach the age of ninety and whose vitality of mind and body were still so great in 1932 that, recording recollections of her noted relative, she wrote gallantly: "Next birthday, I'll be eighty-eight years young!"[110]

To candid young Sue, her Virginia cousin seemed quite homely in face and feature. But otherwise she found her very attractive. She was gracious, a witty and brilliant talker, and had "the most perfect

*Martinsburg.

form or figure I ever beheld." She rode horses fearlessly and magnificently, danced wonderfully, and was so merry and light-hearted that she seemed without a care or responsibility in the world. Somewhere, evidently, she had resolutely put behind her all thoughts of her first and unfulfilled romance.

With all who visited the Boyd home, the gay Virginian girl was very popular—especially with the Confederate officers and soldiers who were welcomed there. On occasion, she matched the attire of the latter for she proudly displayed in the home of her Knoxville kin the fine riding habit which was the uniform of a Confederate captain. For months she enjoyed herself thoroughly but, inevitably, she again grew restless, and though she often told Aunt Susan sincerely that she had never been happier she at length confided to Sue that she was tired of home life, and "wanted something more ex-ci-ting and 'new fields to conquer.' "[110]

Soon after reaching this decision, she took reluctant and affectionate leave of her Tennessee relatives, and went on to visit friends in Alabama and Georgia. There, as in Tennessee, she was welcomed warmly as the "Virginia heroine." While, in her own words, the incessant kindnesses of her countrymen made her trip through the South one long ovation, she explained carefully that it must be borne in mind that the war period furnished such exciting extremes of peril and pleasure and grief and joy as to justify such outbursts in a people naturally warm-hearted and sensitive. She was deeply moved and highly grateful, but her appreciation of the compliments paid her was disarmingly free of egotism or complacency.

In Alabama Belle had a long and delightful stay in Montgomery, and then, at the beginning of May, went on to Mobile. Here, at the Battle House, she received a telegram which she opened casually. For a moment or two after she had read it she still failed to grasp its terrible significance. Then she felt the full impact of the terse message, "General Jackson now lies in state at the Governor's mansion."

There had been no merciful premonition to soften the shock of General Jackson's death. True, before reaching Mobile, she had heard a rumor that he had been wounded at Chancellorsville. But it had been reported that the wound was trifling. She had probably reflected then that nothing could happen to "Stonewall." After all it was then a custom with the Northern press to kill off or disable prematurely all the Southern leaders it particularly feared and such rumors were now rarely credited in the South.

Yet "Stonewall" was really dead. Due to the belief of Colonel S.

Bassett French, aide-de-camp to both General Jackson and to Governor Letcher of Virginia, that Belle already knew of it, the news had come in a particularly abrupt and shocking fashion.

Belle's grief at the loss of the famous commander, who had condescended to be her friend, was most poignant. Its sole outward expression was the band of crape upon her left arm which she wore for the next thirty days, in conformity with the military rules as to mourning. But inwardly the intensity of her grief was such that she found it too painful to discuss the death of the military idol of her Valley. Even later in her memoirs she could only bring herself to say that she left to abler pens the honor of tracing his career and describing his virtues.

It was with a heavy heart that she left Mobile and continued to Charleston, South Carolina, where she remained but one day. This gave her time, however, to go aboard two gunboats in the harbor and to make out with the aid of sea-glasses nearly all the ships of the Yankee blockading squadron. That evening she dined with General Beauregard, who was in charge of the harbor defenses, and several of his staff officers.

CHAPTER EIGHTEEN

With the Southern Forces to Martinsburg

HEN Belle finally reached Richmond, she was extremely anxious to get home. Though Jackson had left the Valley forever, the Federals were still there and his warning to her to remain out of their hands continued to dictate her movements. It was therefore with intense satisfaction that she learned from the best authority in the Southern Capital that Confederate troops were about to advance down the Valley with the capture of Winchester as their immediate objective. So ardently did she long to see her parents and her village again that she decided instantly to follow the Confederate advance closely.

This she did, and that the Valley had no doubts of her loyalty, is convincingly related in the *Rockingham Register* of Harrisonburg, Virginia, of Friday, June 5, 1863:

> "Miss Belle Boyd, the Confederate heroine, and the victim of Yankee persecutions, has been in Harrisonburg for a few days past. She is stopping at the American (Hotel), and is probably en route for her home in Martinsburg."

On June 14th, when the attack on Winchester began, Belle was only four miles away and most impatient to cover that small remaining distance.

In fact, it was not her fault that she had not already set foot in Martinsburg. For when Major Harry Gilmor, known as one of the bravest and most reckless Southern officers, set out with ten men early in June to scout within the Northern lines he found her on his path and most insistent on going with him.

Gilmor, warm friend of Harry Douglas, to whom Belle had given her vital message at Front Royal, had been ordered to scout the Yankee position at Winchester where the Federal commander Milroy had his headquarters. Whatever information he obtained was to be delivered to General Jenkins in command of the Valley District and used to pave the way for the advance of Ewell's army.

It was in the Valley at Woodstock, as Major Gilmor relates in his thrilling narrative of cavalry and scouting activity of the war, that he met his old acquaintance, Miss Belle Boyd, whom he had known since the autumn of '61. Immediately, she begged him to allow her to accompany his expedition. He would not and could not consent and she would not and could not be refused. So Gilmor guilefully obtained a temporary respite by telling the determined young woman that she must first secure permission from General Jenkins.[111]

The next morning, to get an early start and to elude Belle, the leader of the scouting party rose before daylight. But when he was ready to slip off, he found that Belle, knowing he would try to do so, had carried off his sabre and pistols to her room to prevent his departure without her. There was nothing to do but wait for her. Soon, down came Miss Belle, fully prepared for the raid, wearing her neat-fitting riding habit, with a pretty little belt around her waist from which the butts of two small pistols emerged, cased in patent-leather holsters.

But the intrepid young lady did not go on the scout. According to Gilmor, the incident ended in the following fashion:

> "She rode with me to the quarters of General Jenkins, to whom I had to report before passing out through his lines. We found him sitting before his tent, and after dispatching my business, Miss Belle presented her request. I fixed myself rather behind her, that I might give a signal to the general not to consent. The fact is, I did not care to be accompanied by a woman on so perilous an enterprise; for, though she was a splendid and reckless rider, of unflinching courage, and her whole soul bound up in the Southern cause yet she was a little—mark you, only a *little* headstrong and willful, and I thought it best, both for her sake and mine, that she should not go. I hope Miss Belle will forgive this little ruse. The general, of course, refused, which made her furious, but he was firm, and I rode off without her."[111]

Had Belle gone with Gilmor, she would have taken part in a most important scout. Major Gilmor reports that his small party made a complete circuit about Winchester and Martinsburg, both occupied by the Yankees, and did it so thoroughly that he learned the exact position of every stationary Federal force, and an accurate count of their numbers. This intelligence was immediately sent to General Ewell by courier, and the official records of the battle show that that Southern commander was indeed remarkably well informed as to the enemy's positions and placed General Early's men accordingly.

When the Confederate attack started, the sound of artillery fire awakened Belle's memories of her part in the battle of Front Royal. Prevented from having a share in the events leading up to the combat, she resolved that she would at least witness the engagement. So, accompanied by a disabled officer, she rode out to a hill commanding an unobstructed view of the field and became absorbed in the struggle taking place below. They were soon joined by several civilians, both men and women, who seemed to consider the hilltop a place of complete security.

But Belle was mounted on a white horse which evidently was conspicuous enough to attract the notice of a Yankee battery about three quarters of a mile away, and suddenly the guns of the battery were turned in their direction. When a screeching shell came in among them, a wild rush for shelter followed. Belle relates frankly that she joined in it wholeheartedly.

That she observed the battle of Winchester is evident from another source. Some time in January, 1865, on a train taking Confederate prisoners from Washington to Fort Delaware, Lieutenant C. of Major Harry Gilmor's battalion asked a comrade casually, "By the way, did you ever hear tell of Miss Belle Boyd?" When the man he questioned, who happened to be Belle's husband, admitted cautiously that the name was not unfamiliar, the officer confided:

> "Well, there isn't a Southerner who would not lay down his life for her. When I was at the battle of Winchester, I was wounded and she came into the hospital where I was and inquired if there were any Maryland boys there. Amongst other delicacies, she gave me some very nice peach-brandy. She and Mrs. G. were in the fort, if I err not, cheering us on when we made a charge and drove the Yankees back."[112]

The Confederates not only succeeded in capturing Winchester and Martinsburg, but also pursued the Federals vigorously toward Maryland. This permitted Belle to return to her native village which was now once more within Southern lines, and she lost no time in doing so. Her father, whose health had been broken by the hardships of campaigning with Jackson, was on leave, and thus she had the great pleasure of being welcomed home by both parents.

That campaigning with General Jackson had been too arduous for forty-six-year-old Ben Boyd is not surprising. The fame of the Stonewall Brigade was achieved by men who had to undergo terrible hardships. They marched incredible distances with feet bruised and maimed by ill-fitting footgear, and in cold weather suffered frightfully because of want of warm uniforms and overcoats. They fought with weapons inferior to those of the enemies who outnumbered them, they were always undernourished and often completely lacked food. They camped without adequate shelter or equipment and had insufficient medical attention and sanitary protection. Sickness and sheer physical exhaustion produced as many casualties as the battlefield, including the mortally weakened Private Boyd, and in the years immediately after the war added to the toll of deaths. Many of the victims of these conditions were young and sturdy men, but most were older soldiers, like Belle's father, whose spirit, unlike their bodies, was unconquerable.

Though Belle did not return to her native village before June 14th, it is believed today by many in Martinsburg that she was there two months earlier and had been arrested by the Yankees. In proof they point to strange notations on the margin of Chancery Book No. 1 in the County Court House in Martinsburg. One of these reads, "Isobel Boyd, Confederate Spy, April 7, 1863." Another is worded, "I wonder if I will be shot tomorrow. B. Boyd. April 1863."

There seems to be no valid reason to consider these interesting items authentic. Neither Belle Boyd nor anyone else has recorded that she was ever imprisoned in the County Court House. Both she and her cousin, Sue Boyd of Knoxville, have indicated that she was farther South and deep within the Confederate lines in April, and Belle's daughter, Mrs. Michael, who has examined these writings, states they are not in her mother's hand. Moreover, Belle invariably signed her name as "Belle Boyd" and insisted on being so designated.

While Belle did not accompany Harry Gilmor on his scouting trip in early June, it is possible that about then she managed to get within the Federal lines on some other mission. At any rate, her presence in the region was not unsuspected by the inhabitants. Five days before the Federals were hurled out of Winchester and Martinsburg, it was being whispered that she was in Front Royal. When this rumor came to the ears of Miss Lucy Buck, she jotted down in her diary,

> " 'Tis said Belle Boyd is in town tonight. What next?"[113]

CHAPTER NINETEEN

Captain Kellogg of Ohio Arrests Belle

LATED by their June successes, the Confederates marched into Pennsylvania. The hearts of Southerners beat high with hope. It was said that Baltimore and Washington were about to be attacked, and with the fall of the Northern Capital it was generally felt that the War would come to a successful conclusion for the Confederacy.

The happiness and fair prospects of the South were short-lived. The terrible battle of Gettysburg was fought in the first days of July, and once again the bloody tide of conflict reversed its course. As the great stream of Confederate wounded flowed back, Martinsburg was promptly transformed into a vast sanitary camp. There being no established hospital facilities in existence, churches, public buildings, and even many private residences were pressed into use. The Boyd home was filled with wounded men, and Belle gave all her time and thought to their needs.

That the Yankees would come again to Martinsburg was obvious. It was equally plain that Belle should leave before their arrival and seek safety within the Southern lines. But she had been away so long and had been at home so short a time that she and her parents could not reconcile themselves to her departure. Reason counseled her to go, and affection urged her to tarry. Keenly aware of the probable consequences, she decided to stay and she closed her mind to all but the frail hope that if she remained quiet the Yankees would neither notice nor molest her.

On retiring from Gettysburg, the Confederates had marched through the village, but for some time their cavalry retained control of it and the adjoining region. Eventually even these Southern troops left and there remained no obstacle whatever to Yankee reoccupation. Even then Belle could still have gone. But as the cavalry withdrew, her mother, who was about to have another child, became very ill. Nothing could now have caused Belle to leave.

For a short time all was tranquil in their region. But when her baby sister was only three days old, and Belle sat in her mother's room, there came the old familiar cry from a servant of: "Oh, here comes de Yankees!" Belle went to the window, and what she saw took her back abruptly and terrifyingly to a similar scene a year earlier at Front Royal. A large unit of mounted troops had halted in front of the house, and, as she looked, two officers advanced to the Boyd door and one rang the bell.

Her father went to meet them, and sent word to her that Major Goff and Lieutenant . . . wished to see her. She descended to the drawing room, and, after introductions, the Major said: "Miss Boyd, General Kelly commanded me to call and see if you really had remained home, such a report having reached headquarters. But he did not credit it, so I have come to ascertain the truth."

General B. F. Kelly, to whom Major Goff referred, had recently been appointed military commander of the Federal Department of West Virginia. Having doubtless heard of Belle's skill in duping Yankee officers, the General had not chosen his deputy carelessly. He had selected from the Third West Virginia Infantry, which had become a mounted unit in May, a young major of unusual ability with earlier service as lieutenant and adjutant. This officer, Nathan Goff, had already demonstrated possession of the great qualities which were to characterize his post-war career as Federal District Attorney, Congressman, candidate for Governor of West Virginia, and Secretary of the Navy. On such a man General Kelly could indeed rely "to ascertain the truth."[114]

Major Goff's blunt announcement of his mission made no visible impression on the daughter of Ben and Mary Boyd. Feigning ignorance that she had anything to fear, she demanded coldly: "Major Goff, what is there so peculiarly strange in my remaining in my own home with my parents?"

The Federal officer countered in turn with questions: "But do you not think it rather dangerous? Are you then not really afraid of being arrested?"

"Oh, no!", answered Belle, "for I don't know why they should do so. I am no criminal!"

"Yes, true," conceded her visitor, "but you are a rebel and will do more harm to our cause than half the men could do."

"But there are other rebels beside myself," she protested.

"Yes," he agreed, "but then not so dangerous as yourself."

This inconclusive and courteous verbal fencing continued for a few moments more, and then, with no indication as to the action to be taken, the two Northern officers withdrew. That their call took place on July 18th or 19th is suggested by the history of the Third West Virginia

Infantry which not only shows that it was "near Hedgeville and Martinsburg" on those days but also that it had been made a mounted regiment in May.[115]

For several days no more was heard from the invaders and the Boyds ventured to hope that Belle would be subjected to no further annoyance. But on the fourth day, probably July 23rd, an order was issued for her arrest. When the arresting party, headed by Captain Horace Kellogg of Company B, One Hundred and Twenty-Third Ohio Volunteer Infantry[116], came for her, Mrs. Boyd was still very ill. Mr. Boyd, fearing that his daughter's removal might prove fatal to his wife, begged that Belle be allowed to remain at home during her mother's convalescence. He also felt that within this period of grace he could bring pressure to bear at Washington which might result in her outright release.

Obligingly enough, the Yankees granted his request. Belle was placed on parole, Private John B. Fairchilds of Company C of Captain Kellogg's regiment was detailed to guard her, sentries were stationed about the house, and so strict a watch was kept that she was not even permitted to go out on the balcony.

The hot July weather, her mother's illness, and her imprisonment in her own home combined to make her thoroughly miserable. And this unpleasant situation was aggravated by the requirement that all entering or leaving the house must have passes.

Craving fresh air and exercise, Belle succeeded one day in obtaining a special permit from the commanding officer. This read:

> "Miss Belle Boyd has permission to walk out for half an hour, at 5 o'clock this a.m., giving her word of honor that she will use nothing which she may see or hear to the disadvantage of the U. S. troops."

But the Yankees still feared their captive would communicate vital news to the Southern forces, so some high authority decided that granting her permission to walk about was unwise under no matter what restrictions. A patrol sent out immediately took her into custody only a few blocks away and she was hastily escorted back to the house with guards, armed with loaded muskets, on each side of her. About an hour after this unceremonious return to her home, she received a note from the general's headquarters informing her that, although she was on parole, she was "not allowed to promenade freely in Martinsburg."

For nearly a month she lived in a constant state of anxiety and suspense as to her fate. Then Provost-Marshal Kellogg called upon her with a detective and told her that she must get ready to go to Washington, for Secretary of War Stanton had so ordered. The time of departure was set for eleven o'clock the next morning. While the exact date is unknown, it must have been between August 15th and 20th, allowing for the passage of almost a month after July 23rd when she was formally arrested.

Mrs. Boyd, whose condition had greatly improved, immediately suffered a serious relapse upon learning that her daughter was to be taken to Washington. Despite this, Mr. Boyd decided to accompany Belle and the detective. Probably he had in mind that he could hasten the negotiations he had under way there, and bring Belle back with him.

Some thirty-five years later, Belle again met Captain Kellogg, Private Fairchilds, and another member of their regiment at Norwalk, Ohio. The occasion was a gathering of veterans before which Belle gave a recital of her adventures. A few weeks after the meeting she related to a reporter:

> "It was at the conclusion of my entertainment, and a large number of the audience had remained to be introduced, an informal reception as it were. Among others, I was presented to Captain Kellogg of the 123rd Ohio who arrested me at Martinsburg, Virginia in 1863 after the Gettysburg fight. He in turn introduced Mr. John Fairchilds whom he had detailed to stand over me until the arrival of secret service men from Washington. Just to make the chain complete, they introduced me to Mr. Walter Perrin, who belonged to the reserves and who stood guard over me at the Old Capitol Prison in Washington."[117]

For both Belle and her former enemies, this meeting released a flood of memories. "We old vets were like a lot of children as we talked over the events of those days." One thing she must have told the former Provost Marshal was that in June, 1863, the month before her arrest, she had watched the battle of Winchester from a hilltop. In turn the Ohioans must have related to her that it was in that battle that the One Hundred and Twenty-Third Ohio had been very badly used up, and most of its members captured and taken to Richmond. Kellogg, Fairchilds, and Perrin were not among these prisoners, however. They had managed to evade capture, had contrived to make their way to Maryland and, when they had rejoined the main Federal force, a small detachment of survivors from their regiment had been stationed at Martinsburg on provost and picket duty under command of Captain Kellogg.[118]

CHAPTER TWENTY

A Rose, an Archer, and the Rubber Ball Mail

UPON arrival in Washington, Belle was taken to the Carroll Prison, a building adjoining and connected with the Old Capitol Prison. Not realizing that she would never see him again, she said adieu to her father at the gates, and was then conducted to the "room for distinguished guests." The room acquired its distinction solely from its inmates and in no respect from its furnishings. Among the Southern ladies who had already occupied it were Miss Antonia Ford, and Nannie T. and her aged mother.

For Belle, the familiar, monotonous routine of prison life began again. The days and nights were interminably long and she spent hours gazing listlessly through her grated windows. To those who looked up from without and nodded in friendly greeting, she must have seemed just as appealing and forlorn as the attractive young lady George Lawrence saw at another Old Capitol window earlier in that year.

In fact, legend asserts Belle was the charming girl he worshipped, and is convincingly abetted by two powerful aides. In his introduction to Belle's book, Mr. Sala quotes extensively from Lawrence's exquisitely delicate portrayal of his nameless heroine and sincerely believes she was Belle Boyd. And in *Secret Service Operator 13*, Robert W. Chambers, assuming Mr. Sala to be correct in this assumption, describes Belle in almost the identical words used by the lyrical Lawrence.

George Lawrence, a young, romantic Englishman with an enviable literary reputation, had come to North America to gather material for books, and to write articles for the *Morning Post* of London. Sympathizing ardently with the South, he was unwilling to see the war solely from behind the Northern lines or to accept uncritically the Federal attitude regarding the issues involved. As he journeyed from one side to the other, his sentiments swayed him so powerfully that he tried to help the Southern cause with too much enthusiasm and too little discretion. A natural consequence was that one day he found himself a prisoner in the Old Capitol. There, no whit perturbed, he recorded his experiences for future publication.

He relates that one day, as he walked gloomily in the court-yard, he glanced up casually and unexpectantly at the bars of a second story window. The vision he was at first not at all sure he actually saw there was a slight figure arrayed in the freshest summer toilette of cool, pink muslin. Tight braids of dark hair shaded clear, pale cheeks; eyes meant to sparkle held a very sad look; and the languid bowing down of a small head betrayed the sadness as something caused by more than weariness.

In the background of this amazingly pretty picture in so rude and strange a setting stood a mature lady—the mother, evidently. That their crime had been abetment of the South he knew instinctively even before he detected the ensign of her faith that the demoiselle still wore undauntedly—a pearl solitaire fashioned in a single star.

For days he was content to lift his cap ceremoniously, and the ladies punctiliously acknowledged his salute. But one evening, as he loitered with understandable restlessness under their window, "a low significant cough made me look up; I saw the flash of a gold bracelet and the wave of a white hand, and there fell at my feet a fragrant rosebud nestling in fresh green leaves." The flustered and delighted Briton conveyed his thanks inadequately with an expressive gesture and a dozen hurried, awkward words, and so proud was he of this graceful gift to a hitherto unlucky stranger that he wrote: "Other fragrant messengers followed in their season, but, if ever I 'win hame to mine ain countrie' I make mine avow to enshrine that first rosebud in my *reliquaire* with all honor and solemnity, there to abide until one of us shall be dust."[119]

Legend's insistence that Belle was the imprisoned damozel who enchanted Lawrence is readily understandable. And she should indeed have been, for Harry Douglas has told so well how she, too, could bestow a rose upon a cavalier with all the grace and charm of any fair lady of the medieval age of chivalry. But, nevertheless, she tossed no floral avowals to Mr. Lawrence from her prison window. And this is true, not only because her hair was never dark, but also, regrettably, because she was not in the Old Capitol Prison at the time that George Lawrence was there.

When the bewitched Englishman's story is carefully examined, its relation to outside events shows his imprisonment began about April 3, 1863, and the affidavit he signed upon release is dated June 5th of that year. Belle did not reach the Old Capitol until late August. In April, her cousin, Sue Boyd, has said she was still in the South, and so she could not have been then either a prisoner in the Old Capitol tossing roses to an admirer or in the County Court House at Martinsburg wondering if she were to be shot on the morrow. In early June she was at Woodstock in the Valley hiding Harry Gilmor's weapons so he would not go scouting without her.

Mr. Lawrence's tactful reference to the "mature lady" in the background suggests that the prisoners he knew may have been Nannie T. and her "aged mother." Moreover, the pearl solitaire with its distinctive shape indicates a belle of the Lone Star State rather than a daughter of the Old Dominion.

Usually, communication with Old Capitol prisoners via jail windows was of a much less idyllic character. Though citizens of Washington friendly to the Southern cause engaged in it freely, it was a serious violation of regulations and therefore a most dangerous pastime. As early as May 28th, 1862, Provost-Marshal Doster caused the following announcement to be published on the front page of the *Washington Star*.

> "The officer of the Guard at the 'Old Capitol Prison' will not allow signals to be made to the prisoners under his charge by men or women passing in front of his building. This practice has led to insubordination, and in one case to a fatal result.
>
> "Any one, without respect of person, violating this order will be sent to the Central Guard House."

But not even the risk of fatal consequences ended the practice, and among the many stories of such occurrences there is a classic jest which emphasizes the grim zest with which the prisoners goaded their guards with both actual and imaginary infractions. It was perpetrated by an inmate who sent for the officer in charge, complained bitterly that the windows of her cell were too dirty, and stated that it was imperative that they be washed. When asked why this was so essential, the lady retorted with finality: "Why? Because my friends outside can no longer make out my signals."

It was an equally bold spirit who began to communicate with Belle by shooting winged messages into her room. Somehow she, as venturesome as ever, managed to procure, and to hurl out of her window, rubber balls containing answers to her aerial correspondent.

This unorthodox mail service began one evening when she sat at her window and sang "Take me back to my own sunny South." A crowd collected on the opposite side of the street to listen, and when she stopped the gathering dispersed. Watching the retiring figures with envy, she rose, lowered the gas-light, resumed her seat and, leaning her head against the bars, fell into deep thought.

She was abruptly aroused from reverie by the sound of something whizzing by her head and striking the opposite wall. Her first reaction was that a shot had been fired at her. Recovering from this momentary fear, she turned up the light and found that the missile was an arrow to which a note was fastened.

This note assured her that she had many warm friends in Washington with whom she could now correspond if she desired. On Thursdays and Saturdays just after twilight the archer would enter the square opposite the prison and whistle "Twas within' a mile of Edinbro'town." If alone, and safe from observation, she was to lower the gas-light as a signal and stay away from the window. He would then shoot an arrow into the room with a message attached.

In order to reply, she should procure a large rubber ball, open it, place her answer within, and sew the halves together. On Tuesdays he would also come into the square and give the same signal. She was then to throw the ball with as much force as possible across the street and into the square. Signed to this intriguing note were the initials "C.H."

For a long time Belle doubted the wisdom of answering this strange note. But natural prudence yielded to delight over so romantic a way of correspondence with one who professed to be a friend. So she began a series of communications with him, and, fortunately, had no cause to regret it. The archer's professions of friendship proved to be honorable and sincere. Through him she secured much valuable information regarding Federal movements. He also passed on to her small Confederate flags made by ladies of Washington and with these, although it was most rash to display them, she decorated her room.

Within the prison, Belle had, of course, promptly established communication with the other captives. It was only a few days after her arrival that she heard the familiar sound of some instrument grating against the wall. When the point of a knife pierced the plaster, she set to work on her side and soon tightly rolled notes were being exchanged.

She had first made certain, however, that her neighbors were actually *bona fide* Southern sympathizers. This precaution was necessary because the prison authorities now had functioning an effective system of espionage as a counter-measure against the highly organized intercommunication network of the prisoners, and often trapped the unwary by using decoy agents and messages. In this particular instance, her correspondents proved to be four men who nine months earlier had been captured while trying to go South to join the Confederate forces.

Her contact with them did not last very long. Mr. Lockwood, officer of the keys, had become particularly adept in breaking up the exchange of messages, and one of his most successful methods was to ...ate openings through which notes were passed. While the hole used ...nd her friends had been artfully concealed, nevertheless he ... was immediately plastered over and the four men were ...m.

... room they had occupied had a new tenant. ... who had been arrested charged with being a ... some reason, Belle was permitted to visit and ...uthorities had probably arranged to have the con... women overheard and doubtless hoped they would ...outes, and members of the Confederate mail service. ...overnment wanted very much to wipe it out and must ...Belle was well informed.

...s may have been talkative but they do not seem to have ...mative. Had they been, the privileges given them would ... have been continued indefinitely. Instead, Miss P. was soon ... and Belle learned that she had given her parole to engage in no fu...er activity against the Yankees.

As Major Doster has revealed, the monotony of imprisonment was well-nigh unbearable for the high-spirited girl. It was therefore natural for her to resort to strange and even desperate means to enliven the deadly routine of her inactive existence. So at times she found distraction in fastening one of her Confederate flags to a broom-handle and then suspending her improvised flagstaff outside the window.

This invariably produced results of a lively character. The banner would attract the attention of a sentinel and he would promptly bellow: "Take in that . . . . flag, or I'll blow your . . . . brains out!"

Having carefully withdrawn from range, Belle would pay no attention to this profane command, but would be on the alert for the next development. This was generally a musket shot, the ball hitting her ceiling or wall with a most ominous thud. Then, giving the sentinel no time to reload, Belle's next move was to step quickly to the window and look out casually as though nothing had occurred. This tormenting of the guards was not only aggravating but also highly dangerous. The Old Capitol records show at least one case of a prisoner being fatally shot by a guard under conditions involving far less, if any, provocation.

But Belle soon lost her zest for such diversions. The heat, the rigors of confinement, and the noxious fumes of the prison combined to sap her strength. She became seriously ill of typhoid fever, grew steadily worse under the awkward and unwelcome treatment of Dr. F., surgeon of the prison, and improved only when attended by a Confederate physician among the captives.

After three weeks of care by the Southern doctor, he pronounced her convalescent and a week later she could walk about. During her illness, relatives and friends had tried to gain access to her but all requests to visit her were referred by his order to Secretary Stanton and denied. One application that she be removed from the Old Capitol during her illness drew from him the comment: "No, she is a . . . . rebel; let her die there!"

After her recovery, one of the chief prison officials, Captain James B. Mix of the Eleventh New York Infantry[120], stopped in to tell her that a most beautiful woman had arrived and was in a room at the farther end of the passage on the floor below her. Ill and listless, Belle received this information without interest.

However, a day or so later, while walking down the hall, Belle came face to face with the new inmate. Both women stopped short in amazement and gazed at one another in immediate mutual and angry recognition. To Captain Mix the new prisoner was "most beautiful." But to Belle she was only "Miss Annie Jones" the woman she had befriended at Front Royal in May, 1862 and who had repaid her kindness by denouncing her to the Federals and causing her arrest as a dangerous rebel and malignant enemy.*

After this momentary halt, Belle continued on her way. Why Annie Jones had been arrested, she was not able to learn. But Annie was believed to be a Yankee camp-follower and it was commonly said in the Old Capitol that she was insane. Measures soon taken for her removal elsewhere seem to indicate that the rumor was not wholly without foundation.

Recovering some of her energy, Belle now felt keenly the need of outdoor exercise. Accordingly, she wrote General Martindale, commandant of the forces in and about Washington, asking for the privilege of walking daily in Capitol Square. To her astonishment, a gracious

*See p. 56.

reply granted permission on condition that she promise on her honor as a lady to communicate with no one verbally or by letter while walking. She agreed gladly, and was allowed to walk in the Square every evening from five to five-thirty followed by a corporal and a guard carrying loaded muskets.

This concession was soon withdrawn, however, for when it became known in Washington that Belle Boyd could be seen walking in front of the prison, Southern sympathizers—"and their name was Legion"—gathered to see her and manifested their interest and concern so strongly that Secretary Stanton revoked her parole.

On one occasion some young girls passing her dropped a piece of Bristol board with a Confederate battle flag and the name of Belle Boyd worked on it in worsted. The corporal commanding the guard noticed the incident and picked up the memento before Belle could do so. He immediately stopped the girls and, but for his prisoner's entreaties, would have arrested them. Instead, cajoled and mollified, he dismissed them with a light reprimand. Not content with this victory over her escort, Belle, after promising not to implicate him if the article were found in her possession, secured it from him for five dollars and wore it proudly for a long time after leaving Washington.

CHAPTER TWENTY-ONE

Belle Assists Prisoners to Escape

IN October Belle engineered the escape of three prisoners from the Old Capitol. She first learned of their intention when, as she sat one evening by her door, a note was tossed to her behind the sentry's back. It was from a Mr. K. of Virginia begging her to aid him and two friends to get away, and asking for financial assistance. She replied at once that she would do all she could, and at the first opportunity handed Mr. K. forty dollars.

She then enlisted the aid of her archer correspondent, C. H., and via arrow and rubber ball made arrangements for outside help. As soon as all was ready, the plan agreed upon was carried out.

Above Mr. K.'s room was a garret occupied by two friends, and the initial step provided that K. was to proceed to the garret with them upon returning from supper. An observant sentry, however, almost prevented the escape at its very inception.

The sentinel, seeing K. mounting the garret staircase, ordered him back. "You don't belong there," he shouted, "so come down!" Standing in her own door-way, Belle promptly called out to the guard in simulated surprise, "Sentry, have you been so long here, and don't know where the prisoners are quartered? Let him pass on to his room." Taking the hint, K. declared boldly, "I know what I am about!" It being so evident that he did, the guard became convinced he had made a mistake, and let K. proceed.

K. now being in the garret, Belle hurriedly dispatched a note to Superintendent Wood saying she would like to see him. When he came, she detained him in conversation until from around the corner of the prison facing the street came a loud cry of "Murder! Murder!" Though it represented only the ruse agreed upon to draw attention away from the place where the attempt to escape would be made, the shout was so realistic that it caused Belle's heart to beat violently. The moment he heard it, Mr. Wood rushed to a window and flung it open to find out what was happening. As he did so, soldiers lounging below as they awaited their turn of duty ran hurriedly in the direction from which the cries continued to come.

Taking advantage of this diversion, K. and his companions removed a part of the roof, scrambled out upon the eaves and, descending to the street by means of a lightning conductor, made off into the darkness. Meanwhile the cries of "Murder!" led their investigators nowhere. The next morning the guards finally understood what had occurred when the prisoners were mustered and K. and his two associates were missing. Suspicion fell upon Belle, in view of her unwarranted interference with the sentinel and her note to Superintendent Wood. But nothing could be proved against her and she felt amply repaid later when she learned that the fugitives had reached Richmond safely.

This detailed story of escape is not without confirmation. The War Department records admit that three prisoners got away from the Old Capitol that month. And the all-seeing *Washington Star* tells of the method of escape, although it evidently believed that only one person was involved.[121]

The *Star* relates that a young man named J. G. Thompson, son of a Washington restaurant keeper, and charged with being a rebel mail carrier, escaped from Carroll Prison on the night of October 1st. "Thompson was confined in the upper part of the prison, and succeeded in getting upon the roof of the building, on the corner of Pennsylvania Avenue and First Street East, used as a boarding house, and escaped by going down the lightning rod to the ground."

Throughout Belle's captivity, official proceedings against her were conducted under the direction of Major Levi C. Turner, a noted investigator of the Judge Advocate's Department.[122] She characterizes them as a trial by court-martial. While it is quite possible that she was brought before a military court, it is more likely that her case was handled with greater privacy by a military commission without charges being filed. There were innumerable military courts and commissions in session at this time and the records regarding them are far from complete. Those available do not include her case.

Advance notice of her fate came to Belle bluntly and indirectly. One day, as she was standing in the hall, Captain Mix informed "Miss Annie Jones" that she must leave for an insane asylum on the morrow. This curt announcement caused Miss Jones to scream hysterically and to rush away from him. She came directly toward Belle, and it may be that she held the latter accountable for her fate and meant to attack her. As Annie drew near, Belle turned away cooly to leave, but as she did Captain Mix gave bad news to her also with equal abruptness and directness. What he said was: "Oh you need not put on airs by getting out of the way for you've got to go to Fitchburg Jail during the war. You have been sentenced to hard labor there."

Unnerved by the suddenness of the blow and the screams of Miss Jones, Belle fell fainting to the floor. Taken to her room, she suffered a relapse into fever. Her father, learning of her sentence and her second illness, promptly came back to Washington and resumed his efforts on her behalf. Eventually his exertions succeeded and his daughter's sentence was commuted. In its modified form, it was "banishment to the South—never to return North again during the war."

She was to leave for Fortress Monroe on December 1st. Her father was still in Washington and staying with a niece, but had become so ill himself that he was unable to visit Belle before her departure. He had even planned to accompany her at least part way, but just before she was to leave a message was brought to her that though not dangerously ill he was confined to the house by a serious indisposition. Greatly distressed, she begged to be permitted to see him before going to Fortress Monroe, but her request was refused.

Meanwhile, a Confederate colonel in the prison gave her letters of introduction to the Honorable Alexander Stephens, Vice-President of the Confederacy, and to the Honorable Bowling Baker, Chief Auditor of the Confederate Treasury Department, commending her to their "kind care and protection." Realizing that such communications were contraband, she determined nevertheless to get them through, if possible.

Early on the morning of December 1st, she left the Old Capitol. The following day the *New York Tribune* stated briefly that Captain James B. Mix of General Martindale's staff had left Washington for City Point "with the notorious Belle Boyd, who is to be delivered to the rebel authorities at that place." And on the 4th the *Washington Star* published an Associated Press dispatch from Fortress Monroe stating: "Miss Belle Boyd arrived last evening from Washington in charge of a lieutenant." Confirming the nature of the amended decision she stated was taken in her case, it added, "She is to be sent over the lines, to remain during the war."

It is remarkable that regarding her second imprisonment in Washington, the Northern press only ventured to print two items about her and these after her departure. Perhaps its silence was requested by the War Department which may have considered publicity about her second captivity undersirable in view of the public interest her presence had aroused in 1862. It may even have been that knowledge of her imprisonment was kept from the press.

She was certainly, both in 1862 and 1863, a special and secret prisoner of the War Department as to whom no charges were filed and as to whom the prison authorities had evidently received instructions from Secretary Stanton to make no official records whatever. Under normal procedure in the Old Capitol, all prisoners were registered. Failure to do so in the case of Belle Boyd on two widely separated occasions points to intentional omission rather than to oversight. "No entries for Belle Boyd were found in the registers of Old Capitol and Carroll Prisons which are in the National Archives."[123]

A further indication of her importance as a secret prisoner of state is that Captain Mix was detailed to escort her to Fortress Monroe. This gentleman commanded President Lincoln's bodyguard in the summer and fall of 1862. He achieved considerable distinction and earned the North's gratitude when he risked his life and incurred injuries, which disabled him temporarily, in rendering effective aid to the President who had lost control of his horse returning from the Soldiers' Home to the White House. Captain Mix was assigned to duty at the Old Capitol in May, 1863, rejoined his regiment in April, 1864, and later became Lieutenant-Colonel of the Seventh New York Infantry. Though efforts were made to oust him from presidential favor, his enemies failed, and he received an autograph letter from Mr. Lincoln stating he was greatly attached to him and had no reason to change his opinion.[120]

That this prominent officer was selected to take Belle Boyd to Fortress Monroe suggests that this duty was important enough to require someone in whose ability and fidelity the highest authority had the utmost confidence.

Had the *New York Tribune* and the *Washington Star* both failed to mention Belle's departure from Washington, the Federal Government would still have failed to conceal her second imprisonment. In 1879 a magazine article appeared recording her among the secret agents and spies of the rebel government held in the jail in 1863. The author of the article was Colonel N. T. Colby, military commandant of the Old Capitol early that year.[124]

To this officer, Belle was an undeniably good-looking woman with a fine figure and a merry disposition who could, he thought, have been very dangerous to the Federal Government had she possessed as much good sense and judgment. As it was, she impressed him as governed more by romance and love of notoriety than by actual regard for the Southern cause. And, in his opinion, all the damage she ever did the North was to tempt, some months later, the Federal naval officer she subsequently married to be disloyal. As secret agents, he considered Belle and her husband, who was also later a prisoner in the Old Capitol, just "lightweights."

Like Wood, Baker, and Doster, he noted her flippancy. Unlike them, he saw nothing else, and again like them, he failed to perceive that this disarming quality and the assumed inability to be really dangerous were the very weapons she had used successfully against officers who had carelessly reached similar reassuring conclusions. Moreover, he had no real opportunity to appraise her talents seriously for he was merely in charge of the prison as a military post and of the military personnel stationed there. He had no part in official investigation of secret service activities of prisoners. He was primarily a line officer with a splendid battle record, and was given an invalid's post at the Old Capitol because he had been incapacitated for further field service. The following description of him by Belle's husband reveals the casual nature of his contact with the prisoners.

> "Colonel Colby, the military commandant, who has charge of this post, I saw but little of; but we all liked him, for he was ever courteous and polite, and always had a good word for us."[125]

Colonel Colby evidently never realized the strange trend of his conclusion that all the damage Belle did the North was to tempt a naval officer in 1864 to be disloyal. Yet it suggests plainly that he believed she had done nothing whatever to justify her imprisonment in 1862 and again in 1863. Secretary Stanton would hardly have relished learning the military commandant of the Old Capitol held this subversive viewpoint. And it was, of course, no mean or pointless achievement for a prisoner to convince her jailer by any means that she had done no harm and was not dangerous.

Legend will have it that the original sentence imposed upon Belle Boyd in Washington in the latter part of 1863 was the death penalty, and that it was commuted through President Lincoln's clemency. The kernel of truth from which this myth grew was undoubtedly an informal warning, like that given her in Martinsburg in July, 1861, that a repetition of her offence would be punished by the supreme penalty. After having been sent South once with the expectation that she would remain there, she had been found within the Northern lines in July, 1863 and this time a specific condition of her release, as the *Washington Star* confirmed, was that she must remain outside the Union lines for the rest of the war.

In *Forgotten Ladies*, Mr. R. L. Wright refuses to take seriously the warning given Belle that "the next time she stepped across the lines would mean a firing squad." He dismisses this caution contemptuously as an empty threat because neither side shot a woman spy during the entire war.[126] The effectiveness of this observation is marred, however, by two significant facts. One is that Belle, with her own life often at stake, could hardly perceive clearly in the future what Mr. Wright finds so obvious in the past. The second is that right after the War the Federal Government proved unmistakably that women offenders were not immune. When a military commission ruled that Mrs. Surratt (held by General Baker to be "as lithe a rebel as Belle Boyd") must be hanged for her part in the conspiracy resulting in the assassination of President Lincoln, the sentence was carried out.

It has also been said repeatedly that Belle's second imprisonment ended with her exchange for General Nathan Goff. Nothing is found to confirm this. It is quite possible, though, that in releasing her the Federal Government secured some reciprocal advantage. Naturally it would have been dramatic to exchange her for the noted Nathan Goff who called on her in Martinsburg and was to become Secretary of the Navy. However, *General* Nathan Goff was not this distinguished Virginian of the Martinsburg encounter but was an officer of the same name from Rhode Island.[127]

That President Lincoln intervened to reduce Belle's sentence is not improbable. There is no actual evidence that he did, but only he or Secretary Stanton could have made the change. Although Stanton was not given to leniency, it is known that the President was highly susceptible to requests for clemency and that Stanton was not always successful in preventing favorable presidential action.

CHAPTER TWENTY-TWO

Belle Meets "The Beast"

HEN Belle and Captain Mix arrived at Fortress Monroe, which was about nine o'clock on the morning of December 2nd, she was more than pleased to have to suffer his company no longer. She had made no conquest of him and, for that reason, perhaps, found him most annoying and ungentlemanly. In fact, he seemed to go to a great deal of trouble to make everything as disagreeable as possible.

At the Fortress, Captain Mix went ashore to report to Captain John Cassels of Company C, Eleventh Pennsylvania Cavalry[128], who was Provost Marshal there and also aide-de-camp to General Benjamin F. Butler, the departmental commander. It was to the care of this Federal general of formidable reputation that Belle was to be committed until the exchange boat left for Richmond, and she fervently hoped that she would not attract his baneful attention before departure.

When Captain Mix returned, he was accompanied by Major John E. Mulford of the Third New York Infantry[129], then the Federal exchange officer. The Major, an elegant and courteous gentleman who subsequently became a brigadier-general, escorted Belle ceremoniously to the Provost-Marshal's office. From there she was taken to General Butler's headquarters and, after a short wait, conducted into his presence.

To understand the import of the conversation that followed between the Southern girl and the general known through the South as "The Beast," some details on sturdy Ben Butler are essential. No Federal commander ever contrived to get himself more bitterly hated by the Confederacy—not even Sherman. A very strong and forceful personality from New England, he lacked completely any consciousness of sectional or cultural inferiority, and the ordinarily successful Southern social tactics to make Northern leaders feel that they were but unmannerly louts impressed him not at all.

It was Butler who, when in command at New Orleans, enraged the South by carrying out the first execution there in eighteen years. A man named Mumford had led a body of men to the Federal Mint where they pulled down a United States flag placed there by Farragut, trailed it on the ground through the streets, tore it into pieces, and distributed bits as keepsakes. Mumford was arrested and, despite every effort made to save him from death, was hanged by order of the inexorable Butler.

But it was another incident in the same city that earned him the title of "Butler, the Beast." This was his famous or infamous General Order No. 28. The ladies of New Orleans being given to manifesting in every conceivable way their contempt for Federal officers and men they met in the streets, this order provided that, "when any female shall, by word, gesture, or movement, insult or show contempt for any officer or soldier of the United States, she shall be regarded and held liable to be treated as a woman of the town plying her avocation."

The resultant storm that shook the town and the rest of the South disturbed Butler not at all. When the order was commented on unfavorably in the House of Parliament, he merely pointed out that he had borrowed his proclamation from the Ordinances of London.

This Federal commander's personal appearance was hardly calculated to make those appearing before him feel that the reports of his terrible severity had been exaggerated. According to one of them, Mr. E. A. Pollard, editor of the *Richmond Examiner*, Butler was a short, well set-up man with a large peaked head and a well developed chest. His eyes, under his slanting forehead, were small, muddy, and cruel. They had an unpleasant, smothered glow which, in one, was curtailed by a drooping lid, and the rest of his features were concealed by enormous chops of flesh with little webs of red veins in them. When he smiled, he used only one side of his mouth and displayed bad, projecting teeth. The effect, Mr. Pollard says reasonably enough, was not even remotely reassuring.[130]

When Belle was brought before this dread personage, he looked up and exclaimed: "Ah! so this is Miss Boyd, the famous rebel spy. Pray be seated."

"Thank you, General Butler," she replied, "but I prefer to stand."

Although she fought desperately for self-control, Belle was greatly agitated, possibly as much by anger as by apprehension, and she trembled violently. The General, noticing this, said again: "Pray be seated," and inquired, "But why do you tremble so? Are you frightened?"

Despite her anxiety, Belle could not resist taking advantage of such an opening. So she answered: "No, . . . ah! that is, yes, General Butler. I must acknowledge that I do feel frightened in the presence of a man of such world-wide reputation as yourself."

This seemed to please him immensely. Rubbing his hands together, and smiling benignly, he insisted: "Oh, pray do be seated, Miss Boyd," and added, "But what do you mean when you say that I am widely known?"

Summoning all her courage, Belle eyed him coldly, and replied with emphatic firmness: "I mean, General Butler, that you are a man whose atrocious conduct and brutality, especially to Southern ladies, is so infamous that even the English Parliament commented upon it. I naturally feel alarmed at being in your presence."

The Yankee commander, who had evidently expected some graceful compliment, did not take this forthright rebuke calmly. As Belle concluded her statement, he rose quickly and angrily ordered her out of his office.

This anecdote, which is related only by Belle Boyd, has met with one seemingly effective objection expressed vigorously by Mr. R. L. Wright in *Forgotten Ladies* and the uncritically imitative Mr. W. O. Stevens in *The Shenandoah and Its Byways*.[131] This is that Belle could not have seen Ben Butler at Fortress Monroe because he was stationed elsewhere.

This argument would be conclusive—if correct. But neither the War Department nor grim Ben Butler supports these critics. In his memoirs the General himself records that he was appointed to command the Department of Virginia and North Carolina on November 2, 1863, and shows that on the 18th he wrote Secretary Stanton from Fortress Monroe about the exchange of prisoners.[132] That he was there on December 2nd, the day Belle relates she saw him, is clear from an item in *The National Intelligencer* on December 8th reporting that General Butler and staff left the Fortress on the 4th on a blockade mission.

Actually, Mr. Wright and Mr. Stevens do not claim General Butler was not at Fortress Monroe on December 2, 1863. Confusing Belle's second release in December, 1863 with her first release in August, 1862, they maintain in effect that her tale of seeing General Butler in December, 1863 is false because in August, 1862 General Dix had replaced General Butler at Fortress Monroe and the latter was then at New Orleans.

One such absurdity, when unintentional, would be excusable and even mildly amusing. But this one, unfortunately, is typical of numerous other unjustifiable inaccuracies and distortions by Mr. Wright and

Mr. Stevens regarding Belle Boyd which, as shown in Chapter Thirty-five, make their critical essays on her unreliable.

From General Butler's headquarters, Belle was taken to a hotel, and required to give her word that she would not leave the premises without permission. Here among other involuntary guests she noticed the Misses Lomax, sisters of General Lomax, Miss Goldsborough of Baltimore, and several other persons whose names she did not dare to reveal. Waiting with impatience and anxiety in such agreeable society for the next step in her homeward journey, she reflected uneasily that her vengeful and tactless retort might lead "The Beast" to take revenge by sending her back to prison.

For some reason, the Misses Lomax were sent back to Baltimore.* But for Miss Goldsborough, like Belle, there could be no return. That very day the *Richmond Examiner* told the South why:

> "Miss E. W. Goldsborough of Baltimore, of wealthy parents, beautiful and refined, has been detected in correspondence with 'rebels' and sentenced to banishment."

The two ladies were ordered to be ready to leave that night, and when the time for departure came were taken to the Provost-Marshal's office. Belle's baggage consisted of two Saratoga trunks and a bonnet box and upon her arrival she was asked for the keys. A man and two women then went through her luggage thoroughly, although she assured them that this was unnecessary as she had just come from prison. They were astonished, therefore, and she was greatly chagrined when they found two sets of private clothing, a uniform for Major-General W—, a dozen linen shirts, several pairs of army gauntlets, some felt hats, a pair of field glasses (formerly General Jackson's), and many items of wearing apparel. Most of these items Belle had smuggled into the Old Capitol. Asked how this had been accomplished, she refused to tell but begged to be permitted to retain the fieldglasses. Being contraband, like all the other articles, they were confiscated, however, and were given eventually, she said, to General Butler.

The discovery of this contraband in her baggage caused the Federal agents to suspect that she had more concealed on her person, so she was told that she must submit to a personal inspection. This news was most disturbing for she carried $20,000 in Confederate notes, $5,000

*Their mother, Elizabeth Lindsay Lomax, intimates on p. 226 of *Leaves from an Old Washington Diary*, (E. P. Dutton & Co., N. Y. City, 1943), that they were paroled by General Butler at Fortress Monroe about December 6, 1863.

in Federal greenbacks, and nearly $1,000 in gold, as well as the letters she was to present to Confederate officials.

Insisting that she had nothing contraband on her, she objected vigorously to the search. As it was getting late, Captain Cassels said impatiently: "Well, if you will take an oath to the effect that you have nothing contraband upon you—no letters or papers—you shall not be searched."

Being unable to make such a statement under oath, she handed him the letters. As she did so, he asked her if she had any money. She made no verbal reply, but merely handed him about $3,000 in Confederate funds which were in her pocket. This he regarded as valueless, and sneeringly informed her she could keep "that stuff." Possible further inquiry as to the more valuable currency was side-tracked when the Captain began to examine the papers she had handed him.

Upon reading the passage about her services to the Confederacy, her kindnesses to fellow-prisoners, and other matters, the impatient Captain became very angry and informed her that he would send the papers to General Butler the next morning.

However, he took no immediate measures to postpone her departure. Why? Perhaps because the call of romance was more urgent. According to the diary of Mrs. Lomax, her daughter Nannie, held at Fortress Monroe, and the Provost-Marshal felt very tenderly toward one another. The Captain may, with reason, have decided that Ben Butler rather than Miss Nannie would have to wait.

Throughout Belle's examination, Miss Goldsborough, who had been subjected to a similar ordeal earlier in the day, sat nearby, a thoroughly interested and sympathetic spectator.

After Captain Cassels' statement that he would report to General Butler, the two women were taken to the wharf, placed on a tug, and sent off to the Federal exchange boat, the *City of New York.* Major Mulford received them kindly, conducted them to the salon, and presented them to his wife—a very charming lady. The boat remained at anchor all night, but got under way the next morning at seven. It ran aground an hour later, but was soon freed, and headed for City Point.

As they resumed way, Belle noticed that the tug had again put out and was apparently in pursuit of their vessel. Her heart sank for she feared this meant that General Butler had ordered her detention. But Major Mulford, angered by the delay caused by the accident and anxious to proceed, paid no heed to the tug and the *City of New York* quickly left it far behind.

Later, Belle learned that her fears had not been unfounded. When General Butler, already smarting from the sting of her sarcastic parting shot, saw the letters Captain Cassels had taken from her, he ordered that she be taken into custody again and sent to Fort Warren in Massachusetts Bay. In issuing these instructions, she states he remarked he would now indeed play a leading rôle in "Beauty and the Beast." When the tug returned without her, he was beside himself with rage at being thwarted. "This I had from such good authority," she wrote later, "that I am confident the General will not feel it worth his while to contradict the statement."

The exchange boat arrived at City Point late in the evening of December 4th. The next morning the two ladies were taken on board the Southern flag-of-truce vessel of which Captain Hatch, Confederate exchange officer, was in charge. On the way up the James, he had to proceed cautiously through military obstructions between Chapin's and Drury's Bluffs, intended to prevent hostile ships from proceeding upstream. In spite of all his precautions, the boat became entangled with one of these obstacles and was forced to put in at Drury's Bluff. Here the ladies were transferred to a tug which took them to Richmond. They arrived in the Confederate Capital at eight o'clock in the evening and put up at the Spotswood House.

At breakfast the next day, friends and acquaintances of Belle expressed surprise on seeing her for her release was totally unexpected. However, the morning papers announced her return and thereafter she was besieged with company. This warm friendly reception pleased her greatly, but the happiness it gave her was of short duration.

On Saturday, December 12th, one week after her arrival, she was a joyous and light-hearted guest at a dinner party. Two days later, on the morning of the 14th, before rising, she received a note from Captain Hatch expressing great sorrow at being the bearer of mournful tidings and stating that when she was dressed he would call upon her accompanied by the hotel proprietor's wife. She dressed hurriedly, and sent for him.

Holding a newspaper in his hand, Captain Hatch approached her and said: "Miss Belle, you are aware that you left your father ill?" There was no need for him to continue. Grasping the import of his call instantly, she exclaimed: "My God! Is he dead?" and fainted.

While she recovered consciousness quickly, the shock of her father's death and her greatly weakened condition combined to cause another spell of severe and prolonged illness. Despite her weakness and the

Federal sentence of banishment, she felt she must rejoin her mother immediately. Several Southern Senators, officers in charge of exchange of prisoners, and other influential persons wrote to the Federal Government urging that she be granted permission to return to her widowed mother. At the suggestion of friends, she herself wrote to President Lincoln and Secretary Stanton and appealed to them as the daughter of a brother Mason. But all these requests were refused.

Her health finally became so bad that it was necessary for her to go farther South. In February she left Richmond for Mobile, Atlanta, Augusta, and other points. During this trying time, she was the grateful recipient of every possible attention and kindness. She records:

> "I cannot express one half the gratitude that I feel to the many kind hosts whom I met in my journey through the South. During my illness in Richmond I was well cared for; and among the warmest of my friends must be ranked the wife of the world-renowned Captain Semmes, afterwards Admiral Semmes, of the ill-fated *Alabama*.
>
> "Mrs. Semmes treated me with as much attention as though I had been her own daughter and invited me to visit them at their home in Mobile."

Later she learned the details of her father's death. Her mother wrote that, upon hearing that his daughter had been sent South, Mr. Boyd's condition became steadily worse. When it became evident that death was certain, relatives in Washington sent for Mrs. Boyd and the children and they reached his side just before he passed away. He was conscious to the end and spoke often of his absent daughter. He declared she was hovering about his couch, became quite restive if anyone in the room approached a certain spot, and complained that Belle was being kept from him. He died on December 6th, the day after her arrival in Richmond.

While her father's death was totally unexpected, she felt subsequently that a strange dream should have prepared her for this grievous blow. On the night her father died, she had retired earlier than usual, and soon fell asleep. She awoke suddenly, or seemed to awaken, but found she had neither the power nor the desire to move. In the center of her room stood General Jackson, whose eyes rested sorrowfully upon her. Beside him stood her father, who looked at her but said nothing. As she stared at them standing together, General Jackson turned and said to Mr. Boyd: "It is time for us to go." Then, taking her father's hand, the General led him away, adding, as he did so: "Poor child!"

CHAPTER TWENTY-THREE

Dispatches for England, and Capture at Sea

IT was March, 1864, when Belle returned to Richmond from her second tour of the South. Although her condition had improved, her constitution had been badly undermined, and her health required much care. To go home was impossible, and as, since her father's death, she felt more restless than ever, and very unhappy, she decided to go to Europe. When she made this plan known to President Davis, he readily approved.

The reason he so readily approved was doubtless that Belle was to carry Confederate dispatches to England. Her later words, "I knew that the venture was a desperate one" indicate that the pretext of a Continental voyage on the ground of ill-health was used primarily to secure for her the more privileged status of a private person on a personal errand in case of capture by the Federals.

For a private individual to cross the Atlantic on a purely private matter was then very difficult. The Southern ports were blockaded and the only vessels operating were blockade runners carrying Southern goods to Europe to sell and returning with desperately needed materials bought abroad. Ostensibly privately owned, the blockade runners were often owned fully or in partnership by the Confederacy and, though registered usually as British in the name of a nominal British owner and flying the British flag at sea, they generally displayed the Confederate flag when not in danger of capture as prizes of war. These ships had practically no accommodations for passengers. Those they carried had to be approved by the Confederate Government and most of them were on official business to and from Southern agents and connections abroad.

Orders were given to the Secretary of State to make Belle a bearer of dispatches, and she began her preparations for the ocean voyage. The dispatches were ready on March 25th, but a brief recurrence of illness prevented her departure, and as the papers she was to take were too important to be delayed, they went forward by some other messenger. On March 29th she left Richmond with other dispatches. But her train arrived behind schedule at Wilmington, North Carolina, and she found that the blockade runner on which she expected to sail had left several hours earlier.

To her dismay, she learned that no ship would sail thereafter for at least two weeks. Not only was there no available boat in port, but had there been it would not have invited capture by making its departure visible to the Federal blockaders during the period of the full moon.

After a prolonged wait at Wilmington, several ships arrived. Among them was the steamer *Greyhound* commanded by an officer to whom Belle referred only as Captain "Henry." He invited her to take passage on his ship. As she was acquainted with his family, she accepted gratefully and felt particularly secure because he was a skillful naval commander. According to her, he had held a commission in the United States Navy for many years, had resigned at the beginning of the war to enter the Confederate Navy, and, strange indeed to relate, had also served on "Stonewall" Jackson's staff.

But Belle was not the only passenger upon whom the *Greyhound's* mysterious master made a most favorable impression. In one of his books, Mr. Pollard, editor of the *Richmond Examiner*, mentions that Captain "Henry," about whose name and nationality he states blockade runners could have no impertinent curiosity, had been wounded while serving with "Stonewall" Jackson. Then he adds: "What a splendid fellow he was; a graceful dash of manner which yet beamed with intelligence, an exuberant hospitality, a kindness that when it did a graceful thing so gracefully waived all expressions of obligation."[133]

It was on the evening of May 8th that Belle bade farewell to her friends in Wilmington and went on board the *Greyhound*. It was then an anxious moment for her, she revealed, for she knew that the venture on which she was embarking was a desperate one. "But I felt sustained by the greatness of my cause," she added, and thus stressed that the improvement of her health was but a pretext for her real mission.

The reason for such a tenuous fiction is more readily understandable when it is realized that Belle Boyd was forbidden, under penalty of drastic punishment, to go North again during the war, and that she was taking the precaution to travel under the alias of "Mrs. Lewis" on a theoretically neutral ship that might nevertheless be captured by the Federals and taken North. A civilian passenger traveling for purely personal reasons on a contraband-carrying commercial ship taken as a prize by a war vessel might be simply a witness detained for prize-court proceedings, and not a prisoner of war. A Confederate courier on a vessel commanded by a former Confederate naval officer could only expect to be treated as an active foe.

Excluding servants, there were several passengers on board Captain Henry's ship. In addition to "Mrs. Lewis," these included Mr. Pollard and a Mr. Newell. Belle knew that Mr. Pollard was the noted editor of the Richmond paper, but he, through gallantry or actual ignorance, mentions nothing in his writings to indicate that he knew her real identity.

On the night of the 8th, all was in readiness for immediate departure, but the ship remained at anchor, waiting for the moon to go down. Only six miles out, the Yankee blockading fleet lay waiting patiently. Its larger ships were anchored, but its lighter vessels cruised about inquisitively in all directions.

At ten o'clock orders came at last to get under way. The anchor was raised, lights were extinguished, steam was gotten up, and the *Greyhound* moved slowly toward her destiny. Her deck was piled high with cotton, and on the highest bales men were perched with instructions to keep a sharp lookout for Yankee blockaders. The passengers who, until then, had been nervously exchanging meaningless pleasantries, fell silent, and no one thought of sleep. "It was," says Belle, "a night never to be forgotten—a night of almost breathless anxiety."

That anxiety would have been much greater and akin to despair had Captain Henry and his passengers known how well informed the Yankees were regarding the recent movements of the *Greyhound* as a blockade runner.

On February 3rd the U. S. Consul at Liverpool had reported to the United States Navy that the owner or holder of the steamer *Greyhound,* cleared from Liverpool on January 5th, was one Henry Lafone. (Not to be confused with "Captain Henry.") On February 27th Commander (later Commodore) George H. Preble of the U. S. S. *St. Louis* informed the Secretary of the Navy that among blockade runners coaling and clearing at Funchal, Madeira, was the screw steamer *Greyhound* which had left for Nassau the day before. To this he added: "The owner of the *Greyhound* died of delirium tremens on the 22nd inst." And on April 2nd, the commander of the U. S. S. *Galena* listed among the Confederate and blockade running vessels at Nassau, "a three-masted propeller, called the *Greyhound*, nearly new, painted lead color, with red streak; has three fore-and-aft masts and wears the Confederate flag; about 400 tons; a fast sailer."[134]

When dawn broke on Belle's twentieth birthday anniversary, many eyes scanned the horizon fearfully. To the great joy of all, not a sail was in sight, and they began to hope that they had eluded the blockaders.

As they ran close by the wreck of the Confederate ironclad *Raleigh,* the passengers lost all interest in the Yankees for they became sea-sick. Their sufferings were great, but there was no solace in the sudden shock that cured their ailment and was caused by the alarming sight of a hostile vessel bearing down on them.

This took place at about noon when a thick haze on the water lifted and the lookout at the masthead sang out: "Sail ho!" As everyone rushed aft to gaze in dismay at the Yankee ship, steam pressure was increased feverishly and more sails were set. The object of this latter step was not only to add speed to the *Greyhound* but also to steady her.

Despite these measures, the distance between prey and pursuer lessened visibly every minute. The masts of the latter grew higher and higher and its hull loomed larger and larger. It was quite evident that unless some misfortune befell the enemy, the *Greyhound's* immediate destination was sure to be a Northern port. When this thought occurred to Belle, she also realized that, as she carried dispatches, capture and recognition would mean a third imprisonment and further indignities and suffering.

As the chase continued, the enemy cruiser still gained steadily and eventually came within shooting range. How long Belle watched and waited for a shell to be sent after or into the *Greyhound*, she could not recall. But it came at last.

> "A thin, white curl of smoke rose high in the air as the enemy luffed up and presented her formidable broadside. Almost simultaneously with the hissing sound of the shell, as it buried itself in the sea within a few yards of us, came the smothered report of its explosion under water."

Shots now followed each other in rapid succession. Some fell very close, while others, wide of the mark, burst high over the heads of those on the *Greyhound*. Meanwhile, her crew rushed upon the bales of cotton and began to roll them overboard. As they vanished beneath the waves, the epitaph uttered for each bale was: "By —— there's another they'll not get!"

Upon the captain's deck, the *Greyhound's* master paced to and fro, alternately looking hopefully at the compass and demanding desperately: "More steam! More steam!" At last, he turned to "Mrs. Lewis" and cried vehemently: "Miss Belle, I declare to you that, but for your presence on board, I would burn her to the water's edge, rather than those infernal scoundrels should reap the benefit of a single bale of our cargo."

"Captain Henry," she replied with spirit, "act without reference to me. Do what you think your duty. For my part, sir, I concur with you; burn her by all means. I am not afraid. I have made up my mind and am indifferent to my fate, if only the Federals do not get the vessel."

The ship's master did not answer, but turned abruptly and walked swiftly aft where he held a hurried consultation with his officers. Then he came back to her and said bitterly: "It is too late to burn her now. The Yankee is almost on board of us. We must surrender!" And so, at his command, the *Greyhound* luffed up into the wind and her engines were stopped.

The enemy's fire still continued. With the Yankee ship but half a mile away, a missile from its long gun amidships came hurtling with a deep humming sound between Belle and the captain and just above their heads. "By Jove!" cried Captain Henry, "don't they intend to give us quarter, or show us some mercy, at any rate? I have surrendered."

At that moment, came a stentorian hail: "Steamer ahoy! Haul down that flag, or we will pour a broadside into you."

The captain of the *Greyhound* reluctantly ordered the man at the wheel to take down the British ensign. But the sailor, a Briton, sturdily refused. He answered stolidly that he had sailed often under the colors overhead, that he had never seen them hauled down, and added doggedly: "I cannot do it now."

The Yankee ship impatiently hailed the *Greyhound* again and demanded immediate compliance. For a tense moment, it seemed that defiant refusal might be their answer. But at length one of the members of the crew executed the captain's order. The *Greyhound's* colors slowly fluttered down.

Meanwhile sailors were hurriedly rolling toward the ship's side, a keg containing some $20,000 or $30,000. As they reluctantly heaved it up and cast it overboard, Belle realized the need of disposing of the dispatches and letters of introduction of "Mrs. Lewis." Immediately she rushed below and thrust these papers into the ship's fires. As soon as they were completely consumed she hurried back on deck.

As the colors came down, a boat put out from the Yankee ship, and it quickly pulled alongside. From it, the executive officer of the Federal vessel, Lieutenant Louis Kempff, boarded the *Greyhound*, greeted Captain Henry politely and asked to see the ship's papers. Captain Henry replied curtly that he had no documents. Thereupon the unperturbed Lieutenant Kempff, ceremoniously attended, says Mr. Pollard, by an ensign with his hair parted in the middle and wearing lavender kid gloves, told the *Greyhound's* master formally that he would have to accompany him on board the U. S. S. *Connecticut* for investigation by its captain, Commander John J. Almy.

This strict observance of naval punctilio was not new to Captain Henry. It was part of the ritual of the regular establishment of the United States Navy from which he had resigned. He was now a prisoner of two of his seniors in that service. In subsequent years when Commander Almy and Lieutenant Kempff attained the rank of rear-admiral, Captain Henry's thoughts must have reverted sadly to this moment.[135]

In their respective essays on Belle Boyd, Mr. Wright and Mr. Stevens are highly critical of her account of the capture of the *Greyhound.* Both make much of the fact that Mr. Pollard does not mention her in his description of the affair. Mr. Stevens, by not conceding at all that she was on board, implies that Mr. Pollard's omission means that she was not. The more astute Mr. Wright, though he still considers Mr. Pollard's failure to mention her as significant, grudgingly admits that the Boston papers recorded her on board when the *Greyhound* reached that town.[136]

In trying to show that Belle attached too much importance to the occurrence, Mr. Wright contends that Mr. Pollard treated the *Greyhound's* capture lightly. However, the Richmond editor's narrative is strikingly like Belle's in most particulars, including the destruction of papers and of some of the cargo. He, as does she, reveals that Captain Henry had meant to resist capture, and adds: "But for that peculiar nuisance of blockade runners—women passengers—the *Greyhound* might have been burnt."[137]

Mr. Pollard also used a false name—probably "E. A. Parkinson"—and considered later that he could have escaped trouble had he suppressed his true identity. But after being removed from the *Greyhound* he insisted that the Federal naval authorities place him back on board and allow him to go on to Boston to represent the ship's owners in prize-court proceedings. There he was thrown into Fort Warren and held prisoner for ten weeks. During that period he conducted a spirited correspondence with the British Ambassador as to his rights aboard a "British" vessel. He was paroled, but in December was taken into custody again and placed in solitary confinement at Fortress Monroe on orders from Secretary Stanton to General Grant. He might have rotted there until the war ended had not the unpredictable and contumacious General Butler sent him South in open defiance of an order to hold him. *Observations in the North* is in essence a vehement denunciation by Mr. Pollard of the taking of the *Greyhound* and the treatment accorded him.

The aggressive and assertive journalist may have known Belle Boyd on board the *Greyhound* merely as "Mrs. Lewis." By the time he wrote his book, however, he had surely learned her actual identity from the numerous items about her in the very Boston papers that denounced him. Nevertheless, he chose not to mention her name. Whatever his reason, his omission is of no service at all to Mr. Wright and Mr. Stevens. What they should have consulted to learn the facts is the log of the U. S. S. *Connecticut.*

This official record shows that the Anglo-rebel steamer *Greyhound* was boarded at 1:40 p. m., May 10th (Belle says the 9th), had run the blockade the night before from Wilmington en route to Bermuda, was loaded with cotton, tobacco, and turpentine, had "among her passengers, the famous rebel lady, Miss Belle Boyd, and her servant.", and that between 6 and 8 p. m. a prize crew was placed aboard in charge of "Acting Ensign Samuel Harding."[138]

Supplementing the log is Commander Almy's personal report. In this, in unmasking the *Greyhound's* master, he states: "the Captain represents himself as George Henry, but his real name is George H. Bier, whom I formerly knew as a Lieutenant in the U. S. Navy, and his name appears in the Confederate Navy register as a lieutenant in that service." Further, George Bier's Federal service is confirmed by the official records.[139]

This unexpected disclosure of his identity shows that the naval record of Captain Bier was just what Belle said it was. Was she equally accurate regarding his alleged service with "Stonewall" Jackson? A list of General Jackson's staff contains the following data: "Major George H. Bier, (C. S. Navy), C. O., Sept., 1862, released January 12, 1863."[140]

Commander Almy's knowledge that he had captured "the famous rebel lady, Miss Belle Boyd," was no secret on board the U. S. S. *Connecticut.* This is evident from the text of a letter sent by a seaman on the *Connecticut* to his father. From that ship at the Norfolk Navy Yard on May 15, 1864, Lawrence Priestman wrote: "we have had some fast running for the last two weeks, chasing blockade runners down the Gulf." And he remarked that the captain of English men-of-war lying at Fortress Monroe "seemed rather surprised to see us towing a Steamer with the English flag at her main peak, after sending one in the day before with an English flag flying on her too."[141]

The *Connecticut* had captured these two ships, Lawrence explained, since he had last written his father. One was the *Minnie*, taken on the 9th, and the other the *"Grey Hound,"* (*sic.*) taken on the 10th. There had been a rebel lieutenant on the *Minnie* who seemed a nice sort of fellow. As to the *"Grey Hound,"* there were on board among the prisoners

> "two females, one named Belle Boyde, a spy for the Rebels. She was at the battle of Fredericksburg, encouraging the soldiers and giving the Rebel General a great deal of information with regard to how our armies were situated, and it was she who won the battle of Bull Run. This makes the 4th time she has been captured and what they will do with her I do not know. I guess they will keep her until 'this cruel war is over.' "

What did the young Federal sailor think of this enemy of the North? In the very last sentence of his letter Lawrence Priestman passes judgment upon his feminine foe:

> "I think she must be a second Joan of Arc, The Maid of Orleans."[141]

CHAPTER TWENTY-FOUR

Belle Meets Samuel Hardinge

HEN Captain Henry was told that he would have to go on board the *Connecticut*, he donned his coat. Mr. Kempff and he then stepped into the waiting boat and were rowed to the Federal ship.

Lieutenant Kempff left Acting Ensign William M. Swasey[142] in charge of the *Greyhound*. Looking at the ensign, Belle decided: "An officer as unfit for authority as any who has ever trodden the decks of a man-of-war."

Swasey's subordinates treated him with ridicule, and despite his routine issuance of disciplinary orders he was soon coaxed by an Irish sailor to permit him to take a bottle of whiskey from the spirit-room. Thereafter he allowed others the same privilege.

It was not long before Mr. Swasey caught sight of "Mrs. Lewis." The moment he did, he roared out: "Sergeant of the guard! Put a man in front of this door, and give him orders to stab this woman if she dares come out."

As Belle said later in her memoirs: "This order, so highly becoming an officer and a gentleman, so courteous in its language, and withal so necessary to the safety and preservation of the prize, was given in a menacing voice, and in the very words I have used."

To her astonishment and disgust, the Federal officers and men were allowed to walk into her cabin at their pleasure. Over the protests of the sentry at the door, who seemed to her better qualified to exercise command than his superiors, they helped themselves freely to Captain Henry's private store of wine. Swearing and swilling by both officers and men of the prize crew are also recorded by Mr. Pollard, who points out that their gross behavior drove a Negress on board to vow that she hadn't seen a Christian since leaving Petersburg.

As Belle watched the Yankees in amazement, Acting Ensign John M. Reville[143] walked up and said with studied insolence: "Do you know that it was I who fired the shot that passed close over your head?"

"Was it?" she replied icily. "Should you like to know what I said of the gunner? 'That man, whoever he may be, is an arrant coward to fire on a defenseless ship after her surrender.' "

The discomfited ensign withdrew hastily. Belle's attention was then drawn irresistibly to another Federal officer who had just come over the side of the ship. Crossing the deck by the wheel, he approached the cabin. As he came closer, she knew instinctively that this officer, the first gentleman she had seen in this hour of trial, was made of finer stuff than his comrades.

> "His dark-brown hair hung down on his shoulders; his eyes were large and bright. Those who judge of beauty by regularity of feature only could not have pronounced him strictly handsome. Neither Phidias nor Praxiteles would have chosen the subject for a model of Grecian grace; but the fascination of his manner was such, his every movement was so much that of a refined gentleman, that my 'Southern proclivities,' strong as they were, yielded for a moment to the impulses of my heart, and I said to myself, 'Oh, what a good fellow that must be!' "

To her intense disappointment, this fine-looking young officer passed by the cabin without entering or making any inquiry about her. But she lost no time in inquiring about him. Turning to one of the *Connecticut's* officers standing nearby, she asked the name of the new arrival and was told he was, "Lieutenant Hardinge."[144]

Hardinge had sought the officer left in charge and soon Belle overheard the following conversation.

Mr. Swasey hailed the newcomer with: "Hallo, Hardinge, anything up? What is it?"

"Yes, sir;" Hardinge answered, "by order of Captain Almy, I have come to relieve you of command of this vessel. It is his order that you proceed forthwith on board the *Connecticut*. You will be pleased to hand over to me the papers you have in relation to this vessel."

The disgruntled Mr. Swasey did not take this change calmly. "It is a lie! It is a lie!," he exclaimed. "It ain't no such thing! I won't believe it. You have been lately juggling with the captain. Confound it! That's the way you always do!"

Young Hardinge put an immediate stop to this tirade. "Mr. Swasey," he said quietly, "I am but obeying my orders. You must not insult me. If you continue to do so, I shall report you."

Mr. Swasey glumly handed over his papers, flung himself into the boat alongside and was rowed to the *Connecticut*. As soon as he had left, Mr. Hardinge called the sergeant of marines, and instructed him as to the posting of the men. Later, Belle heard the sergeant tell an officer of the *Greyhound* that though Mr. Hardinge was a strict disciplinarian on duty, there wasn't a finer young fellow in the Navy.

Once he had taken over command and issued his orders, Mr. Hardinge promptly indicated that "Mrs. Lewis" had not escaped his notice. Coming aft, and bowing, he requested permission to enter the cabin.

"Certainly," replied the lady with assumed meekness, "I know that I am a prisoner."

His courteous rebuke assured her that her heart had indeed not misled her. "I am now in command of this vessel," he said, "and I beg you will consider yourself a passenger, not a prisoner." In the light of subsequent events, he might well have added: "Indeed, from now on, consider me your prisoner."

At eight o'clock in the evening the *Greyhound* was ordered to get under way and proceed north, keeping just astern of the *Connecticut.* Earlier in the day, all those originally on the *Greyhound* had been removed to the Federal ship except Captain Henry, Belle Boyd and her maid, the steward, the cook, and the cabin-boy. Shortly after the ships headed north, Belle retired but sleep was impossible. Throughout the night her imagination conjured up feverishly the walls of the Federal prison toward which she felt certain she was now proceeding, and it is more than likely that they resembled those of the Old Capitol.

The next morning at daylight she heard loud hails from the *Connecticut.* A boat was sent over from the latter and she then learned that their immediate destination was Fortress Monroe, so well known to her, and that the *Greyhound* was now to be towed by the *Connecticut.* Towlines were quickly secured and both vessels got under way.

By the second night after the blockade runner's surrender, Belle had recovered her customary good spirits and, with Captain Henry, had found that the young and attractive officer in command of the prize was a most congenial companion. That evening, the three were seated together, close by the wheel.

> "The moon shone beautifully clear, lighting up everything with a brightness truly magnificent. The ocean, just agitated by a slight breeze that swept over its surface, looked like one vast bed of sparkling diamonds, and the rippling of the little waves as they struck the boat's side seemed but soft accompaniment to the vocal music with which Captain Henry had been regaling us."

But the *Greyhound's* perceptive and considerate master was soon aware that his companions found their own society even more delightful than his singing.

> "Presently Captain Henry went forward to converse with Mr. Hall, the officer on watch. We two were left to ourselves, and Mr. Hardinge quoted some beautiful passages from Byron and Shakespeare. Then, in a decidedly Claude Melnotte style, he endeavored to paint 'the home to which, if love could but fulfill its prayers, this heart would lead thee!' And from poetry he passed on to plead an oft told tale. . ."

Few women have been wooed more romantically. Captured on the high seas by a Federal cruiser, Belle still hoped to conceal her identity as an enemy agent against whom a sentence of banishment had been pronounced. Meanwhile she was being courted ardently and poetically in the moonlight by the handsome young officer of the Federal navy who had her and the captured ship in his charge. Powerfully drawn to him, her emotions were deeply stirred and urged her to fervent response.

But she could not completely forget in this charming interlude that her situation was desperate. She had known Mr. Hardinge for so short a time! What would happen when he had to choose between his country and his heart? Then came the thought that if he really felt as he professed to feel, he might be useful to the Southern cause. Unwittingly, or willingly? Either way, perhaps, but in her heart immediately blossomed the hope that he might come to love for her sake the ill-used South.

By the time Mr. Hardinge climaxed his declaration of affection by asking her to be his wife, Belle was again mistress of her emotions. With a tantalizing assumption of feminine reserve that yet conveyed she was not at all indifferent to his pleading, she answered quietly that his proposal involved serious consequences. These must be carefully considered, so he must not expect a definite reply until they reached Boston, their ultimate destination.

This seemingly tepid reception of his avowal did not dampen Sam Hardinge's ardor in the least. Throughout the remainder of the voyage, he was as kind and courteous to everyone as though Belle had accepted him. Even Captain Henry took a great fancy to him and swore eternal friendship.

CHAPTER TWENTY-FIVE

Belle Accepts Hardinge and Helps Captain Henry Escape

N the morning of May 12th, the *Connecticut* and her prize arrived off the Capes. After waiting for a fog to lift, they steamed on to Hampton Roads. Here Belle learned from Sam Hardinge that "Butler, the Beast," was still at Fortress Monroe. This made her very despondent for she knew, in view of their last encounter, that she could expect no consideration from him. As they approached their anchorage, the grim outline of the fortress loomed larger and larger. Gazing at it she felt much like a helpless fly nearing a cunning old spider.

When the *Greyhound* anchored, Ensign Hardinge went on board the flagship *Minnesota* to report and was absent for about two hours. Upon his return, the prize ship again got under way and rejoined the *Connecticut* which had kept on to the mouth of the James. To Belle's dismay, Sam Hardinge had been unable to learn what was in store for her, and his failure made him as unhappy and desperate as she.

The *Greyhound* was now under orders to stop close by the ironclad *Roanoke*, commanded by Captain Guert Gansevoort[145], then acting in place of Admiral Lee. As they came up with the *Roanoke* and anchored, a gale of hurricane proportions sprang up, followed by a heavy rain. The *Greyhound* began to drag toward a lee shore and for a moment Belle and Captain Henry, disregarding their own danger, enjoyed the hope that the Yankees were about to lose their prize. But this pleasant expectation was quickly disappointed, although Belle presumably found solace in Captain Henry's professional comment that "the vessel was admirably handled by Mr. Hardinge."

After the storm, Captain Gansevoort came aboard to inspect the captured ship. As he entered the cabin, he greeted "Mrs. Lewis" jovially. "So this is Miss Belle Boyd, is it?"

Before she could respond, Captain Henry came in. The Federal captain turned around and, recognizing him, exclaimed: "What! By ——! George, old fel—" Then, suddenly remembering his own official status, and the delicate position of "George" as master of a blockade runner, he cut his friendly greeting short.

However, champagne was now brought in, and as the golden liquid circulated, Captain Gansevoort resumed his friendly air. He swore Captain Henry should have a parole extending as far as Boston and asked for pen, ink, and paper so it might be granted at once. These materials Belle produced swiftly. The Captain's executive officer wrote out the parole, and Captain Gansevoort signed it. Mr. Hardinge then requested that he be given the original document or a copy but the Captain refused. His orders, he said, were sufficient.

As Captain Gansevoort rose to depart, he turned to Belle: "You, Miss, when you arrive at New York, can go on shore, provided Mr. Hardinge accompanies you. And," he added gallantly, "I will not enforce a written parole with you, but will take a verbal promise. Don't be at all alarmed. You shan't go to prison."

Unfortunately, the Captain's visit did not end on this cordial note. The *Greyhound* when she entered Hampton Roads displayed the United States flag at the fore of the boat but at her stern the English ensign was still flying. When Captain Gansevoort saw this, he ordered the latter ensign lowered immediately. Mr. Hardinge ventured to suggest that this was a violation of law respecting neutral vessels captured in time of war. The ruffled Captain brushed this aside roughly with the emphatic rejoinder: "I don't want any sea-lawyer's arguments!" Upon his return to his own ship he sent Mr. Hardinge a written order forbidding him to fly the foreign ensign.

Later, a boat from the *Roanoke* brought an order for the *Greyhound* to be brought under the lee of the Federal ship. Once there, various contradictory orders were received. Mr. Hardinge grew increasingly restless, and upon receipt of an order to leave his station, he had the *Greyhound* steam off instantly. However, Commander Almy of the *Connecticut*, observing her departure and that a gale of wind was blowing, stopped her farther down.

The following day a tug from Fortress Monroe went alongside the *Connecticut* and, with one exception, all officers, passengers and members of the crews of the *Greyhound* and the *Minnie* then on the *Connecticut* were transferred to the tug and taken ashore. The exception was Mr. Pollard who was returned to the *Greyhound*.

Belle, to her surprise and elation, was not disturbed aboard the *Greyhound* and thus did not have to face General Butler again. Yet it was probably known at Fortress Monroe that she had been captured, for Commander Almy knew who she was and she had learned from Captain Henry how her secret had been revealed. Commander Almy had been informed by someone on board the previously captured *Minnie* that the *Greyhound* was ready to leave port and that Belle Boyd would be a passenger.

What probably saved her from the personal attention of "the Beast" was the fact that she was a prisoner of the Navy and that the Navy Department instead of the Secretary of War had immediate jurisdiction over her. Even this was not at all reassuring for the Navy would undoubtedly consult the War Department regarding her.

After Mr. Pollard had been brought aboard, the ship finally put out to sea and headed for Boston with an intermediate stop to be made at New York for coaling. As the prize ship entered New York harbor, Belle, from the vantage point of a seat on the deckhouse, gazed at the sight spread out before her and enjoyed "a panorama of sea and shore scarce equalled in beauty by the approach to any other city in the world."

Off Quarantine in The Narrows, the *Greyhound* was boarded by a health officer. When his inspection was ended, the ship proceeded up the East River and anchored off the Navy Yard. Mr. Hardinge promptly went ashore to report the *Greyhound's* arrival, and when he returned in the afternoon the dock was crowded with persons who had gathered to witness the landing of the female rebel spy. They were disappointed, however, for a Navy Yard tug came alongside the *Greyhound* and took the lady, Mr. Hardinge, and Captain Henry to the foot of Canal Street on the New York side of the river.

Here Belle procured a carriage and drove to the house of a friend where she enjoyed the great relief of removing from her person the gold coins she had concealed about her and the burdensome weight of which had at times almost caused her to faint. This gold belonged to her and to Captain Henry. It was not, as some of the Yankee papers subsequently claimed, part of the funds the Confederate Government had shipped on the blockade runner.

On this day Belle visited Niblo's Theatre and saw a performance of *Bel Demonio*, the romantic drama of John Brougham in which the noted lyric *artiste*, Mademoiselle Vestivali, was then appearing.[146] The following morning Mr. Hardinge called for his prisoner, and, after she had finished shopping, they returned to the *Greyhound*, now in midstream. Mr. Pollard, who had been paroled by Mr. Hardinge, and Captain Henry had both rejoined the ship earlier.

At about four o'clock in the afternoon the ship sailed for Boston via Long Island Sound. Shortly after, Sam Hardinge came to Belle's cabin to repeat with even greater fervor his earlier declaration of affection. Belle could no longer withstand his plea. So generous and noble had he been in everything that she had to acknowledge to herself and to him that her heart was his. The intimate details of the tender conference that followed she kept secret. But she wrote later that in promising to be his wife she realized keenly how much their political principles differed. Against the perils and unhappiness that these fundamental differences might create, she once more set up the hope that for her sake he might in time come to love the South. It was probably expecting too much. Yet had not Sam Hardinge dared to declare to Captain Gansevoort that the *Greyhound* was a neutral vessel?

The first person to learn of the engagement was Captain Henry and he was delighted. Joining their hands, he said: "Hardinge, you are a good fellow, and I love you, boy! Miss Belle deserves a good husband and I know of no one more worthy of her than yourself. May you both be happy!"

Despite this romantic development, the thought of escape was constantly in Belle's mind. In fact, shortly after the *Greyhound* was captured it had been agreed that an attempt should be made to seize control of the vessel from the prize crew. This plan was abandoned, however, for the aid of the chief engineer of the blockade runner was essential to operate the ship. Wisely Commander Almy had refused to let that officer return to the *Greyhound*.

But another plot succeeded admirably, and was carried out as they came to anchor off the Boston Navy Yard. At the time when Mr. Hardinge was forward, busy giving orders, Captain Henry, Mr. Pollard and Belle were aft in the cabin. The latter engaged the attention of the two pilots on board by asking them if they would take a glass of wine. When they accepted, she nodded significantly to the Confederate naval officer.

Receiving this signal, the master of the *Greyhound* casually put on his hat, picked up his umbrella, and strolled out on deck. He walked slowly toward the stern of the boat and stood there for some moments. Over the side was a harbor-boat which Mr. Hardinge had summoned in order to go ashore to report their arrival, but just before going, he had re-entered the cabin to get certain papers. When he failed to find them, he asked his fiancée where they might be. She suggested the lower cabin where he had been dressing.

The instant he went below to seek the papers, Captain Henry

stepped quickly into the waiting harbor-boat. Aided by the tide, it disappeared rapidly astern. By the time Mr. Hardinge had regained the deck, Captain Henry was on shore.

Finding his boat gone, the unsuspecting Hardinge assumed the man had grown tired of waiting and had rowed off, so he called another, and went ashore to make his report. Three hours elapsed before he returned. Then he was accompanied by several gentlemen, including United States Marshal Keyes. The observant Mr. Pollard records him as "a little Yankee with gimlet eyes" who wore "a long-tailed coat, scrupulously blue, and garnished with immense metal buttons marked 'U. S.' "

Marshal Keyes soon asked for Captain Henry and in an offhand way Belle replied, "I think he is on deck."

Mr. Hardinge and the Marshal went out to find him. Almost immediately they were back to announce excitedly that the blockade runner's master was not aboard. They were certain he had escaped.

CHAPTER TWENTY-SIX

Belle is Exiled. The Navy Dismisses Hardinge

HE mere arrival of the captured *Greyhound* aroused much interest in Boston and Washington. When it became known that the dangerous Belle Boyd and the hated Mr. Pollard were among the passengers, public excitement succeeded general interest. And when Captain Henry made his dramatic escape, the affair of the *Greyhound* became a sensation.

On May 20th, the *Boston Post* recorded the arrival of the captured "British" steamer *Greyhound* on the 19th:

> "The steamer * * * had on board as passengers the somewhat famous rebel spy, Miss Belle Boyd, and Mr. Pollard of Richmond, author of a Southern history of the Rebellion. Miss Boyd came on board the steamer at Wilmington as Miss Lewis, and her deportment on shipboard is described by the officers as very lady-like."

On the same day the *Washington National Republican* in announcing the arrival of the *Greyhound* at Boston stated: "The famous Belle Boyd is a passenger."

The following day, the 21st, the *Boston Post* had much more to say for it had succeeded in interviewing Belle. This had not been achieved without considerable difficulty as, said the paper, "There is much curiosity to see her, but the Marshal is so choice of his charge that but few are gratified."

The *Post*, revealing that the Confederate spy had taken passage for Nassau, commented that the armed intervention of Uncle Sam had supplied a vastly different destination. Instead of being welcomed at Nassau, she had been politely waited upon in Boston by Marshal Keyes and "invited" to take lodgings at the Tremont House until the pleasure of the Government became known.

The *Post's* reporter found the Southern girl to be a tall, blond, well-formed woman, graceful in her manners, who conversed freely and well and was obviously a person of intelligence and quick understanding. She was also very well attended for she was accompanied by three servants—a white woman, a black girl, and a black boy.

Could such refinement be real in a person the Associated Press, the *Washington Star, Leslie's Weekly,* and others had stridently assured the North was a female desperado and an immoral character? The *Post* sought evidence from different sources as to her behavior on board ship. What it learned and related was that her bearing in action and speech had been strictly becoming and proper in all respects. But was she courageous? How had she acted during "the attack on the *Greyhound*"? The answer was that "Miss B. came on deck, took a seat upon a bale of cotton, and quietly sat fanning herself and watching the explosion of the shells."

By now the *Post* was sufficiently impressed by her quality to ask the youthful Confederate agent her views as to the issues involved in the war. It found that she held and expressed freely, but not in offensive terms, strong admiration of and sympathy with the South. That was hardly surprising, but what the *Post* learned next most certainly was.

How, the *Post's* man asked, did she think the conflict would terminate? The twenty-year old Virginian girl did not hesitate or quibble. In her opinion, the outcome of the struggle then going on between Lee and Grant would also decide the war. These two Generals, she maintained, were the two ablest in the country.

More than ten months later, her prophecy was vindicated at Appomattox, and today eminent historians enjoying the inestimable advantage of hindsight are unanimous as to the military greatness of Lee and Grant. But when Belle spoke with such prescience and assurance, Grant had commanded the Union forces for only two months. Yet she had already perceived his ability, and felt that the North would have to make no more changes in command. It was to be to the death between Lee and Grant. Was this her purely personal conviction, or did she echo what she had learned in Richmond?

In concluding its article, the *Post* expressed the belief that she would be paroled and "Boston left without a Belle." As to Captain Henry, it had, as yet, but little to say. However, it did mention that on May 19th, when the *Greyhound* arrived, he could not be found. It added, with unjustifiable optimism, "he will, probably, soon turn up."

Five days after his disappearance, it became quite apparent that he would neither turn up nor be turned up. So Boston, in the following telegraphed item which the *National Intelligencer* in Washington printed on the 24th, admitted his escape and revealed that, as the Navy

Department subsequently confirmed, it had occurred because the taking of necessary precautions had been neglected.

> "The captain of the captured blockade runner *Greyhound*, which reached Boston on Thursday noon, escaped during the excitement incident to her arrival. The ship was surrounded by boats from the shore and there being little or no lookout kept the captured captain availed himself of the neglect, and got ashore, dodging his captors."

There was no negligence, however, with respect to pursuit of Captain Henry. Detectives were hot on his trail, and Marshal Keyes' gimlet eyes peered frantically into every possible hiding place. The Boston police were also exerting all their skill but found themselves bewildered and baffled by a wealth of identification data.

The trouble was that there were conflicting descriptions of the fugitive on every point. For example, some persons were certain he wore a black hat. Others were equally positive it was white. As to his nose, it was asserted by many that it was definitely aquiline. Yet there were several who were convinced it was decidedly *retroussé*. With such evidence to mislead them, and much of it furnished by Belle and others with intent to confuse, the authorities were exasperated.

While the search was at its height, Captain Henry lay *perdu* at a Boston hotel under an assumed name, and Belle received several communications from him. Two days later, when the hue and cry had subsided somewhat, he left for Canada by way of New York. In the latter town, he was imprudent or impudent enough to put up at a large hotel on Broadway. With almost fifteen years of service in the United States Navy, it was not improbable that he might see there many old friends of pre-war days. Fortunately, not one recognized him and eventually he made his way north and crossed the border into Canada.

Only one thing could have made Captain Henry's escape more dramatic. That would have been for Belle to have vanished with him. This omission legend has tried desperately to remedy in the form of the strange tale of Captain James H. Reid of Medford, Massachusetts, who, in his time, was dean of the Boston harbor pilots.

In 1864 Reid, as his story was still being told in 1914[147], was an employee of a news association competing with the Associated Press. His particular assignment was to row out to incoming boats, gather news, and take it back to town. One evening at dusk a remarkable adventure befell him when he went out to meet the blockade runner

Bat which had been captured off Charleston, South Carolina, and brought to Boston by a prize crew.

When he first reached the *Bat*, nothing unusual happened, and he went about gathering news tranquilly. But, as he was about to shove off, a man in the uniform of a naval officer hailed him. Would he accept twenty-five dollars to row a woman ashore? He consented immediately. A woman and the officer got into his boat and he took them to land.

The following day he learned to his great astonishment that the woman was the Confederate spy, Belle Boyd. Questioned by the authorities regarding her escape, Reid told his story. As his explanation that he thought the lady was some officer's wife seemed convincing, no action was taken against him for his part in the escape. She was, he recalled distinctly, one of the handsomest women he had ever seen, "with jet black eyes and raven hair, with a lace mantilla thrown over it."

All efforts to capture Belle Boyd failed, goes the tale, and she eventually reached England. As to her male companion, his identity remained a mystery forever.

James Reid undoubtedly had a thrilling, profitable, and even pleasant experience. Perhaps he was the man who took Captain Henry ashore from the *Greyhound*, and in later years he may have enjoyed embellishing that incident a bit. Or he may have taken a naval officer and a woman off the *Bat* at some time and subsequently convinced himself and others that the lady was Belle Boyd. But Captain Henry left the *Greyhound* alone. As for the *Bat* and what may have happened aboard her, that blockade runner was not captured until October 1864, more than four months after Belle reached Boston aboard the *Greyhound*.[148]

So, despite the gallant service Captain Reid rendered some black-eyed and raven-haired beauty, the blue-eyed and light-haired Belle was still a prisoner aboard when Captain Henry left. After Hardinge and Marshal Keyes had made sure the Confederate officer was no longer on board, the ship was brought alongside a wharf and the Marshal took Hardinge's fiancée ashore. Here a large crowd had gathered to see Belle Boyd debark for, while the Boston papers had not yet announced her presence, word had been wired from New York that she was a passenger.

At the Tremont House, Marshal Keyes most amiably ushered his prisoner to the rooms provided for her. With an awkward attempt at gallantry which could hardly have raised her spirits, he assured her that in a few days he would have either the very great pleasure of taking her to Canada or the decidedly unpleasant task of entrusting her to the tender mercies of the commandant at Fort Warren.

As time went on, the Boston press continued to discuss Belle and what might happen to her. Soon it announced somewhat prematurely: "Belle Boyd has been sent to Fitchburg Jail." The distraught Sam Hardinge could stand it no longer. He feared the news might eventually prove correct and so he dashed off to Washington to attempt to bring about her release. He carried with him letters of introduction to many influential persons and succeeded in inducing several to exert themselves on behalf of Belle.

Her own none too abundant patience now became exhausted. Since her capture, she had had no indication of the action to be taken in her case and probably feared that unless pressure were brought to bear she would be allowed to languish in captivity indefinitely and perhaps permanently. So, supplementing Sam Hardinge's endeavors in Washington, she wrote directly to Secretary of the Navy Welles admitting that, though she had used another name, she was actually Belle Boyd, and wished to go to Canada. The *Washington National Republican*, learning that this letter had been received by the Secretary on May 24th, and acquiring a knowledge of its contents, printed this item on the 25th:

> "A letter was received in this city today from the notorious female spy 'Belle Boyd,' forwarded to the Secretary of the Navy by United States Marshal Keyes, of Boston, at 'Belle's' request. She is the 'Mrs. Davis' captured on board the Greyhound. She says she was allowed to leave the South for a foreign land to recover her health, which had been much impaired by former imprisonment; that she was on board a *British* ship (the Greyhound) when captured, and was intending to go to Canada to settle until 'this cruel war is over' in order to be as near to her mother, who lives somewhere in this vicinity, as possible. She says she assumed the name of Davis 'in order to escape newspaper notoriety.' This declaration is *positive evidence of insanity*, upon which Belle's earnest plea to be released from imprisonment will undoubtedly receive favorable consideration."

By this time, Sam Hardinge had done all he could in Washington to secure Belle's release. On the 26th he left the Capital by train for New York. But his fiancée and her plight were very much on his mind and he expressed his views freely en route. According to a Navy Department record[149], although he was in uniform he did not hesitate to make himself quite conspicuous in the use of language and the expression of sentiments considered disloyal and unbecoming an officer. Concerning the captivity of Belle Boyd, he was most outspoken and indignant, and boasted that he would have her released. He had with him a little silver-mounted revolver which he said had belonged to her.

The same official record indicates that one reason for Hardinge's trip to Washington was to apply for a month's leave of absence. His purpose in asking for leave is unknown, but it can be hazarded that he planned, if Belle were released, to accompany her to Canada and make her Mrs. Hardinge. He would then have had a most difficult decision to make. Should he, already involved in the escape of a Confederate officer, attempt to return to Federal naval duty as the husband of a Southern agent, and face the obvious consequences? Or should he neglect to return and thus, by deserting the military service of the United States, become an exile from his native land?

In less than two weeks after Belle had written Secretary Welles, Washington acted. Marshal Keyes received a telegram ordering that Miss Boyd and her servants be escorted to Canada. She must leave within twenty-four hours, and if caught again within the United States or by the United States authorities, she would be shot. The Marshal brought her this message on a Sunday evening, and it was decided that she should take the next train at five o'clock on Monday afternoon.

While this satisfactory outcome no doubt pleased Sam Hardinge immensely, his own affairs now took a turn for the worse and any prospect of a Canadian honeymoon vanished. On Monday morning he was sent for by Admiral Stringham, the Navy Yard commandant. Late that afternoon he sent Belle this letter from the Receiving Ship *Ohio*.

> "My dear Miss Belle:
>
> It is all up with me. Mr. Hall, the engineers and myself, are prisoners charged with complicity in the escape of Captain H—. The Admiral says that it looks bad for us; so I have adopted a very good motto, viz: 'Face the music!' and, come what may, the officers under me shall be spared. I have asked permission of the Admiral to come and bid you goodby. I hope that his answer will be in the affirmative."

To Belle it must have seemed that she would have to leave Boston without seeing him again. But the Admiral paroled him and the other officers until sundown, and he met her at the station in time to say a sad goodby. It was only goodby, though, and not farewell, for she trusted he would soon rejoin her. But she could not have been too certain of that. The charges against Hardinge were most serious, and that the Federal Government could be as harsh to others as it had been lenient with her had been made manifest on Sunday morning. It was then that Mr. Pollard, against whom the Boston papers had been exceedingly vituperative, had been imprisoned in Fort Warren. Now, as Belle sped toward Canada, it was Marshal Keyes, and not her fiancée, who accompanied her. Among the many unhappy thoughts that harassed her the dominant one must have been that Sam Hardinge was in trouble because her devotion to the South had compelled her to trick him to enable Captain Henry to escape.

As to the outcome of the charges against Hardinge, Belle—to whom the subject was no doubt a very painful one—said nothing definite in her memoirs. Some writers have claimed that Hardinge went to Washington and prevailed upon his superiors to accept his resignation, and in *Reveille in Washington* Margaret Leech says ambiguously that he was "discharged."

The Navy Department makes no mystery of what happened. Hardinge was arrested by order of the Secretary of the Navy on June 8th, was confined on board the *Ohio* until July 8th, and on that day dismissed from the service in the following terms:

> "For your neglect of duty, in permitting the Captain of the prize steamer GREYHOUND under your charge to escape, you are hereby dismissed from the Navy of the United States as an Acting Ensign on temporary service."[150]

Hardinge was guilty of inexcusable negligence but not of dishonorable complicity. The essence of his offence was that as a young officer, inexperienced in the finer points involved in the paroling of prisoners, he did not recall on arrival at Boston that Captain Henry was under parole only until Boston was reached. With the dropping of the anchor, the parole ended. The prisoner should then have been placed under adequate guard or paroled again by competent authority.

According to the Navy Department, the pilot of the U. S. Supply Steamer *Newbern*, who assisted in taking the *Greyhound* to Boston, reported that "Harding allowed Captain Bier and Miss Boyd to go ashore in New York while they were detained there by bad weather." Apparently the *Newbern's* pilot considered this was improper. But it was not if, as Belle asserted, both prisoners had been placed on parole by Captain Gansevoort. As to Captain George Henry Bier's parole and the propriety of allowing him ashore in New York, there can be no question whatever. The Navy Department states definitely that Captain Bier and Miss Boyd were sent in the *Greyhound* from Hampton Roads to Boston, "Captain Bier being paroled on his promise to obey all the orders of the prize master, Mr. Harding, until he reached Boston Harbor. There he made his escape while still in charge of Harding."[151]

Why was Belle allowed to go to Canada? Even the *Washington National Republican* knew better than to take seriously her pleas that she wished to settle there to be as near her mother as possible, and that she had been traveling for her health on a *British* ship. As to the latter assertion, the well-informed newspaper pointed out on the 25th that while it was being said the *Greyhound* was a British vessel commanded by a British captain with a British master's certificate, it so happened that "George H. Brier" was well known to Captain Gustavus Fox, Assistant Secretary of the Navy. The paper added that Captain Fox had sailed in the same ship with him before the war, and that "Brier," who had entered the rebel navy after the rebellion began, was, at the time of his capture, a rebel naval officer.

From Belle's standpoint, her request was plausible enough. For months her letters from the South to her mother in territory occupied by the North had been intercepted, and her mother, who had telegraphed Marshal Keyes, had recently been refused permission to come to Boston. Belle certainly did not want to be imprisoned in the North; she knew the Federal Government would hardly let her go home to Martinsburg; and she surely doubted that they would simply ship her back South a third time. It would be much better to be sent to Canada. There she would be as near as possible to her mother with respect to unobstructed communication but, above all, if the North proved foolish enough to let her go, she could sail to England and fulfill her mission verbally.

The proper course was surely to detain "Mrs. Lewis" like Mr. Pollard and, in view of her past activities, to hold her for the duration of the war. That she was permitted to go to Canada suggests strongly either unusual stupidity in handling her case or that the influence she claimed to possess and to have used was potent enough to insure not only her release but also what was equivalent to official authorization to proceed on her Confederate mission. She was too discreet, of course, to reveal the identity of those who helped her so effectively. But in an amiably ironic comment on the *National Republican's* articles she expressed appreciation that the promised shooting had been deferred until they caught her again, and added: "I felt much obliged to members of Congress and others who used their influence in my behalf."

The treatment accorded her in this instance was much like that given her at Winchester on May 22, 1862, when she and Lieutenant H. (Hasbrouck?) were apprehended as she was taking papers and messages to Front Royal. On that occasion she talked her way out of a serious predicament and was released and allowed to go on to Front Royal where her activities the next day were highly disastrous to the Federal forces. In both cases it is significant that the ire of the Federal authorities was felt solely by the Union officers she had duped.

It is generally understood that Mrs. Rose O'Neal Greenhow, one of the most potent of Confederate female secret agents, had many influential connections in Washington, even on the Senate Military Affairs Committee, which proved invaluable in gathering vital information and in warding off punishment. It is quite likely, too, that it took similar influence to induce the Federal authorities to speed Belle Boyd on her Confederate mission to England via Canada under the escort of a courteous and solicitous United States marshal. Nothing suggests this more than the great contrast as grimmer Federal officers dismissed Ensign Hardinge from the Navy, pursued the fugitive Captain Bier even into Canada, and threw into Fort Warren and then into "solitary" at Fortress Monroe the Richmond editor, Mr. Pollard, whose own political weapons were certainly not negligible.

What may have served greatly to protect Belle was her wide knowledge of undercover activities of politicians in Washington who professed Northern allegiance and had Southern sympathies, or had furtively cast anchors to windward. She did not betray them in her memoirs, but merely hinted that she had such knowledge and could be driven to use it.

In his introduction to Belle's book, Mr. Sala reveals that later she received in London intimations threatening that the life of Sam Hardinge, then in Federal prison, depended upon the suppression of her story then about to be published. Regarding these intimations, he quotes a reader of the *New York World* as writing of officials high in power at Washington concerning whom Belle knew more than was generally known: "They fear the truth." Belle herself wrote: "Many have advised me to suppress this volume, urging that its publication will probably cause my life-long banishment. But I cannot—I will not recede."

Apparently she could have added that she need not recede. For, though the book was not suppressed, Sam Hardinge was released as mysteriously as Belle ever was, and when her memoirs appeared, Mr. Sala's preface included the warning passage that Belle Boyd

> "is in possession of a vast amount of information implicating certain high officials at Washington both in public and private *scandals*, which she deems it imprudent at present to publish. '*The time is not yet.*' "

CHAPTER TWENTY-SEVEN

Canada, England and Marriage

T Montreal, Belle stopped at the St. Lawrence Hall. Learning that Captain Bier and his wife were at Niagara, she set off to join them. In Niagara she registered at the Clifton House, and from her windows had a clear view of the American Falls. Lower down she could see the Suspension Bridge crossing over to the States and offering a constant and almost irresistible temptation to venture back. An even more powerful deterrent, however, was the news given her on good authority that more than one hundred thousand dollars would be paid if she and Captain Bier were captured, and that Federal agents were stationed at the bridge to trap them if they tried to enter.

She and Captain Bier soon discovered that even in Canada they were subject to constant surveillance by Federal detectives. They watched closely two very foppishly dressed men with waxed mustaches who were apparently very much interested in them, and became convinced that they were Yankee agents. Not long after this, they started for Quebec. When they stopped at Toronto en route they found the same sleuths at the railroad station. As the supposed Federal operatives also took passage with them on the steamer for Montreal, Belle and Captain Bier determined to make certain that they were both being followed.

At Montreal Captain and Mrs. Bier went to the Donegana Hotel and Belle stayed again at the St. Lawrence Hall. She immediately found one of the Federal men at her hotel and Captain Bier reported the other at his.

When the Biers and Belle went on to Quebec, the two agents still accompanied them. It was only when Belle sailed for England that the one trailing her was shaken off. However, he did try to secure passage on the same boat but failed to obtain accommodations.

In Liverpool Belle remained for a few days at the Washington Hotel and then went to London. There she visited Mr. Hotze, the Confederacy's commercial agent, for whom she had been given in Richmond communications from the Secretary of State. She reported to Mr. Hotze that these dispatches had been destroyed and she states that this ended her connection with the Confederate Government for the time being. What she does not state and yet is more than probable is that she gave Mr. Hotze verbal information which she could not have delivered had she not been permitted to continue her trip to England.

Mr. Hotze turned over to her a letter which had been left with him and the important news it contained was of a highly personal and pleasant nature. Sam Hardinge had come to England to join her and not finding her had gone on to Paris to look for her. Realizing that she might have been delayed en route, he had left word for her in London. She communicated with him immediately and he quickly returned to England. Their meeting was joyous and Sam Hardinge resumed his interrupted courtship under far more favorable and agreeable conditions. It soon came to an end again, however, but a more satisfactory one, for they were married on August 25th, 1864.

Among the most interesting accounts of the wedding were those of *Le Moniteur Universel* of Paris and the *Morning Post* of London as set forth in *Belle Boyd in Camp and Prison.*

The French paper mentioned, among other matters, that the young bridegroom was to leave shortly for the Confederate States to volunteer as a private. This was one of the conditions, it was said, that the bride had imposed to prove her husband's present devotion to the cause he had so recently been fighting. And it was added that the Federal Government had already placed a price on his head.

The *Morning Post,* then the official organ of the British Prime Minister, devoted a long article on August 26th to the Hardinge-Boyd nuptial ceremony. According to its columns, the marriage, which took place at St. James's Church in Piccadilly and was performed by the Reverend Mr. Paull of St. James's Chapel, drew a considerable number of English and American sympathizers with the Confederacy. These were most anxious to see "the lady whose heroism has made her name so famous and to witness the result of her last captivity, the making captive of the Federal officer under whose guard she was again being conveyed to prison." There were many prominent guests in attendance, and the notables included the Honorable James Williams, formerly United States Minister at Constantinople, the Honorable John L. O'Sullivan, former United States Minister at Lisbon, Mr. Henry Hotze,* Major Hughes, C. S. A., Captain Fearon, C. S. A., Mr. Keen Richards

*Spelled "Henry Hogde" in the *Morning Post.*

of Kentucky, Mr. C. Warren Adams, Mr. Edward Robinson Harvey, and Mr. Henry Howard Barber. Among the ladies were Mrs. Paull, Mrs. Harvey, who attended the bride, and Madame Cerbelle Reay. At the conclusion of the impressive ceremony, Mr. and Mrs. Hardinge and their guests adjourned to the Brunswick Hotel in Jermyn Street for a wedding luncheon.

Legend is most insistent that the Prince of Wales was at the wedding, and this statement is often found, with graphic pictorial embellishment, in the more imaginative articles about Belle Boyd. But there are two good reasons why His Royal Highness could not have been present. One is that the official "Court News," as published in the *London Times* on August 30th, shows that on the 25th the Prince attended a picnic given by the Countess of Fife at the Falls of Moich in the Highlands of Scotland.

The other reason is that it would have been an exceedingly grave *faux pas* in international relations for the heir to the British throne to have attended, even incognito, a wedding at which the bride was a recognized Southern agent, the groom was a dismissed officer of the United States Navy, and three of the guests were the leading Confederate agents and propagandists in England. England was then doing everything possible to help the Confederacy unofficially while avoiding any semblance of official recognition or entanglement. For the Prince to have been present at the ceremony or at the reception would have been uncomfortably close to official endorsement by the British Government of the Confederacy and its cause.

But far more significant than the absence of the Prince of Wales was the presence of Henry Hotze, James Williams, and John L. O'Sullivan. When it is realized who these men were, and the importance of their Confederate missions abroad is understood, it becomes abundantly clear that Belle Boyd ranked exceptionally high as a confidential and trustworthy agent of the South. Had these men not known beyond question that the Confederate Government had the utmost confidence in her, not one of them would have been in St. James's Chapel or at the Brunswick Hotel on August 25th.

Henry Hotze, a native of Switzerland, had worked on the staff of the *Mobile Register* before the War. In 1862, at the age of twenty-seven, he became the Confederacy's propaganda agent in England. At first he was given limited funds, but when he quickly produced results and Secretary Benjamin came to think highly of him, these were greatly increased. One of his early achievements was to have opened to him the columns of the *London Morning Post*, then the official journal of the Prime Minister, Lord Palmerston. Gradually other English papers extended him a similar courtesy and, as inspired articles in the English press began to gain more and more sympathy for the South, his status soon approached that of an unofficial and highly respected ambassador of the Confederate States at the Court of St. James.

Intellectually honest and a most successful propagandist, it is claimed that he showed far more insight into public opinion than the more publicized Confederate representatives, Mason and Slidell and, in fact, possessed a masterly *finesse* in resourcefulness which would have done honor to Bismarck or Cavour. His fastidiousness, deftness, and lightness of touch in a delicate situation were remarkable.[152] For Henry Hotze to go to Belle's wedding was to bestow deliberately upon her the highest honor within his power.

As for James Williams, he had been made Minister to Turkey by President Buchanan. When the War began, he went to Europe as a Confederate minister at large and propagandist and gave Mr. Hotze highly effective aid. His articles in various newspapers played an important part in swinging the English middle and upper classes to the Southern cause. It was he who visited Emperor Maximilian at "Miramar" and persuaded him it would be advantageous to ally himself with the Confederacy, or at least to recognize it. Further, Mr. Williams kept Mason and Slidell fully posted and carried on a secret correspondence with Jefferson Davis.

But what must have mattered most to Belle Boyd and James Williams in London in August, 1864, was that they were in a sense "home folks" and could talk for hours of relatives and friends in Knoxville and of gay private and official parties in the old Blount Mansion. Williams, a Tennesseean, had founded the *Knoxville Post* in 1841, and had edited it for several years. He had also founded the Deaf and Dumb Asylum in Knoxville, and in 1843 had been elected to the State House of Representatives. He must have known Belle's cousin, Judge Samuel Beckett Boyd, who was mayor of Knoxville from 1847 to 1852. And he must have known her first cousin of the same name who had left Martinsburg, settled in Knoxville, and married a Boyd cousin there, for this Samuel Beckett Boyd, in whose Knoxville home Belle's grandmother had died in 1857, became in 1859 a trustee of the Asylum Mr. Williams had established.[153]

John L. O'Sullivan, the third Confederate official at the wedding, was a prominent journalist and diplomat. Coiner of the righteous term "Manifest Destiny" to express American imperialism, he had been United States Minister at Lisbon from 1854 to 1858. Having established the *United States Magazine and Democratic Review*, his contributors included his warm friend Nathaniel Hawthorne, Thoreau, Poe, Bryant, and other great writers and poets. Later, with Samuel J. Tilden, he founded the *New York Morning News*. As a Southern "rebel" he held the official position of Special Agent of the Confederate Government in London.

History records also an earlier association of their names in flagrant "rebellion" which Belle Boyd and John L. O'Sullivan could hardly have failed to recall and discuss. Mr. O'Sullivan's great-grandfather John had been adjutant-general of the army of "Bonnie Prince Charlie" in 1745. The following year he fought at Culloden where the Duke of Cumberland defeated the unhappy Stuart prince. It was on that historic field that the English captured a probable kinsman of Belle's, William Boyd, fourth Earl of Kilmarnock, who was taken to the Tower of London, convicted of high treason, and beheaded.[154]

News of the Hardinge-Boyd marriage reached the States quickly. On September 8th the *New York World* reprinted a long and highly inaccurate account from the *London Shipping Gazette* of August 26th. This gave the readers of the New York paper an amazing amount of misinformation.

They learned, for instance, that the Federal vessel that had captured the *Greyhound* was the "Connactuca"; that Belle's father was a general who owned vast estates in Virginia; and that Belle, who had accompanied him throughout his campaign with "Stonewall" Jackson, had heroically led troops to battle. They were told, too, that she and Hardinge had escaped from the *Greyhound* together; that Belle had enlisted her husband's support for the South; and that both intended to run the blockade to join the service of the Confederacy.

Possibly this imaginatively embroidered tale gave Captain Reid the germ of his story about Belle Boyd escaping with a naval officer from a ship in Boston Harbor. When it came to the attention of the Federal authorities, who doubtless had already read in French and other foreign papers that Belle expected her husband to fight for the South, it surely induced in them a not unnatural desire to take Sam Hardinge into custody on sight. They did not have to wait very long to gratify this wish.

CHAPTER TWENTY-EIGHT

Hardinge in Old Capitol Prison and at Fort Delaware

ARDINGE was to leave England late in September. He did not sail until November. Then, instead of boarding a blockade runner he took a ship for Boston.

Why Hardinge did not sail directly to the South is not clear. If he carried Confederate dispatches, that should have been his course. According to Belle, the sole purpose of his trip was to communicate with her family. This was hardly an adequate pretext, even if coupled with a desire to see his own parents. After all, neither Belle nor he could fail to realize, in view of the *Greyhound* episode, their marriage, and the printed foreign reports regarding his intention to serve the South, that he would be arrested, if only for investigation, when found on Northern soil. And Boston, where he was now so well known, was seemingly the worst possible choice as a port of entry. There must have been some other reason for the trip. Perhaps something had been left unfinished at Boston.

On leaving Boston, Hardinge first visited his parents in Brooklyn. He then left for Martinsburg via Baltimore. Upon arrival at his wife's home, he found that Mrs. Boyd and Belle's sister were visiting about ten miles away. He was received by his wife's grandmother, Mrs. Ruth Burns Glenn, and the servants, and given Belle's room. The widow of old Captain Glenn shed tears when she learned his identity, welcomed him affectionately, and spent the entire evening in conversation with him. Later, he wrote in the journal he kept for Belle, and which is contained in her memoirs.

> "When, at last, I retired to sleep, it was in your own room; and as I entered in at the door, I uncovered my head and thought of you.
>
> "This was your room. Here you had been held a prisoner, and had suffered the torture of an agonizing doubt as to your fate. Here lay your books just as you had left them. Writings, quotations, every thing to remind me of you, were here; and I do not know how long a time I should have stood gazing about me in silence, had it not been for my revery being disturbed by the little

> negro servant, who broke the silence by saying, 'No one's ever sleep in dis room since Missy Bel' been gone—missus says you're de only purson as should.'
>
> "So, when I retired to bed that night and Jim had been dismissed from further attendance upon me, I lay for a long time thinking, looking into the fire, that glimmered and glared about the room, picturing you here, there, and everywhere about the chamber, and thinking of you sadly, far away from me in England —the exile, lonely and sad."

Sam Hardinge remained in Martinsburg until the next afternoon and left for Baltimore at five-thirty o'clock. Apparently, Mrs. Boyd had not returned before his departure, and it is strange indeed that he went off without seeing her. Surely, unless something was amiss, he would have waited.

Possibly he received a warning and left hurriedly. At any rate, he got no farther than Monacocy Station where he was arrested and charged, he recorded, with being a deserter. This could only have been a pretext to take him into custody, for he had been dismissed from the naval service. At Harper's Ferry, where he was sent, he was questioned at some length by General Stevenson who called him a spy and asked him to produce the Confederate dispatches he was believed to be carrying.

Hardinge's arrest caused quite a stir, said the *Washington Star* on December 6th. He was made prisoner on Friday, the 2nd, and when questioned as to his motive in visiting Martinsburg, said he had intended to take his sister-in-law, Mamie Boyd, North to educate her. The military authorities, naturally, did not believe this and feared Belle was "lurking somewhere in the vicinity in which Hardinge was captured."

When taken into custody, the prisoner, a medium-sized man with dark hair, dark hazel eyes, and a thin, smooth face, was dressed tastefully in broadcloth, wore a tall beaver hat, and carried a cane. The *Star* observed he could not be called handsome. But he evidently thought highly of himself, had the gift of "gab" in abundance, and "while being conveyed to the Old Capitol, he conversed freely with the officer having him in charge and boasted of his wealth and education." He also asserted that his wife was still in Europe, writing the history of her adventures, and that he was engaged upon a novel which would be called "The Wreck."

Taken to Washington, he was first imprisoned in Forrest Hall, better known as "The Last Ditch" because it was considered the worst

Federal prison. Removed to the Old Capitol, he was finally placed in Room 35 of Carroll Prison. Here on December 24th, Mrs. Boyd wrote him lamenting that the authorities would not let her call.

Hardinge's journal, written primarily for his wife's eyes, gives many details of his life in the prison so well known to her, and reveals how hard it was for him to adapt himself to his new situation. He describes Superintendent Wood well, tells several stories about him, and confides that Wood claimed he had a notebook of reminiscences about the Old Capitol which, if published, would equal any of Reynolds's novels of the Tower of London. But, in general, Hardinge's experiences were unpleasant, and it is clear that his imprisonment weakened him physically and depressed him mentally. However, he derived great comfort and satisfaction from the constant consideration accorded him by Confederate prisoners when they learned he was Belle Boyd's husband.

That he loved her very deeply is certain. And he was extremely sensitive to the slightest criticism of her. But Belle relished flaying her Northern critics and was far more concerned with what she thought of them and their cause than with their reflections upon her. The *Washington Star,* in a nostalgic editorial on May 8, 1943, discloses that, after marrying Sam Hardinge, Belle sent the *Star* a letter from London recounting her experiences. That the contents of this letter are not now available is much to be regretted for, comments the *Star.* "Miss Boyd's literary style was as compelling as her personality. To say that she wrote 'like a prairie fire' is to be guilty of 'a masterpiece of understatement.' "

The editor to whom Belle wrote was Crosby Stuart Noyes. He was probably still editor when, a short time later, Hardinge, then in the Old Capitol, was deeply hurt by some rather scornful allusions to his wife and himself in the *Star.* He, too, wrote the editor. But his note was a formal challenge to that startled gentleman to make good his words on the field of honor.[155] No duel followed, of course. Yet no one, and least of all the newspaperman, could have doubted that Sam Hardinge was in deadly earnest.

Meanwhile the prisoner's parents had learned of his arrest and where he was confined. They came to Washington, and tried to see him. They succeeded only after calling on Secretary Stanton and obtaining a pass.

During their visit Hardinge discovered he was to be sent to Fort Delaware near Wilmington. At this point in his journal there is much confusion for though he is then supposed to be at Fort Delaware he continues to write as though still in Carroll Prison.

It was on the train to Wilmington that Lieutenant C. of Major Gilmor's command asked him if he knew of Miss Belle Boyd, and, relating her presence at the battle of Winchester, said feelingly, "Well, there isn't a Southerner who would not lay down his life for her."*

The Confederate cavalryman then added it was said Miss Belle had married a Yankee, asserted he would not believe it, and insisted the fortunate man must be a rebel. At this point, Hardinge identified himself as Belle Boyd's husband. Lieutenant C. apologized for his personal remarks, Sam Hardinge assured him he saw no grounds for offense, and the two were the best of friends for the remainder of their journey.

The conditions of Hardinge's imprisonment in Fort Delaware were seemingly even more severe than in Washington, and it is highly probable that they seriously impaired his health. When finally released without explanation on February 3rd, 1865, by Special Orders, No. 62, Headquarters, Fort Delaware, he was so weak that he could barely move. Yet he was simply put out of the prison to make his own way as best he could to town, sixteen miles away. He could procure no transportation and trudged on swollen, rag-encased feet for four pain-filled hours in bitterly cold weather until he reached Wilmington.

The orders under which he was freed term him a "political prisoner." This indicates he was not arrested as a deserter. As the attitude of the general who questioned him shows, he was suspected of carrying Confederate dispatches. In addition, the Federal authorities must have expected Belle to harass them further and accordingly had welcomed the advantage secured by holding her husband. In fact, at the Old Capitol when Major Turner of the Judge Advocate's Department interrogated Hardinge, he assured the prisoner that he was held as a hostage for his wife's good behavior with the thought that the possibility of reprisal against him would deter Belle from resuming her harmful activities.

Why was Hardinge released? It may have been because the end of the war was in sight, and further detention would serve no useful purpose. But under the surface there may well have been another clash of wills in which Belle was again triumphant. She had been warned that her husband's life depended upon the suppression of the

---

*Fully quoted, p. 121.

book she was ready to publish. And her answer, when her own life-long banishment was intimated, had been, "I cannot—I will not recede."

It would have been characteristic of her to counter the Federal threats by demanding the release of Sam Hardinge and threatening in turn to print *all* the material in her possession if he were not freed. She had sacrificed Hardinge once to help Captain Bier escape, but now loyalty no longer asserted precedence over affection. If, as seems quite possible, there was an exchange of threats, it is significant that Hardinge was released suddenly before the book was published and that when the book appeared it contained a warning that Belle still held a vast amount of information about high officials in Washington which it was not yet time to publish.*

Upon Hardinge's release, he lost no time in getting out of the Northern States. From Wilmington, he journeyed to New York, called at his brother's place of business, went home to Brooklyn, bathed, and then left immediately for England. A terse notation of his precipitate departure is significantly the last entry in his journal. How anxious he was to leave America, and how eager to rejoin his wife, is eloquently shown by the fact that on February 8th, only five days after leaving Fort Delaware, he sailed for England.

In *Reveille in Washington*, Miss Leech relates that Hardinge died in the United States, and did not rejoin Belle. Belle's cousin, Sue Boyd of Knoxville, seemed to recall in her eighty-seventh year that Hardinge was drowned when a White Star steamer went down in the Atlantic. But in May, 1865, Mr. Sala, Belle's English sponsor, quoted in his preface to Belle's book, a *New York World* reader's comment that Hardinge had sailed on February 8th. The only New York sailing for England on the 8th was that of the *Cuba*, a Cunarder.[156] This vessel reached Liverpool safely on February 19th.

*Warning quoted, p. 173.

CHAPTER TWENTY-NINE

Mother, Widow, Author, and Actress

WHILE Hardinge was held as a political prisoner, and possibly as a hostage in America, his wife's situation in London became critical. For some time she got along on funds she had brought with her, but later she had to dispose of her jewels. By the time she was driven to make her appeal to Mr. Sala, she was in great difficulties.

This noted British writer says: "I found the lady in very great distress of mind and body. She was sick, without money, and driven almost to distraction by the cruel news that her husband was suffering the 'tender mercies' of a Federal prison."

He discloses that her agent at home had forwarded her almost eight hundred pounds sterling but that the Federal Government had extracted the drafts from her mail. Eager to help her, he wrote a communication headed, "A Word to Confederate Sympathizers" which outlined her desperate position and suggested that assistance should and would be forthcoming. The letter appeared in the *Morning Herald* and, according to Mr. Sala, another London paper reprinted the item, adding the remarkable assertion that it was in a position to verify what had been stated, and making this further comment:

> "Probably, the history of the world does not contain a parallel case. Her adventures in the midst of the American War surpass anything to be met with in the pages of fiction. Her great beauty, elegant manners, and personal attractions generally, in conjunction with her romantic history before her marriage, which took place three months ago at the West End in the presence of a fashionable assemblage of affectionate and admiring friends, concur to invest her with attributes which render her such a heroine as the world has seldom, if ever seen, in a lady only now in her twentieth year."

Some writers have indicated that this appeared in the *London Times*. No such passage is found in that paper, and Mr. Sala's discretion in not naming the paper "in a position to verify what had been stated" suggests that the journal so greatly concerned for her was the *Index*. This was a newspaper published in London with Confederate funds as part of Mr. Hotze's propaganda.

Mrs. Hardinge's friends and admirers were prompt and generous in response and her financial problems were temporarily solved. But her temperament would not permit her to be dependent upon others and inactive on her own behalf. It did not take her long to decide that there must be something she could do right away. And so, even before Mr. Sala made his plea for aid, the thought of writing the story of some of her services to the South had occurred to her, and had been carried out.

The end of the war was in sight, and probably the book was written so as to be ready when peace came. *Belle Boyd in Camp and Prison* is a simple narrative, written hurriedly and, when read carefully, betrays that a strong discretion dictated what could then be told and what could not. Belle contented herself chiefly with describing the shooting of the soldier in Martinsburg, the episode involving Lieutenant H. at Front Royal and Winchester, her rôle in the battle of Front Royal, her arrests and her two imprisonments in the Old Capitol, her travels throughout the South, the taking of the *Greyhound*, Captain Bier's escape, her romance with Samuel Hardinge, and her wedding in London. To this she appended extracts from her husband's journal.

These were incidents that could then be discussed for they were all to some extent publicly known. Her part in them she told vividly in a style which some critics have found too theatrical. It is, however, in the authentic dramatic mood of most Southern actors in our great historical tragedy.*

Belle Boyd in Camp and Prison appeared in London shortly after the middle of May, 1865. According to the *London Times*, in which it was advertised, its two volumes sold for twenty-one shillings. (About $5.15 today.) Typical of its reception is this comment from the *London Saturday Gazette:*

> "Belle Boyd in Camp and Prison is one of those books into which the whole soul and spirit of the writer have evidently passed —which are too earnest for artistic construction, too real and heartfelt either for self-concealment or self-display * * * The darling of the entire South, Belle Boyd may be regarded as the female genius or impersonation of the Confederacy in which her name has been a household word from almost the beginning of the war."

At this time, Sam Hardinge was still alive, for Mr. Sala's introduction, dated May 17th, makes no later reference to him than his sailing

---

*See Foreword, first line.

from America on February 8th. And the addition of his journal to the book is another indication of his safe arrival in England. But Belle's husband did not long survive. When and where he died is uncertain. It has been said that he remained in the United States instead of going to England, and also that Mrs. Hardinge rejoined him and nursed him devotedly throughout illness that ended in his death about 1868. This is inconsistent with the inception of her theatrical career in England. It is more likely that Samuel Wylde Hardinge, Jr., seriously weakened by his imprisonment, died in England no later than July, 1866, and probably before the end of 1865.

There is also much doubt as to when and where Grace Hardinge was born. By some, the year of the birth of the daughter of Belle and Samuel W. Hardinge has been fixed as late as 1868, and the place as somewhere in the United States. But Belle's living daughter, by her second husband, Mrs. Marie Isabelle (Hammond) Michael, is certain that her half-sister, Grace, was born in England. As this must have been before Belle went on the English stage, the child was evidently born in the latter part of 1865 or the first half of 1866.

The English edition of Belle's book was quickly followed by one in America, and her income from both must have been substantial. But, as the author surely realized, this could only be a temporary resource. For a young woman in a foreign land, with an infant daughter, and who was a widow or obviously about to become one, some permanent occupation was imperative. What should it be?

Inevitably, it must have occurred to her or to someone among her influential friends that she could play a rôle on the stage as dramatically as in real life. Moreover, the attention she had received in the press abroad and at home, and the publication of her book, were bound to be helpful.

Mr. Sala knew everybody and enjoyed using his excellent connections to help anyone. It so happened that at about the time Belle's book came out Mr. Sala was particularly enthusiastic about the playing of one of London's noted dramatic actresses, and his memoirs record that he went to see her play repeatedly. This lady was Kate Bateman. Mr. Sala knew her father, Colonel H. L. Bateman, well, and the latter—the well known theatrical producer who had managed Sir Henry Irving in Sir Henry's most brilliant early successes—was then in London. It is likely that Mr. Sala brought Colonel Bateman and Belle Boyd together, stressed her possibilities as an actress, and sought the Colonel's assistance in starting her stage career. That the producer who presented her in her first appearance in New York City was H. L. Bateman justifies this inference.

Belle Boyd, the actress, made her debut at the Theatre Royal in Manchester, England, late in 1866. She and her sponsors obviously hoped that she would have a great stage career. Her opening rôle was that of Pauline in *The Lady of Lyons*. This was a famous starring part in which many great English and American actresses earned their laurels, and it is a remarkable tribute to the ability and versatility of Belle Boyd that she could undertake so prominent a part in her first public appearance at the age of twenty-two. Great credit for her achievement must also be given to her intensive training under the highly competent coaching and guidance of Avonia Jones and Walter Montgomery.

These two capable coaches were then at the height of their own successful stage careers. Miss Jones, born in Richmond, Virginia, in 1839, had spent most of her twenty-six years in the theatre, for her father was manager of the Avon Theatre in the capital of Virginia. As a young actress of great talent, she played throughout the United States before the War and registered notable successes in Richmond, Memphis, St. Louis, New Orleans, and numerous other cities. By 1860 she was considered one of the best dramatic performers the nation had produced. She then played in Canada and Australia, and in 1861 arrived in London and soon appeared at the Drury Lane Theatre. By 1865 she had become a great favorite of the English stage, and her multitude of admirers claimed she had no superior.[157]

Walter Montgomery was primarily an eloquent interpreter of Shakespeare. He had achieved great distinction in *Hamlet, As You Like It, King John*, and other plays, had toured extensively in England and the United States, and enjoyed quite a vogue in the latter country. As late as 1870 he appeared in some of his favorite rôles at the Boston Theatre, and at the Academy of Music in New York.[157]

At the end of 1866, evidently fearing no persecution by the victorious Northerners, Belle returned to the United States with her daughter, Grace, and made her first appearance in her own country at Ben de Bar's Theatre in St. Louis. Ben de Bar, a noted English actor, was also a well known producer and manager who operated several theatres in the United States and on occasion acted in his own productions. From St. Louis, Belle proceeded on a starring tour of stock houses in the South and Southwest. For this swing around the circuit, her manager was John P. Smith. Born in Richmond, Virginia in 1832, Mr.

Smith began his career by managing Artemus Ward. He then directed tours of many leading theatrical figures, including Clara Morris and Barney Williams, and played an important part in the successes of his charges. Later he managed the Brooklyn and the Park Theatres in Brooklyn, New York.[158]

On January 9th, 1868, Belle played in New York City for the first time. The press on the 7th and 8th announced that on Thursday the 9th there would be an English Comedy Night at the Theatre Français (14th Street Theatre) on which occasion BELLE BOYD of Virginia would make HER FIRST APPEARANCE IN NEW YORK in the comedy *The Honeymoon* and in the comedietta *Faint Heart Never Won Fair Lady.* Belle Boyd would play the part of Juliana and Robert Johnston that of Duke Aranza in the comedy. There would be a full and efficient dramatic company in support, and music by "the full grand orchestra of the Ristori performances under the direction of Mr. Robert Stoepel."[159]

This particular performance does not seem to have attracted much attention. In 1927, George Odell, Professor of Dramatic Literature at Columbia University, wrote cryptically in his history of the New York stage: "I do not know what urged Belle Boyd to make her debut on January 9th as Juliana in *The Honeymoon* and in *Faint Heart Never Won Fair Lady*, nor can I imagine why she brought Robert Johnston from the Bowery to play Aranza. In fact, I do not know who Belle was; I only know that the deed was done."[160]

Professor Odell was too easily puzzled. Colonel Bateman had simply seized an opportunity to give Belle a New York tryout, and Robert Johnston, an idol of the Bowery, had been made an added attraction.

At the beginning of January, the distinguished artist Adelaide Ristori was appearing daily in *Marie Antoinette* and other plays produced by Colonel Bateman at the Theatre Français. But on the 9th she evidently was graciously willing to allow her engagement to be interrupted for one night in favor of Belle Boyd. This unusual concession becomes understandable when it appears that a capacity house on 14th Street was out of the question for anyone on January 9th because of the competition furnished by another theatrical event that evening. This was the highly advertised opening of the newly erected and magnificently decorated Pike's Opera House (later the Grand Opera House) at Twenty-Third Street and Eighth Avenue. Everyone planned to go there, and only those who could not get in went elsewhere.

It seems odd that Professor Odell did not know "who Belle was." For while there were undoubtedly persons in 1927 who had never heard of her as the noted Confederate scout and spy, so great an authority on dramatic literature and the New York stage should have known that Belle Boyd was the person whose adventures were dramatized in Dion Boucicault's *Belle Lamar*, which opened August 10th, 1874, at Booth's Theatre in New York.

Unlike Professor Odell, the great Irish dramatist knew about Belle Boyd. Boucicault was quite active in the theatre in London in 1865, and probably met her. Her book must also have come to his attention then or later. Other than the text of his play, he has left no record that he based it on Belle's rôle in the battle of Front Royal. But the text itself, although he takes a playwright's liberties with the actual facts, is ample proof. In one scene, after Belle Lamar has procured information regarding the plans of McDowell, Fremont, and Banks, "Stonewall" Jackson says to her:

> "The intelligence you have obtained is of vital value and saves our army from impending disaster. The presence of McDowell at Front Royal betrays a design to overwhelm us by the concert of these three advancing forces; if they unite we must be annihilated. Rhett, you will ride tonight for Gordonville; beg General Ewell to join me and put heart into his speed. Combined we can fall on McDowell's division; that broken, Banks at Strasburg will find himself outflanked and must fall back. Do not lose an hour."[161]

Belle Lamar, considered by some critics to rank high among Boucicault's works, did not enjoy a long run. Had Belle Boyd been available to play the title rôle, it would probably have aroused great public interest. That she did not play it is truly regrettable. But legend, ignoring that she was then in retirement, willfully pretends that what should have happened actually did. When Belle's daughter Byrd died in 1932 no less a paper than the *New York Times*, in reviewing Byrd's stage career, aided legend by confusing the dramatic recitals her mother began in 1886 with *Belle Lamar* and reported incorrectly that Belle had appeared in that play for fifteen years.[162]

What Belle's single performance in New York revealed was that she had not yet attained the first rank in her new and exacting profession. In order to obtain more experience in stage detail, she soon joined the Miles & Bates Stock Company at Cincinnati, and assumed the stage name of Nina Benjamin. This change of theatrical identity had a definite sentimental significance. "Nina Benjamin" was a combination of the Christian names of two persons very dear to Belle—her special chum at school in Baltimore, and her father.

After a short stay in Cincinnati, Nina Benjamin was engaged by Maurice and Henry Greenwall as stock star for their theatres in Galveston and Houston. From Texas, she went to Louisiana where she played for David Bidwell in his New Orleans Theatre.[163]

At New Orleans in March, 1869, she gave gave her last performance and retired from the stage. Her theatrical career had been brief and highly varied, and for the immediate future it offered much to a talented young woman who had not yet reached her twenty-fifth birthday. But she gave up the theatre and the fame she expected to win in it to reach for the greater happiness inplicit in the insistent wooing of a most ardent admirer.

CHAPTER THIRTY

Belle Marries Again

EARLY in 1869, John Swainston Hammond, seeking diversion, attended a performance at the New Orleans Theatre and found a wife. So fascinated was he by the acting, appearance, and personality of Nina Benjamin that he sought a mutual acquaintance and arranged to be presented. At close range offstage, he found the lady even more attractive, promptly laid siege to her heart, and conquered it. On March 17th they were married in New Orleans.

According to the Hammond children, their father was born in England, educated at Oxford, served as an officer in the Crimean War, and was wounded twice in that conflict. Coming to the United States later, he was commissioned in 1861 as a first lieutenant in Company H, Seventeenth Massachusetts Infantry. At the time of his marriage, he was a man of considerable means, and traveled extensively as sales representative of a firm in the tea and coffee business.

The official war records add little to this. They reveal that he was a merchant, enrolled in July, 1861, was made a first lieutenant that month, and resigned May 15, 1862. One military history gives his age in 1861 as thirty-four and another as thirty. At the time of his resignation his regiment was in North Carolina and he and his company had already engaged in scouting and raiding. Why he resigned is not stated.

The regimental records tend to prove that he had previous service in the British Army. Company H of the Seventeenth Massachusetts Infantry was known as "the British Volunteers" because it developed from a military drill club, and it was at first almost exclusively composed of men of English birth or parentage. Several had been in the British Army and it was natural to select them as officers. John K. Lloyd, who had been a sergeant in the Coldstream Guards, was made captain of the company. Robert McCourt, who had also been a sergeant, was made second lieutenant. That John S. Hammond was made first lieutenant suggests that he, too, had had foreign service as a noncommissioned officer, but not as an officer. Service as an officer would seemingly have resulted in his ranking Captain Lloyd.[164]

Although he came to be known as Colonel Hammond, there is no indication that he saw further service after May 1862. Probably he was called "Colonel" merely in courteous appreciation of his service in a lower rank. It is also possible that he actually acquired that grade in some National Guard regiment following the war.

After their marriage, the Hammonds went to California, and their first child was born there some time between 1870 and 1872. This was a son, Arthur, who died in his first or second year.

Thereafter the Hammonds, as required by Mr. Hammond's business, moved about the country. They remained in the larger cities for appreciable periods and took an active part in the social life of these towns. A daughter, Byrd Swainston Hammond, was born February 26, 1874, at the Butterfield Mansion in Utica, New York; a second daughter, Marie Isabelle Boyd Hammond, on October 31, 1878, in Baltimore; and a son, John Edmund Swainston Hammond, on August 30, 1881, in Philadelphia. In the last named town the family seems to have lived on North Thirteenth Street.

It was while the Hammonds lived in New York State that the Southern lady who had told her daughter stories of Belle Boyd bringing quinine through the land blockade finally met her heroine.* According to "A. C. C.," it was in the '70s that a man arrived on business, accompanied by his charming and beautiful wife, in the small New York town where her mother, the only Southern woman in the community, then lived. The two ladies, drawn together by their Southern origin, became acquainted quickly. On two or three occasions the beautiful Mrs. Hammond said to her new-found friend: "I want to tell you something that will interest you—well, not now; perhaps some other time." But what she intended to reveal was still untold when she and her husband left.

Before their departure, however, a strange incident occurred which increased the mystery surrounding the couple. When the Bishop of Albany visited the small community, the Hammonds were "paying guests" in the home of the leading physician of the town. At a dinner given by the doctor in honor of the Bishop, they and the parents of "A. C. C." were present. The glamorous Mrs. Hammond—lady of mystery—soon dominated the dining table, and when she spoke of England the Bishop was delighted. He knew that country well and wanted to discuss it. But the lady became embarrassingly confused.

---

*See page 26. Incident from a letter signed "A. C. C." published in the *Washington Evening Star*, May 14, 1943.

The guests, not knowing that her limited knowledge was based only on a short stay abroad, concluded she had never seen England.

It was not until years later when the Southern lady in the small New York town read a newspaper account of Belle Boyd's career that she recognized the name under which she had been introduced to that community. Only then did she realize that "the fascinating woman she had known for a few months was the same one who had been beloved of many malaria victims for the quinine she successfully had smuggled across the lines."

In Baltimore the Hammonds doubtless often saw the man who was police commissioner from 1874 to 1879. He had known Belle since the autumn of '61 and held her in very high esteem for her reckless courage and her great devotion to the South. Belle must have been glad to meet Harry Gilmor again and probably forgave him for having induced General Jenkins to refuse to let her go on the scout before Winchester in June of '63.

The Hammonds also traveled farther South. Belle's cousin, the former Sue Boyd and her husband, Alvin Barton, had the pleasure of receiving Colonel Hammond at their home in Knoxville.

For almost sixteen years the Hammonds led an unusually happy existence. Colonel Hammond was greatly devoted to his wife and the children, including Grace Hardinge, and provided liberally for them. But in 1883 or 1884 some serious disagreement occurred, and in 1884 Mrs. Hammond brought suit for divorce. Whatever misunderstanding or difficulty arose, its exact nature must remain unknown. The loyalty of their living daughter, Mrs. Michael, to both her parents bars further inquiry.

On November 1st, 1884, the United States District Court in Dallas, Texas entered a decree granting Mrs. John S. Hammond (born Boyd) a divorce from her husband on the ground of cruel treatment, and awarded custody of the children to the mother.[167] The ground assigned was purely technical. That Colonel Hammond was never guilty of cruelty toward his wife or children, is revealed by his daughter, Mrs. Michael. He submitted to the divorce solely because the woman he still loved wished it. Until his death in 1886 at Syracuse, New York, he continued to demonstrate in every way honorably open to him his continuing affection for her.

When the divorce was granted, he gave Mrs. Hammond a substantial financial settlement and turned over to her the large residence they had been occupying in Dallas, Texas. Later he created trust funds for his children to provide means for their education.

The story of the Hammond divorce is sometimes told differently in Martinsburg. This is because the *Martinsburg Independent* on October 18, 1884, printed an item under a Dallas date-line which it credited to the "Pkil Press."

According to the "Pkil Press," Mrs. Hammond, living in Dallas, had fired upon and wounded a young man calling on her daughter "Maria" because he refused to marry that young lady to whom Mrs. Hammond claimed he was engaged. After elaborating upon the shooting, the paper turned its attention to Mrs. Hammond.

She had married Mr. Hammond, it said, and discovered several years later that he had an undivorced wife. She lived apart from him thereafter until he secured a divorce, and then remarried him. Shortly after this, continued the paper, Mr. Hammond had brought suit against his wife "for the most serious of causes," but "it is understood he has since been reconciled to her."

Mrs. Michael, surviving daughter of the Hammonds, denies that her father had a wife living when he married Belle Boyd Hardinge, and denies that he sued her mother for divorce on any ground. She points out that in 1884 she herself was "Maria Hammond" and was only six years old, that her sister Byrd was only ten, and her half-sister Grace Hardinge about eighteen. She believes that the failure of the "Pkil Press" to say it was Mrs. Hammond who was suing for divorce was deliberate and most reprehensible. Further, her mother's divorce decree, dated only twenty days after the newspaper article appeared, is today in Mrs. Michael's possession.

Under the circumstances, how accurate was the article attributed by the *Martinsburg Independent* to the "Pkil Press."? Most relevant and significant is the report of the State Librarian of Texas, after searching for local comment in the files of various regional publications, including the *Dallas Herald* which in 1884 was the leading Dallas paper. No mention of the incident was found.[168] No less significant and relevant is the fact that the Library of Congress, the Library of Southern Methodist University, the Dallas Historical Society, the Dallas Public Library, the Dallas *Morning News*, and Dallas "old-timers" in the publishing business are all unable to find any record of or to recall any local publication that could have been the "Pkil Press."

CHAPTER THIRTY-ONE

Third Marriage, and Belle's Dramatic Recitals

ON January 7, 1885, Belle Boyd married again. Her third husband was Nathaniel Rue High, son of the Reverend and Mrs. Nathaniel Rue High of Toledo, Ohio. Nat High's father, rector of St. John's Episcopal Church in Toledo, had died in 1884.

In 1885, Nat High was only twenty-four years old. When he first met Mrs. Hammond he was playing juvenile leads for a stock company. Very handsome and possessing a most attractive personality, he was considered to be in his youthful rôles even more fascinating than John Barrymore, the great idol of a later generation.

Despite Mr. High's theatrical prestige, he and his wife soon had to face a financial crisis. While Mr. Hammond had left funds to educate his children, Belle Boyd still had to rear them, and support her daughter, Grace Hardinge. In 1886, Grace was twenty years old, but Byrd was only twelve, Marie Isabelle but eight, and John only four. Whatever Mr. High earned was inadequate for so large a family. And Belle Boyd High had been away from the stage too long to obtain important rôles again. Apparently, she did try to secure engagements for there is evidence that for a short time she played the part of Daisy Brown in *The Professor*.

But Belle, as always, was not long at loss for a solution of her problems. She determined, probably after discussion with Nat High, to tour the country giving dramatic recitals of her war experiences and adventures, appearing particularly before organizations of war veterans. The problem of a business representative or manager was settled by having Mr. High act in that capacity.

On February 22, 1886, at the People's Theatre in Toledo, Belle Boyd presented for the first time a dramatic narrative of her activities as a Confederate agent. In an attractive uniform of Confederate gray, wearing a broad, low-crowned hat with a large, flowing black plume reminiscent of General "Jeb" Stuart, she came out before a stage background of battle and strife. After the moment of dramatic silence created by her impressive entrance, she fanned into immediate emotional response the memories of veterans who for twenty years had been reminiscing the war. Her opening lines were:

> "Stack arms! Pile up the rails!
> Build up the campfire bright!
> What matter if the canteen fails?
> We'll have a roaring night!"

After a stirring preface, she told of her own adventures, described graphically historical events of the great conflict—such as the immortal charge of Pickett at Gettysburg—and related numerous solemn and humorous incidents of military life. For two thrill-packed hours her audience listened, and relived the misery and suffering and splendor of its martial youth in tears and laughter. When she concluded by stressing the unity of the nation with the words, "One God, One Flag, One People—Forever!", she was acclaimed tumultuously. From then on, for the veterans of the Blue and of the Gray, she was "Our Belle!"

Belle continued these recitals for more than fourteen years. After every one she was surrounded and besieged by comrades eager to discuss some highly treasured personal recollection connected in some way intimately or indirectly with her own memories or experiences. Her appearances brought national recognition as an artist, constant and voluminous newspaper publicity, and a rich financial and spiritual reward.

She not only brought up her children but, as Byrd and Marie Isabelle grew older, took them with her on tour and gave them professional training which proved invaluable later. The basis for their own careers was thus soundly established when their mother, who had by then added other artists to her program, had Byrd appear as "BOYD SWAINSTON, La Belle Petite Soubrette," and Marie as "ISABEL HAMMOND, Vocalist."[169]

In reviving for all veterans the days in which they had played heroic parts, Belle taught incessantly the immediate need for national unity and fraternity. She did this joyously, capably, and sincerely, for she loved her country, her children, and her military comrades with a fierce maternal tenderness, was always an inspired actress, and like James Glenn, her grandfather, and her uncle, James William Glenn, was most happy when talking with veterans of the deeds they had seen and done.

Her recital was usually billed as a thrilling war narrative entitled, "NORTH AND SOUTH; or The Perils of a Spy." According to newspaper comment, it was a graphic tale of daring exploits and adventurous experiences. It was a story of battlefields and the sea; dangerous rides and missions; the outwitting of Federal officers; captures, sentences, imprisonment, reprieves; and, with a real understanding of dramatic values, a notable description of Pickett's charge at Gettysburg.

The highly inaccurate Mr. Stevens, in *The Shenandoah and Its Byways*, implies that there is something strange in the "fact" that Belle Boyd lectured only in the North. Actually, while she appeared more often in the Middle West than elsewhere, she was heard and seen frequently in the East and South as reviews of publications of those sections indicate. And whenever and wherever she appeared under the auspices of a veterans' association, a percentage of the receipts enriched the association's treasury.

Handbills show that she performed in Atlanta, Georgia in August 1895; in Eufaula, Alabama in January 1896; and in Montgomery in the following March. On the latter occasion, W. J. White, a particularly enthusiastic rebel, wired ahead to her next stop:

> "Everybody was well pleased with Belle Boyd. Hope every Confederate veteran will assist her in getting a full house."

Today, in Virginia, Warren County's Commissioner of Revenue, Stephen D. Boyd, probably a collateral relative of Belle Boyd, cherishes a vivid recollection of her recital in the Old Presbyterian Church at Front Royal more than fifty years ago, where a crowded house gave Front Royal's heroine a tremendous ovation.

In Knoxville, Tennessee, Mrs. Mary Reed Boyd Birdsong recalls that Belle Boyd, a first cousin of her father and a second cousin of her mother, visited that town with her theatrical troupe about 1892 and that her husband, Mr. High, accompanied her. Mrs. Michael, daughter of the Hammonds, remembers this visit also, made most memorable for her because at the home of Mrs. Alvin Barton (Sue Boyd), she and her mother met their cousin, Charles Keith Bell.

Cousin Charles, whose father, Dr. William S. Bell, had been mayor of Chattanooga in 1858, and whose grandfather, Judge Charles F. Keith, was a first cousin of Chief Justice Marshall and a connection of Thomas Jefferson and Robert E. Lee, was then an ex-State Senator of Texas and back in Tennessee on a visit. He soon returned to Texas where he was sent to Congress for four years, became state attorney general, and, in 1906, a prominent candidate for the Democratic nomination for governor.[170]

North or South, the dramatic recital of "The Rebel Spy" of "Stonewall Jackson and Shenandoah Valley fame" was enthusiastically endorsed by the press. The *New York Herald* considered her narrative a "wondrous story superbly told." The *Toledo Commercial* termed it "incomparably the best of all narratives of the Civil War." The *Boston Herald* stated Belle Boyd roused her audience to the greatest enthusiasm, and the *New Orleans Times Democrat* reported at great length that her recital had been delivered with such superb dramatic effect that she had concluded and had been gone from the stage for fully a minute before her enthralled audience realized she had finished, and then recalled her repeatedly for a tremendous acclaim. In similar vein, the *Providence Journal* recorded,

> "Her five minute description of the Gettysburg fight was a revelation of dramatic oratory. As she vividly depicted Pickett's charge and its repulse by Hancock's corps one could see the light of battle once more illuminating the eye of many a veteran. Anon from those same eyes fell the tears that trickled down their furrowed cheeks as in tender accents she related some pathetic incident of bloody field or gloomy hospital. Taken in all, it was a master narrative and for real interest and artistic delivery has never been equalled here."[171]

Inevitably, attracted by her success, a number of spurious "Belle Boyds" made their appearance, to the dismay and annoyance of Belle, the Grand Army of the Republic, and the organizations of Confederate veterans. To overcome this nuisance, Belle had to carry special credentials to establish that she was authentic. In the North, one of these was from the R. B. Hayes Post, No. 92, G.A.R., at Washington Court House, Ohio, and dated February 4, 1898, which took "special pleasure in commending Belle Boyd and her great lecture to the comrades of the Grand Army of the Republic, in whose interest she labors."[172]

In the South, the *Atlanta Constitution* on August 19, 1895, informed its readers, "She is the original." And Clement A. Evans at Headquarters, U.C.V., State of Georgia, certified, "The identity of Mrs. B. B. Hammond-High as the true Belle Boyd, the 'Rebel Spy' is complete." Another Southern testimonial was that of the Confederate Association of Kentucky at Louisville, dated November 16, 1897. Its president stated:

> "The bearer of this letter, Mrs. Nat R. High, is the genuine 'Belle Boyd' of Confederate fame. The writer of this letter is a native of the same town in Virginia as Miss Belle, and can vouch

for her; and is personally familiar with her war record and valuable services rendered the cause of the South on the field of battle, and in furnishing secret information of the movements of the Union Army, which won for her what no other woman earned, a commission as Captain in the Secret Service of the Confederate States, and to receive from Stonewall Jackson and other great Generals of the South, special thanks for her services that justly entitle her to rank as the Joan of Arc of the South.

"The Kentucky Confederate Association commends her to the public as the genuine 'Belle Boyd.'

Thos. S. Osborne, JOHN H. LEATHERS,
Secretary. Pres. C. A. of Ky."[172]

Even such documents did not prevent Belle Boyd being challenged on one occasion. It was in the midst of her recital in a town in the Blue Ridge country that a member of her audience arose, asserted that she was not Belle Boyd, and stated that he, Boyd Martin, a friend of the Boyd family and named after Belle's father, could prove that the lecturer was an impostor. Belle quieted the tumult, arranged to meet her accuser after the performance, and continued her talk.

Later, in her dressing room, Boyd Martin soon admitted that she was indeed Belle Boyd for she gave him details of the intimacy of the two families. The Martins had lived in Martinsburg, where they had become great friends of the Boyds, and H. Martin had become a business associate of Benjamin Boyd. So close and pleasant were these social and business relations that Mr. Martin named his son Boyd Martin. Today Boyd Martin's sister, Mrs. W. C. Shulenberger, lives in Hagerstown, Maryland, and the memories of the old friendship are still warm in her heart.

CHAPTER THIRTY-TWO

The Final Curtain

BELLE BOYD arrived at Kilbourn (now Wisconsin Dells), Wisconsin, June 9th, 1900, to give a recital on the 13th for the local G.A.R. post. She came from Portage, Wisconsin, where she had entertained the guests of Rousseau Post, and the papers there had referred to her as a good looking woman with a prepossessing stage appearance who, although fifty-six years old, seemed to be scarcely forty. And one mentioned that her daughter, Byrd, had recently played in Portage the rôle of Nero's wife in *Quo Vadis*.[173]

Early Monday, the 11th, Belle Boyd seemed to be in her usual good health. But she was, for once, somewhat despondent. That evening she suffered a sudden heart attack. Recognizing its probable consequences from its severity, she told her husband, Nat High, that she was dying. A physician was called but Belle died before his arrival.

Mr. High was profoundly affected by his wife's death. He immediately notified Grace, Byrd, Marie Isabelle, and John, and all four came to Kilbourn from Chicago. According to a flamboyant article, CLEOPATRA OF THE SECESSION, in the *New York Daily News* on October 13, 1940, Mr. High could hardly have been present, for, said the paper, Belle's marriage to him lasted less than a year and "they broke up." Actually, Nat High remained Belle's husband and business manager until the day of her death. The text of the wire he sent one of her children reads:

"Miss Isabelle Hammond,
Groveland Avenue, Chicago, Ill.

"Mama died suddenly tonight. Come by Wednesday.

Rue High."[174]

Funeral services were held on June 13th, 1900, in the Episcopal Church. "The church," reported the *Kilbourn Mirror-Gazette* on the 16th, "was filled with people who thus expressed their sympathy for the strangers who came to bury their mother among strangers." Interment was in the beautiful Kilbourn Cemetery, which commands a scenic panorama old soldiers always likened to the field of Gettysburg, and "four veterans of the Union Army and two sons of veterans who also fought in the Spanish War, lowered into the grave the mortal remains of Belle Boyd, the famous rebel spy."

In a later issue of the paper, its editor, who stood pensively beside Belle Boyd's grave as fellow-members of the G.A.R. lowered her to rest, wrote feelingly of the significance of her grave in Kilbourn and that of another grave in Virginia to which he had recently paid a visit of respect.

> "She who sleeps today in that lovely cemetery is a link with that grave in another section of the Union * * * For Belle Boyd, 'the Spy,' was associated with 'Stonewall' Jackson, the General. No reader of the history of that memorable conflict, where one family fought among themselves, where the heroism of either side reflects the glory of the other, will ever stand beside the grave of Belle Boyd in the Kilbourn Cemetery without thinking sympathetically of the grave of 'Stonewall' Jackson, or the graves of the dead of both the Blue and the Gray in the cemeteries of America."

Occasionally there are reports that the United Daughters of the Confederacy have removed or are about to remove Belle Boyd's remains to Martinsburg, and are to erect a suitable memorial. But today this daughter of Virginia still lies at rest at Wisconsin Dells. In this pleasant community so much more faithful to her memory than her native town has ever been, it is to be hoped she will remain undisturbed forever. Upon her tombstone are these simple, memorable words:

BELLE BOYD
Confederate Spy
Born in Virginia
Died in Wisconsin

Erected by a Comrade

When the first edition of this book appeared, the identity of this comrade was unknown. But immediately, in its issue of December 24, 1944, Sterling Sorensen in the *Capital Times* of Madison, Wisconsin solved this mystery. Quoting from a letter of Mr. W. A. Everman of Greenville, Mississippi, in the *Confederate Veteran* of September, 1919, it revealed that he had come across the grave of Belle Boyd on a visit to Wisconsin, and had been impelled to mark her resting place appropriately.

CHAPTER THIRTY-THREE

Was Belle Boyd also Belle Starr?

BELLE'S faithful "Comrade" has undoubtedly passed on. And so, too, have all her comrades from Kilbourn. Yet, while they lived, the local G.A.R. post yearly, in observance of Memorial Day, placed a floral tribute on her grave. She was, of course, a veteran. But there was another intimate tie. Had she not come to their community to speak to them on June 13th? And, instead, had they not sadly buried her on that very day?

On next Memorial Day, on Belle Boyd's grave and on the graves of all other veterans in Kilbourn Cemetery reverent hands will again place floral tokens. For, though no members of the G.A.R. survive, this traditional observance has not been permitted to lapse. Now it is the Harold Larkin Post of the American Legion that assumes the privilege and the duty of honoring yearly Kilbourn's departed veterans, including the Confederate woman who has found eternal peace and sanctuary so far from her Southern Valley.

The death of Belle Boyd received much attention in the nation's press. Unfortunately, the newspapers, with no time to check the miscellaneous material immediately available to them, or even to consider Belle Boyd's out-of-print book, published nation-wide a weird assortment of fact, fiction, and legend. The most conservative endeavored to be as accurate as possible, under the circumstances, but others embellished her already well garbled career with additional imaginative touches.

Two days after her death, the staid *New York Times* devoted a column on its editorial page to recalling "the thrill, the danger, the triumphs, the reverses, the many ups and downs, in the life of the most determined woman foe the United States ever had." It erred, excusably enough, in such matters as stating that her imprisonment in the Old Capitol and Carroll Prisons in Washington had lasted eleven months, that she was related to Charles J. Faulkner, Minister to France under President Buchanan, and that Sam Hardinge had commanded the Federal gunboat that captured the *Greyhound*. But, unlike many papers that said she had been married four or five times, it limited her husbands to the actual number of three.

One exuberant paper which doubled the space given her demise by the *Times* also doubled the number of husbands. It set the figure at six and thoughtfully made two of them full-blooded Choctaw Indians. It named Sam Hardinge as her first husband, forgot to name the one it considered her second, said "Her third husband was Mr. High of Detroit," and added, "Her fourth was Colonel Hammond, and later in Texas she married Sam and Jim Starr, her fifth and sixth spouses respectively."[175]

There was indeed a Belle *Starr*. But she was not Belle *Boyd*. Belle Starr, "Outlaw Queen" of the West, was a notorious character of Texas and the old Indian Territory. Born in Missouri, February 5, 1848, she began her exciting criminal career by associating with Cole Younger, a partner of Jesse James and right-hand man of Quantrill, the guerilla leader. Her life ended abruptly and violently on February 3, 1889, in Indian Territory when someone deliberately fired a charge of buckshot into her back. She has become a semi-legendary figure of the "wild and wooly West." Her actual record, including her strange relations with the Cherokee, Sam Starr, and the Creek, Jim July (known as Jim Starr), with an entertaining resumé of the imaginative folklore about her which is so much a part of our "history" of the West, is set forth fully by Burton Rascoe in his recent and authoritative work, *Belle Starr*.[176]

But the mischief wrought by confusing Belle Boyd and Belle Starr is not going to be easily undone. The statement that Belle Boyd is said to have married two Choctaw Indians is now permanently embedded in the widely used and usually reliable standard reference work, *National Cyclopedia of American Biography*, and is greatly aggravated by its supplemental unqualified assertion that after her marriage to Nathaniel High, and before marrying the Starrs, she married the notorious Cole Younger. Today in the vicinity of Shepherdstown, West Virginia, one may mention Belle Boyd and be asked by those with a tenacious memory for obituarial errata, "Do you mean Mrs. Starr?"

The *National Cyclopedia* seems certain Belle Boyd married Cole Younger. But evidently doubtful about the accuracy of the gossip it repeats about her alleged marriages to the Starrs, it figuratively washes its hands by commenting that it is difficult to disentangle what it is pleased to term "her later matrimonial exploits" from those of an unprincipled woman reported to have assumed her name in order to trade upon her "notoriety." Then, though it insists it seems a fact that Belle Boyd spent her last years among the Choctaws, it lapses into accuracy by conceding that she died at Kilbourn, Wisconsin, June 11, 1900. It is highly regrettable that so disparaging and inaccurate a sketch of Belle Boyd—containing other errors besides those mentioned—should form an ineradicable part of a work accepted as an authoritative source of historical data.

That Nat High was Belle Boyd's last husband is incontestable. It was he the *Kilbourn Mirror-Gazette* meant when it said in describing her funeral that she "seemed to have held the most ardent devotion of the husband who followed her to the grave." As to the wife whose loss he mourned so sincerely, the paper had made certain of her identity. It assured its readers, "In the years since the war there have been several women who claimed to be Belle Boyd, but there seems no doubt of the genuineness of this one. Her husband submitted several instances of proof which could hardly be disputed."

CHAPTER THIRTY-FOUR

Descendants of Belle Boyd

HILE Belle had given up her promising theatrical career to marry Colonel Hammond, their oldest daughter, Byrd, who inherited her mother's dramatic ability and was thoroughly trained by her, quickly achieved the outstanding theatrical success which had been Belle's ambition. Educated in Indianapolis and St. Louis in Roman Catholic convents of the Ursuline Sisters and the Sisters of the Sacred Heart, Byrd married James F. Williams at the age of seventeen. Her first public appearance was in connection with her mother's recitals of her war experiences.

Talented, strikingly beautiful, and graceful, Byrd Hammond won prompt recognition under the stage name of Sarah Boyd. Making her debut in *The Milk White Flag*, she became a noted and very popular actress at the turn of the century, and starred for Charles Frohman in *The Little Minister*. She also starred on the road in *Darkness and Daylight*, and appeared in *Quo Vadis*, and many other plays.[165]

On March 19, 1897, her daughter, Nana Ottilie Williams—grandchild of Belle Boyd—was born. Soon after James Williams died. His widow married H. W. Mowery in 1906 and divorced him fourteen years later. In 1907 she retired from the stage, and died on December 16, 1932, in New York City. She is survived by her daughter, Nana Ottilie, now Mrs. William McCabe, and the latter's two children—Nana Ottilie McCabe, born July 4, 1930, and William Boyd McCabe, born June 16, 1931.

Marie Isabelle, the second daughter of the Hammonds, is still living. As long as she lives Belle Boyd cannot be said to have died, for "Belle Boyd, Jr." is delightfully her mother all over again. Forthright, impetuous, vivacious, and courageous, the years have weighed lightly upon her, and she is still on occasion "Little Hell," as her sisters, Grace and Byrd, and the comrades of her joyously happy youth termed her affectionately and aptly because she was so like her lively, high-spirited mother. She has today the same boundless energy, the same quick intelligence, the same irresistible determination, the same tall, graceful figure and carriage, and the same persuasive and provocative charm. And she alone inherited the fine singing voice which enthralled Dennis

Mahony and Gus Williams in the Old Capitol when Belle Boyd sang "Maryland, My Maryland!" and moved her fellow-prisoners to tears.

Marie Isabelle, educated, as was Byrd, by the Ursuline Sisters and the Sisters of the Sacred Heart in Indianapolis and St. Louis, also attended an Episcopal college near Collingswood, Pennsylvania. She first appeared before the public with her mother and subsequently played in various theatrical parts. In 1903, she married Charles W. Chase, a noted writer and artist, and lived for many years at Chase, Florida. On April 13, 1913, she married her present husband, Adolph Michael. There are no children by either marriage.

Belle's son, John Edmund Hammond, was educated in various private schools and at an Episcopal (military) school in Haddonfield, New Jersey. Little is known as to his later years. War Department records show that John Hammond enlisted September 18, 1899, at Chicago, Illinois, was assigned to Battery O, First Artillery, U.S.A., and was honorable discharged as a private on December 19, 1899, because of disability, at Jackson Barracks, Louisiana.[166]

Mrs. Michael knows that he married and had two sons—John Edmund Hammond, Jr., and Ned Boyd S. Hammond. She recalls further that he also served in the First World War on escort duty in the Atlantic. With no word of him in more than twenty years, she believes he is dead.

Grace Hardinge, brought up with the Hammond children, eventually went to California, married Lee Bennett, and died childless, in 1933.

CHAPTER THIRTY-FIVE

The Verdict of History

HAT will history relate of Belle Boyd? Unless the ignorance, incompetence, and emotional prejudice involved in the attacks upon her are challenged and exposed, it may depict her falsely as a sordid, immoral character of low and obscure origin, disloyal to the Confederacy, and the prevaricating author of a highly imaginative book unsupported by corroborative data.

The first assault against Belle Boyd was launched in 1914, fourteen years after her death, in *The Valley Campaigns* by Dr. Thomas A. Ashby. His virulent attack, culminating in the assertion that she had found no decent place in history, is thoroughly discredited by the evidence furnished in Chapters Eight and Nine.

The second onslaught occurred in 1928 in *Forgotten Ladies* by R. L. Wright, who, in his chapter on "La Belle Rebelle," as Belle was sometimes known, terms her a prevaricator and "debunks" her narrative and career. Probably the most impressive example of Mr. Wright's inaccuracy is his strange revelation that Belle Boyd could not have denounced General Butler at Fortress Monroe on December 2, 1863, because the General was not there on August 29, 1862.* Moreover, his essay contains many inexcusable, inaccurate and even distorted statements of fact which are particularly offensive and distressing when made in bungling criticism of the deceased author of an out-of-print book.

For instance, Belle relates that to overhear the staff conference held by General Shields she used a hole someone had bored for some unknown purpose in a bedroom closet, and indicates plainly her room was in another building. Mr. Wright distorts this by writing that the hole was a generous knothole provided by Nature, that Belle used it often, and that the council chamber was below her bedroom. He then disapproves of the "knothole" as too much of a device of fiction to be taken seriously. He also states that the diary of a Confederate officer reports that on such social occasions as dinner with General Beauregard,

---

*Page 142.

her tour of the South, etc., she was "embarrassed by the novelty of her position." However, this misapplied quotation is from General Ewell's brigade records and is used there to describe Belle's embarrassment in giving military intelligence before troops on the Front Royal battlefield. Moreover, the *dark* blue dress Belle says she wore, Mr. Wright makes "a bright blue gown," and, apparently thinking it more important that she be dressed appropriately than that she convey vital news immediately, he comments feelingly: "the little ninny!"

One more illustration suffices to assess accurately, Mr. Wright's status as historian, analyst, and critic of Belle Boyd. Belle wrote that in June, 1863, she followed the advancing Confederate forces and returned to Martinsburg when *they* occupied it. To discredit her Mr. Wright twists this to: "She calmly returned to her home in Martinsburg, still in northern control, and calmly placed herself once more in the hands of the enemy."

The next unfavorable literary pronouncement was far more formidable in character and extensive in circulation for it appeared in that great reference work, the *Dictionary of American Biography.* Its second volume, published in May, 1929, contains a sketch of Belle Boyd by Marie Kastner. This, aside from stating the year of her birth as 1843 and making Hardinge a lieutenant, gives correctly her own story of her career to and including her wedding, and outlines her subsequent career accurately, making, however, no reference to her children. But immediately preceding Miss Kastner's summary is the damning statement: "The story of her achievements for the South rests mainly on her own none too trustworthy account in *Belle Boyd in Camp and Prison.*"

Not a word in the sketch on Belle Boyd in the *Dictionary of American Biography* justifies the conclusion that Belle's written account is "none too trustworthy." Miss Kastner's stated sources of information for her sketch, in addition to Belle Boyd's book, were obituary items in the *New York Times* and the *Milwaukee Journal, A History of the New York Stage* by T. A. Browne, and B. J. Lossing's *The Pictorial Field Book of the Civil War.* Nothing in any of these items reflects in the slightest upon the accuracy of Belle Boyd's recital. On the contrary, Lossing's book, in quoting Ewell's brigade records, confirms her exploit at Front Royal.

Because it is found in this standard biographical record, the adverse judgment of the *Dictionary of American Biography* is constantly accepted as authoritative by writers, historians, and others who, unable or unwilling to investigate at first-hand, assume the information to be based on adequate research. And some, as will be seen, stretch its implications much further. It is hardly strange that most articles about Belle Boyd now tend more and more to treat demonstrable fact as highly imaginative material akin to fiction.

However, as no one until now has troubled to learn, the story of Belle Boyd's achievements for the South does not rest mainly upon her own account. Her account, when checked exhaustively against official records, newspaper items, and other available data, proves to be an unusually accurate recital. It is impossible, of course, to set forth here the full text of her work and to show how practically every item can be confirmed, but the following record, based on material contained in this book, should suffice.

The high-points of *Belle Boyd in Camp and Prison* are: (1) the shooting of the Union soldier in Martinsburg; (2) Belle's record of service as Confederate scout and agent; (3) the Lieutenant H. incident; (4) her exploit under fire at Front Royal; (5) her arrest immediately thereafter; (6) her arrests in July 1862 and July 1863; (7) her imprisonments in Washington; (8) her tour of the South; (9) her commission as captain; (10) events on the *Greyhound* and at Boston; (11) her wedding. What indicates her truthfulness regarding them?

(1) The shooting of the soldier was referred to by the *Daily Register* of Knoxville, Tennessee, as her "daring defense of her father's house." (2) Her service as scout, spy, mail carrier, and blockade runner is indicated by T. C. De Leon, Major Harry Gilmor, Captain (Reverend) James Power Smith, and Union scout Smitley, and in 1943 "A.C.C." still recalled her mother's stories of Belle running the land blockade with sorely needed quinine. (3) The Lieutenant H. incident is verified in detail by the *Washington Star*, the *Philadelphia North American*, and the *Times* and the *Herald* in New York; and Miss Lucy Buck's diary tells that on that occasion she found Belle Boyd in a carriage with a Yankee officer.

(4) The exploit on the battlefield at Front Royal is confirmed in part by the Associated Press, and in full by General Richard Taylor, Private John Robson, the brigade record made by General Ewell's adjutant, and by Miss Lucy Buck. Since 1940 there has been added the remarkably exact and ample corroboration of Henry Kyd Douglas. Belle Boyd could hardly have a more distinguished advocate than her friend, Harry, who commanded at Appomattox the last Southern bri-

gade to fire, surrender, and stack arms, who became Adjutant General of Maryland, and who, in the Spanish-American War, held the rank of major-general.

(5) That she was arrested right after the battle of Front Royal is recorded by two Federal generals, Nathaniel Kimball and Franklin Sawyer. (6) Her arrest in July, 1862, is clear from the exchange of telegrams between General White and Assistant Secretary of War Wolcott, Moore's Rebellion Record, and Miss Buck's diary. Her next arrest, in July 1863, became public belatedly when the *New York Tribune* and the *Washington Star* reported in December that she was being sent South. (7) Considerable data as to her first term in the Old Capitol is supplied by General Doster, D. A. Mahony, J. J. Williamson, the *Washington Star*, the *Richmond Daily Dispatch*, and the War Department records. Colonel N. T. Colby's brief reference to her relates to her second Washington imprisonment. And a significant estimate of her menace as a rebel appears in General Baker's book on the Federal secret service.

(8) Her visit to Knoxville is described fully in a letter of her cousin, Sue Boyd Barton, now held by the Lawson McGhee Library at Knoxville, and Mrs. Barton states Belle went on to Alabama and Georgia. Belle Boyd wrote that at Knoxville she stopped at the home of her relative, Judge Boyd, and was serenaded by a band. *The Daily Register,* confirming this, names the Florida Brass Band. (9) As to her commission as captain, her cousin Sue's letter recites that Belle showed her relatives a riding habit of grey Confederate cloth "with the rank of 'Capt.' on the collar."

(10) Her presence and capture on the *Greyhound* are attested by the official log of the U. S. S. *Connecticut*, Commander Almy's personal report, and the letter of Lawrence Priestman. Captain Bier's escape, and Belle's detention ashore are recorded by the *Post* of Boston and the *National Intelligencer* and the *National Republican* of Washington. That Sam Hardinge was held accountable for Captain Bier's escape and was deeply interested in Belle Boyd then is apparent from the Navy Department's record of Hardinge's dismissal and other official naval records. (11) Reports of her wedding are based on accounts in the *Morning Post* of London, the *London Shipping Gazette*, and the New York *World*.

Aware that her exciting tale might be challenged, Belle Boyd gave conscientiously the names of the living men who played a part in her adventures. She withheld only, for honorable reasons, those of Lieutenant H., the romantic Captain K., and the soldier she killed at Martinsburg. The official records, indicated by notes at the proper places in this book, show that those she named existed and were where she said they were. Moreover, there is no record that any person mentioned by her ever denied the accuracy of her statements involving him. Even more significant is the fact that until long after she had died, not a voice ventured to claim publicly that Belle Boyd had lied.

There is a wealth of most impressive confirmation of even the lesser details in Belle Boyd's story. For instance, according to her casual statement, it was a "Captain Gwyne" who took her to Federal headquarters early in July, 1861. But it is from the *American Union*, a paper published by the occupying troops, and of which few copies exist, that it is learned Captain James Gwyn, Twenty-third Pennsylvania Infantry, was then third assistant provost-marshal. Similarly, when Belle Boyd says that she learned at daylight on May 11th that the *Greyhound* was to be towed by the U. S. S. *Connecticut*, the official report of Commander Almy sets the time at 5:40 a. m.

In connection with the Lieutenant H. case, Belle Boyd relates that on the morning of May 21st she stopped to pick up a pass promised by Provost-Marshal Tyndale but learned that he had left the village on a scouting expedition and would probably not be back until late that night. She could hardly have foreseen that Major Tyndale's written report of his scout would become part of the official records and confirm her statement as to his absence. And when she ventured the seemingly questionable assertion that Captain "Henry," a Confederate naval officer, had served on "Stonewall" Jackson's staff, she had no knowledge that a future record in the *Southern Historical Society Papers* would effectively prove this odd fact.

On the score of family history, it can least of all be maintained that Belle Boyd was imaginative or even exaggerated slightly. In her book there is no proud recital of her ancestry or of her Tennessee ties. There are merely two factual statements: one is the terse revelation that her mother's father was an old officer; the other is the equally brief comment that in Knoxville she became the guest of her relative, Judge Samuel Boyd. It is from a multitude of far less reticent sources, and not from Belle Boyd, that details about the Glenns, Reeds, Stephensons, and Boyds have been secured.

There are indeed but two items of the story of Belle Boyd as to which no outside proof has yet been forthcoming. These are the two letters written to her by General Jackson in 1862; one, a brief note of thanks after the battle of Front Royal, and the other the communication advising her to go to her relatives in Tennessee. The originals are not among what is left of her personal records. It is known, however, that many of her papers were destroyed in a fire in Lynn, Massachusetts; that others, turned over by her to her daughter, Byrd, and placed in a steel box have been missing since Mrs. Mowery's death; and that Belle Boyd's extensive correspondence addressed to her cousin Hope, and believed to have contained a detailed running account of her war-time adventures, was burned by relatives when Hope Burns died. The official Confederate records are equally unproductive and equally incomplete, and it is probable that when fire destroyed in Richmond the records of the Confederate Signal and Secret Service some information as to the activities of Belle Boyd was lost.

Lack of confirmation that the letters from General Jackson were actually written is not affirmative proof that they were not. Until Belle Boyd's present remarkable record of accuracy can be successfully impeached, it is reasonable to assume that on this, as on other matters, she told the truth.

There are actually six discrepancies in *Belle Boyd in Camp and Prison.* But in five there is cold comfort for any critic. Turner Ashby, her father's Masonic lodge-brother, is mentioned as Henry Ashby. Nine p. m., instead of nine a. m., is stated as the time of her arrival in Washington as a prisoner on August 1, 1862. Thursday, instead of Wednesday, is given as the day of her arrest on July 30, 1862. January 29, 1862, is furnished as the date of General Jackson's letter written evidently in November 1862, and Belle states this letter is headed "Headquarters, Army of Virginia." The first four items are clearly errors of inadvertence by the typographer or by the author. As to the fifth it is reasonable to believe that the omission of a word occurred in the same way. Surely Belle really knew that Lee's command of which Jackson's Second Corps was a part, was the "Army of *Northern* Virginia."

It is only the sixth item upon which the credibility of Belle Boyd can reasonably be challenged. Ironically, not one of the published criticisms of her contains the slightest reference to it.

According to her, soon after her return to Martinsburg in September, 1862, accompanied by a friend of the family, she paid a visit to General Jackson, and found him greatly pleased to see her well and free once more. But in 1920, Captain James Power Smith, who had been an aide-de-camp of "Stonewall" Jackson, revealed that shortly after September 20th, 1862, Belle Boyd appeared at Bunker Hill, escorted by a young Confederate cavalryman, and sought to see the General who refused to see her, not being altogether assured of her loyalty.*

In Chapter Fifteen a possible explanation of this seeming contradiction is offered. But if it cannot be explained, then more important matters are also inexplicable, for the entire subsequent record of Belle Boyd would manifestly have been otherwise had General Jackson's doubt not been momentary and speedily resolved in her favor. It is even questionable that Captain Smith thought the General justified. There is instinctive admiration in his compliment that "She was well mounted and quite a soldierly figure," and there is an absolutely unqualified statement of fact in his description of her as "the notable female scout, Belle Boyd." Probably the reason the critics of Belle Boyd have not quoted Captain Smith against her is that his words act powerfully to destroy their primary claim that there is little evidence, outside her own story, of actual achievement by her for the South.

Following the example of the *Dictionary of American Biography*, the *National Cyclopedia of American Biography* printed in 1933 a sketch of Belle Boyd's career in Volume 23 of its extensive records. This is the reference work which, as indicated in Chapter Thirty-Three, states she is said to have married two Choctaw Indians and that she did marry Cole Younger. It errs in giving her year of birth as 1843, in advancing Hardinge to the rank of naval lieutenant, in not mentioning her second imprisonment in Washington, and in saying that she was imprisoned at Fort Warren and condemned to death. Further, it contributes a new bit of misinformation by declaring that the *Greyhound* was captured by the steamer *Massachusetts*.

By 1936 the verdict of the *Dictionary of American Biography* that Belle Boyd's book was "none too trustworthy" began to bear strange fruit. In that year appeared *The Women of the Confederacy*, a brief but pretentious study based on research financed in part by the Social Science Research Council. In studying Belle Boyd, the authors summarize her book somewhat inaccurately and, while they offer proof that some of her tale is truthful, to show that much of it is suspect they add a note reading familiarly: "The story of Belle Boyd's achievements for the South rests largely upon her own none too trustworthy account." Though they then mention that Miss Kastner in the *Dictionary of*

*Pp. 104-5.

American Biography briefly appraises Belle Boyd's career, they omit to record that what is given as their own curt unfavorable judgment is actually an almost verbatim restatement of Miss Kastner's terse appraisal.

While the authors concede that their subject was, "handsome, charming, and possessed of a deep and tender devotion to the Southern cause," they also assert that, "Her frailities were mendacity, lack of principle, and a flare* for the romantic and spectacular." No evidence is submitted to support the charges of mendacity and lack of principle. And then they damn what they previously considered merely "none too trustworthy" by placing *Belle Boyd in Camp and Prison* in their Bibliography under the far more accusatory heading: "The following works of adventure are of slight value and doubtful authenticity."

But it was not until 1941, almost half a century after Belle Boyd's death, that cumulative inaccuracy and distortion in recording facts about her produced their most reprehensible result. This is a chapter on "Front Royal: The Town of Belle Boyd." in an otherwise meritorious work, *The Shenandoah and Its Byways*, by W. O. Stevens.

While Mr. Stevens does not credit Mr. Wright's *Forgotten Ladies* as the chief source of his misinformation for his summary of Belle Boyd's career, this source seems obvious from the naïve iteration of many of Mr. Wright's highly individualistic mistakes. For instance, he follows Mr. Wright blindly in saying that Belle Boyd could not have seen General Butler at Fortress Monroe because the General was elsewhere on a different occasion, and in saying that she returned to Martinsburg while it was held by the Federals. In addition, he outdoes his mentor with various incredible errors and distortions of his own.

Regarding Belle Boyd's rôle at Front Royal, which he ridicules, his most scholarly comment is: "After that exploit, whatever it was * * *" This contemptuous dismissal of all previous confirmation of her part in the battle is particularly objectionable because it must be understood to include her remarkable vindication by H. K. Douglas, whose newly published *I Rode with Stonewall* was creating a profound impression in historical circles for months prior to the appearance of Mr. Stevens' book.

Mr. Wright and Mr. Stevens both have a clever but unpleasant knack of inflated paraphrase which induces the credulous reader to believe that the original tale must have been fantastic and incredible, and therefore false. For example, when Belle Boyd writes modestly that she dined with General Beauregard, Mr. Wright magnifies this to

---

**Sic!*

a dinner given her by the General, and Mr. Stevens, thinking this twist inadequate, handsomely makes it a banquet tendered her by the General. It is therefore not surprising that when Mr. Stevens comes to refer to the verdict of the *Dictionary of American Biography* that Belle Boyd's account is "none too trustworthy," he asserts that the writer of the material in that reference work actually says that the facts in *Belle Boyd in Camp and Prison* are "highly unreliable."

Throughout Mr. Stevens' chapter on Belle Boyd, there is a flow of such derisive and scornful comment as: "So there is no doubt about her being a real Virginia Lady," and "She was an example of pure Southern Womanhood always." However, Mr. Stevens is no more impressive or convincing in this vein than when, in telling how Belle Boyd overheard General Shields' staff conference at Front Royal, he blunders in thinking this took place at Martinsburg.

In the Valley of the Shenandoah, as well as in historical literature, attacks against Belle Boyd have taken very little note of actuality. A typical instance is a review in the *Evening Journal* of Martinsburg on April 2, 1942, covering an article in the February *Southern Literary Messenger* which briefly outlined Belle Boyd's book and the description by H. K. Douglas of her rôle at Front Royal.

The reviewer, Mrs. M. A. Snodgrass, declares: "We of the older generation in Martinsburg have heard of our parents and friends who lived here during those tragic years of 1861-65, much that contradicts what these and other writers publish about Belle Boyd." Yet all that Mrs. Snodgrass reveals is that the Doll sisters gave her notes they received from their old playmate, Belle Boyd, and that they took the stories she told them verbally with more than a grain of salt. The contents of the notes remain undisclosed.

This critic also asserts: "The older generation dismissed her with one blast—'she was just a camp follower.' " In its least offensive sense, the term "camp follower" used by the anonymous elders means a person who follows or attaches himself or herself to a camp or army without serving in a military capacity. But the Reverend James Power Smith, a reputable Christian gentleman of the older generation, and a former Confederate captain and aide-de-camp of General Jackson, emphatically refutes this scornful characterization. According to him, the well mounted, soldierly figure he saw at Bunker Hill in September, 1862, was: "the notable female scout, Belle Boyd."

The honorable designation of "scout" and the degrading and even scandalous epithet, "camp follower," not only do not mean the same thing, but the former also flatly contradicts the latter. That James Power Smith meant Belle Boyd was officially in the Confederate military service appears from the following definition of the term "scout" by Douglas Southall Freeman in *Lee's Lieutenants:*

> "In explanation of the term 'scouts and spies,' it will be recalled that a soldier engaged in espionage was called a 'scout' in Confederate service, and that a civilian so employed was called a 'spy.' "[177]

Much like others before her, Mrs. Snodgrass states that Belle Boyd's "account of her life * * * is the only basis for the survival of her name." This Martinsburg critic's main objection to such survival is made evident by the statement that a local historian had collected newspaper data of Belle Boyd's later career, "which included three marriages, one divorce, a member of several theatrical companies, and a lecturer on her own war exploits through the West." The reviewer concludes that, "her later life proved that her name should not be forever linked with our town as its 'cause celebre' " and that it is unfortunate that the real heroes of 1861-65 should be forgotten "while one whose life was so sordid and whose adventures were always so shady should be forever recalled."

As to such comments on Belle Boyd, her daughter, Mrs. Michael, asserts, of her own knowledge and on information from her mother, that any actual resentment against her was indeed and still is based upon her marriages to Northerners, her divorce, her adoption of a stage career, and placing her daughters in the theatrical profession. The latter is a typical Southern prejudice.

No one was ever foolhardy enough to criticize Belle Boyd face to face on such matters. But when she returned to Martinsburg after the war, she became aware of and ignored with contempt the birth of this attitude on the part of an antagonistic element. Her first trip home was at the end of 1866. She made another trip later with her daughter, Grace Hardinge, and a third with Colonel Hammond. Her final trip was probably in 1876 when she saw her mother for the last time at Charles Town.

However, Mrs. Michael has been there since. And on her last visit, early in February, 1929, the *Martinsburg Journal*, and the *Mail* and the *Herald* of Hagerstown (Maryland) graciously commented on the arrival of the daughter of the "Famed," "The once famous," and "the most famous" Confederate spy. Despite this welcome in the press, Mrs. Michael learned that in some private discussion and reminiscence her mother's character was still being assailed as bitterly but more subtly than it had been in the Northern press during the War.

Whether Belle Boyd's marriages, her divorce, and her stage career were justifiable from the moral standpoint of her native region is a question for purely local settlement. But what must be challenged as wicked, intolerable, and indefensible are the continuous and determined efforts made by those who condemn her on any pretext to wipe out as imaginary the real record of her service to the South, and to brand as false her own version of her military career without offering actual evidence to bolster their charges or to refute the impressive testimony that proves her story.

What will history relate of Belle Boyd? Will it lump together indiscriminately fact, distortion, and legend, and say, as the *Washington Evening Star* said in its nostalgic editorial of May 8, 1943, "She was a mystery while yet she lived, and she remains a mystery today."? Or will it adopt the judgment of two highly competent authorities—Carl Sandburg and Douglas Southall Freeman?

In 1939, Carl Sandburg accepted Belle Boyd's own story without question in his biographical masterpiece, *Abraham Lincoln—The War Years.* And in 1942, the distinguished historian, Douglas Southall Freeman, related in his notable historical work, *Lee's Lieutenants,* that she was the woman spy who gave news to Jackson's forces of the position of the enemy at Front Royal; and he canonized her historically as, "the renowned Belle Boyd, one of the most active and most reliable of the many secret women agents of the Confederacy."[178]

To the verdict of Doctor Freeman, history might properly add something more. Surely it can record, in the light of the evidence, that the full extent of Belle Boyd's contribution to the cause of the South will probably never be known. As to the unfounded charge that *Belle Boyd in Camp and Prison* is a "none too trustworthy account," should it not be said justly that this work is particularly noteworthy for the *accuracy* of the data a truthful and understandably reticent woman felt it not imprudent to reveal?

Belle Boyd is now at rest beyond all praise and calumny. But if, in the judgment of the living, some enduring tribute is due her, there are two stirring memories of this Southern woman that should not be allowed to perish.

There is the memorable scene on May 23, 1862, when eighteen-year-old Belle, wearing a dark-blue dress and a white apron, raced fearlessly over the fields under infantry and artillery fire, and, as Harry Douglas relates, nearly exhausted, and with her hand pressed against her heart, said in gasps:

> " 'I knew it must be Stonewall, when I heard the first gun. Go back quick and tell him that the Yankee force is very small—one regiment of Maryland infantry, several pieces of artillery and several companies of cavalry. * * * Tell him to charge right down and he will catch them all.' "

And there is that other message Belle gave her countrymen—the message that for the last fifteen years of her life she delivered incessantly with dramatic and sincere intensity to her comrades throughout a reunited nation, a message that on her lips only Death could still. She gave it for the last time to the members of Rousseau Post, Grand Army of the Republic, in Portage, Wisconsin. Her final words are ours for always:

"One God, One Flag, One People—Forever!"

APPENDIX A

Detailed genealogical information is given in the following paragraphs, together with other data of a miscellaneous nature. The genealogical record, compiled from many separate records set forth in the Sources of Information, should not be considered complete as to marriages, or as to issue of the marriages listed.

---

1. Genealogical Data

(*a*) *The Van Meter and Burns Families*

The Van Meters go back to a Dutch ancestor who in 1535 was a historian, and Dutch Consul at London. Descendants settled near Fort Orange (Albany), New York, and later in New Jersey. One ventured into the Valley of the Shenandoah, made friends with the Delawares, and is said to have joined them in fighting the Catawbas. His sons, John and Isaac, secured large grants of land and sold part to the noted pioneer, Joist Hite. Isaac is said to have bounded his land by notching trees with a tomahawk and so to have established his claim by "Tomahawk Right."

Joanna Van Meter, daughter of Johannes and Rebecca Van Meter, and born about 1732 in New Jersey, married William Burns, who came from Scotland and had traveled South with other pioneers. Their son, John Burns, born 1771, married Frances Southwood in 1794. *Ruth Burns, daughter of John and Frances, married Captain James Glenn in June 1823, and was Belle Boyd's maternal grandmother.*

(*b*) *The Reeds*

Lieutenant-Colonel James Reed, of Scottish parentage, was born in Northern Ireland in 1710. In 1730 in America he married eighteen-year-old Margaret Floyd, who, as a child, had escaped from an Indian raid in which her parents and three of their children perished. The Reeds acquired and settled on several hundred acres of land in the Manor of Maske near the Gettysburg of today and Colonel Reed died in Pennsylvania in 1798 or 1799. Their seven sons, James, Samuel (father of Maria Reed Cooper and Eliza Reed Baker of Martinsburg), Benjamin, John, Thomas, William, and Joseph, also served as officers in the Revolutionary forces, James becoming a member of the Society of the Cincinnati and William, Adjutant General of Pennsylvania. Colonel Reed and Mrs. Reed also had two daughters, Sarah and Mary. Sarah married William McKesson, and *Mary, born in 1742, married James Stephenson in 1763. James and Mary Reed Stephenson were great grandparents of Belle Boyd.*

(c) *The Stephensons*

The above mentioned Private James Stephenson, born of Scottish parentage in Ulster, Ireland, probably in 1740, who married Mary Reed in York County, Pennsylvania in 1763, is believed to have died in Berkeley County, Virginia, in 1804. They had three sons, James (born at Gettysburg, Pa. in 1764), William, and Benjamin, and four daughters, Sarah, *Maria*, Isabella, and Margaret. Maria and Isabella married Samuel and John Boyd, brothers, and *Maria and Samuel Boyd were grandparents of Belle Boyd through their son Benjamin Reed Boyd.*

Major James Stephenson, brother of Maria and Isabella, was an uncle of Belle Boyd's father, Benjamin Reed Boyd, and Major Stephenson and Maria Reed Cooper's husband, Alex, were executors of the will of Benjamin's father.

Major Stephenson married Nancy Cunningham and had several children. Their son James R. graduated from West Point in 1822 and at his death in 1841 was a captain in the 7th Infantry Regiment, U.S.A.

(d) *The Glenns*

Captain James Glenn, whose family claimed descent from the Bruces and the Campbells, was born in Frederick County, Va. In the D.A.R. Lineage Book his descendants give his year of birth as 1757 and that of his death as 1832. Other records suggest he was born in 1764 and died in 1827. As his will was dated November, 1832, and probated the following month, the year of death seems conclusively 1832. However, as his son, James William, was born in 1832 shortly before Captain Glenn's death, acceptance of 1757 as the father's year of birth would mean that Captain Glenn was twenty when he joined the 10th Virginia Regiment and seventy-five when his son was born. It is more likely that he was born in 1764, that the story of his running off to enlist at an early age is true, and that he was no more than sixty-eight when his son was born.

By his marriage in 1823 with Ruth Burns, Captain Glenn had four children: Frances Elizabeth, who married James Erskine Stewart, *Mary Rebecca, who married Benjamin Reed Boyd*, James William, who married Susan Earle, and Margaret, who died in infancy and was buried in the garden of "Glenn Burnie."

Mr. and Mrs. Stewart, after leaving Front Royal, lived for a time at Milldale close by the Earle home (Mount Zion), and eventually moved to Luray, Va. where Mr. Stewart became a judge. He died in 1890 and Mrs. Stewart in 1913. Their daughter, Alice, married a Mr. Jennings, and two daughters, Irene and Nettie Jennings, are said to be living in Alexandria. Alice's sister, Frances, married Judge Alexander J. Brand in 1869. The Brands are known to have had one son, Thomas, three daughters, Frances, Alice, and Lillian, and one grandchild, Edith, daughter of Frank Bell and Frances Brand.

Full details are not available as to descendants of Captain James William Glenn and his wife, Susan. One daughter, Elizabeth, became Mrs. Elizabeth Glenn Barnes of Snow Hill, Maryland, and the original commission of old

Captain Glenn is known to have been in her possession. Another daughter, Florence, married Olin Beall, and their son, Hon. J. Glenn Beall of Frostburg, Maryland, former State Highway Commissioner, was elected to Congress in November 1942 from Maryland's Sixth Congressional District.

While Susan Earle, who married James William Glenn, was not directly related already to the Glenns, she was the sister of John Burns Earle's father, Captain A. M. Earle, and Captain Earle's wife, born a Burns, was a first cousin of James William Glenn, whose mother was Ruth Burns Glenn.

As to Benjamin and Mary Rebecca Glenn Boyd, they became the parents of several children, including Belle Boyd.

(*e*) *The Martinsburg Boyds*

Many Boyd families in America cherish stoutly a tradition that they descend from one of three Boyd brothers who came to the Colonies from Ayrshire, Scotland. But since the beginning of the 17th Century, there have been innumerable Boyds coming singly, or in family or larger groups, directly from Scotland, or via Northern Ireland, and sometimes England. Hence there have been many emigrant groups of brothers or other relatives named Boyd, and not all American Boyds can trace their line surely to a specific emigrant Boyd individual or group.

The first American Boyd clearly identified as an ancestor of Belle Boyd is the Samuel Boyd who married Mary Beckett in 1773 and was the father of the Boyd brothers who married Maria and Isabella Stephenson. As the Reeds and Stephensons came from near Gettysburg, Pennsylvania, it seems probable that the Samuel Boyd who married Mary Beckett came of a noted Boyd family living at Marsh Creek, Pennsylvania, near the location of Gettysburg. This Boyd line was founded by William Boyd, born in Northern Ireland of Scottish (Ayrshire) origin about 1700-10, who came over with a large group led by Hance Hamilton—later sheriff of York County, Pa.—which landed at New Castle, Delaware, August 24, 1729. With William were his wife Margaret, several children, and Thomas and John Boyd. Thomas is believed to have been William's brother and John, William's oldest son.

By 1736 William, settled on 200 acres at Marsh Creek, was a blacksmith and farmer. His nine chiildren included two sons, *Samuel* and Robert, born at Marsh Creek. William died in 1767, and provided by will for his children, but no record is found of Samuel and Robert thereafter. (For William Boyd and family, see Source CR, p. 18, et seq., and p. 47.)

It is likely that William's son Samuel was the Samuel Boyd who married Mary Beckett and that Samuel and Mary accompanied or followed James and Mary Stephenson to the vicinity of Martinsburg, Virginia, where later two Boyd sons married two Stephenson daughters. This would make William Boyd Belle Boyd's great-great grandfather and confirm her family's tradition of descent from the Ayrshire Boyds.

Samuel and John Boyd, sons of Samuel and Mary Beckett Boyd, were born in 1775 and 1776—John in Frederick County, Virginia. Samuel married Mary Reed ("Maria") Stephenson in 1798 and died in 1819. John married Maria's sister Isabella in 1803 and died in 1846.

Samuel and Maria Boyd had five children: John William, James Stephenson, *Benjamin Reed*, Isabella, and Anna Maria. James married Elizabeth King Wilson in Martinsburg, had five children (one named Samuel Beckett Boyd), and died in Carmi, Illinois in 1883. Anna Maria married Conrad Hogmire, and one known child was Virginia Reed Hogmire, born in Georgetown, D. C., who married Thomas C. Chalmers. John married Rebecca Southwood, and Isabella married William Compton. *Benjamin married Mary Rebecca Glenn, and they were the parents of Belle Boyd.*

Benjamin and Mary Boyd had eight children. Two girls and two boys died in infancy and were buried in Green Hill Cemetery, Martinsburg, where their father was later buried. The others were *Isabelle (Belle), born May 9, 1844*, William, Glenn, and Mary. Belle Boyd's husbands and descendants are set forth fully in the text. Her brothers went to Kansas and Colorado after the war and are known to have died. William's widow (née Lucy Mills) and her daughter, Mary, were known to be in Seattle, Washington, in 1926. Belle's sister, Mary, went west with William and Glenn, and married Oregon Wentworth Rowland. She was buried in Parsons, Kansas. A son, Robert L. Rowland, Esq., lives in Tulsa, Oklahoma.

(*f*) *The Knoxville Boyds*

After John Boyd married Isabella Stephenson in Berkeley County, Va., in 1803, the couple moved to Tennessee where John died in 1846 and Isabella in 1855. Their children were: Benjamin S., Samuel B., James S., William S., and Sarah. Benjamin Stephenson Boyd married Cynthia Kerr Brooks, Samuel Beckett Boyd married Susan Howard Mason, and William Stephenson Boyd married Mary Kennedy.

Samuel Beckett Boyd attended Blount College (now the University of Tennessee), then studied law, married, and moved to Livingston, Alabama where he practiced law for ten years and became eminent and prosperous. He returned to Knoxville in 1844, where he later held office as chancery court judge, and mayor. He was a first cousin of Belle Boyd's father, and *it was in Samuel Beckett Boyd's home, the Blount Mansion, that his widow, "Aunt Susan," had Belle as a guest early in 1863.*

Four children of Judge and Susan Boyd were: John M., Samuel B., Susan, and Eva. The two sons became doctors. Samuel became president of the Knox County Medical Society and married Maggie A. Baker, daughter of Dr. Harvey Baker. One child was D. W. Boyd.

After Dr. John Boyd's death in 1909 two inscriptions were placed on a large arch over the Knox County Court House entrance. One read, "Our John Boyd. December 23, 1838. May 16, 1909." The other was worded, "OUR BELOVED PHYSICIAN. Dr. John Mason Boyd. Erected by a Grateful Public. Dec. 23, 1838. May 16, 1909."

Samuel was ten years old, Eva fifteen, Susan nineteen, and John twenty-five when Belle Boyd, their second cousin, came to the Blount Mansion in 1863. *It was Susan who became Belle's intimate comrade* and whose recollections of Belle are in the McClung Historical Collection in the Lawson McGhee Library of Knoxville. *It was in the home of Susan (Mrs. Alvin*

Barton) that Belle Boyd and her daughter, Marie Isabelle, met their cousin, Charles Keith Bell of Texas, in 1892. Sue Boyd Barton died in 1934, but her sister Eva, Mrs. E. B. Munson, ninety-five years old, was alive in Knoxville late in 1942.

Isabella Reed Boyd, daughter of Benjamin Stephenson Boyd and his wife Cynthia, was born in 1831. This second cousin of Belle Boyd married Samuel Beckett Boyd of Martinsburg (son of James S. Boyd and Elizabeth King Wilson), who was her second cousin and Belle Boyd's first cousin. This S. B. Boyd (not to be confused with Judge S. B. Boyd or the latter's son, S. B.), was born in Virginia in 1827, went to Knoxville in 1851 and married Isabella Reed Boyd in 1853. Of their eight children two were sons: Samuel Beckett Boyd, who married Julia Harrison, and Benjamin Stephenson Boyd, who married Margaret A. Logan. Their six daughters were: Annie Bruce, who died in infancy, Sarah Sutherland, who married Henry N. Saxton, Jr., Cynthia Irwin, who married James H. McCue, Isabella Reed, who married John M. Allen, Elizabeth Wilson, who married William Caswell, and Mary Reed, who married Albert S. Birdsong. *Mrs. Birdsong, the only surviving child, recalls Belle Boyd's visit to Knoxville in the '90s with Mr. High and a theatrical troupe.*

The S. B. Boyd from Martinsburg, who died in 1920, was a very prominent business man in Knoxville and director of several important financial and public institutions. In the War between the States, this cousin of Belle Boyd was in the Confederate Ordnance Department, took part in the Sander's Raid fighting, and in December, 1864, was captured at Bristol. Taken to Camp Chase, Ohio, he refused to take the Federal "oath of allegiance" and was only released in May, 1865, when New York friends secured a pardon for him from the President. Later, when his wife sought compensation for Federal damage to the Boyd home, the Government refused "because of her pronounced sympathy for and aid of the Southern Confederacy." (Records of Simon Harris Chapter, D.A.R., Knoxville, Tenn.)

(*g*) *The Bells*

James Bell, who was born in Falmouth, Va. in 1796 and died in Knoxville, Tenn., in 1879, married Nancy Stephenson, daughter of William Stephenson and Nancy Kennedy, and first cousin of Benjamin Reed Boyd, Belle Boyd's father. Four children of James and Nancy Bell were: William S., Oscar, Anne, and Margaret. William S. Bell became a doctor, married Elizabeth Douglass Keith, became mayor of Chattanooga in 1858, and was killed in the Confederate service in 1861 at Island Number Ten in the Mississippi River. His wife, Elizabeth, was a daughter of Judge Charles Fleming Keith of Athens, Tenn., and granddaughter of the Captain Alexander Keith of the Revolution whose parents, Reverend James Keith and Mary Isham Randolph of Prince William and Fauquier Counties, Va., were grandparents of Chief Justice Marshall. She was therefore related to Thomas Jefferson and Robert E. Lee, and a third cousin of George W. Randolph, who was Confederate Secretary of War in 1862 when Belle Boyd was arrested by order of the Federal Secretary of War. For Keith-Randolph connection see Note 170.

Dr. and Mrs. Bell had three or more children, two being Charles K., and Anne. Anne married a Mr. Thornton of Birmingham, Ala. Charles Keith Bell, born in 1853, moved to Texas in 1871, became State Senator in 1884, Congressman in 1893, Attorney General of Texas in 1901, and died in 1913. In 1906 he was a candidate for the Democratic nomination for governor. Having the nomination in his grasp, he withdrew his name because his principles would not permit him to approve a trade his campaign manager and Col. House had made to secure support of a major opponent. C. K. Bell married a daughter of John Peter Smith, "the father of Fort Worth." A son, James S. Bell, lives in Tyler, Texas.

(*h*) *D. A. R. Lineage Book*

This lists about thirty persons descended from Lt. Col. James Reed, Captain James Glenn, and Private James Stephenson. These relatives of Belle Boyd include her sister, Mary Glenn Boyd Rowland; her aunt, Frances Elizabeth Glenn Stewart, from whose cottage at Front Royal she rushed to give General Jackson intelligence on the battlefield; Elizabeth Glenn Barnes, daughter of Captain James W. Glenn and Susan Earle; Isabella Reed Boyd, wife of S. B. Boyd; and four daughters of that couple. Some items of the Lineage Book data are contradictory or confusing. Recourse to other stated sources has been necessary to establish that Lt. Col. James Reed had *seven* sons, that the maiden name of Samuel Beckett Boyd's wife was Isabella Reed *Boyd*, and so on.

(*i*) *Year of Birth of Belle Boyd*

Many works state she was born May 9, 1843. Her own book and her own family insist on 1844. At the age of twelve she went to Mount Washington Female College in Baltimore which had no students prior to May 1856. To assert that she was born in 1843 is to maintain that she was twelve in 1855 and attended then a school which was not founded until the next year. (See Source AO, p. 270.) As for official birth records, there are none for Martinsburg prior to 1865.

2. MISCELLANEOUS DATA

(*a*) *Harry Gilmor*

This advocate of Belle Boyd, who extolled in *Four Years in the Saddle* her great courage and her boundless devotion to the South, had, as his final command, the Second Maryland Battalion. Col. Charles T. O'Ferrall, later Governor of Virginia, considered Gilmor one of the most exemplary and conspicuously courageous Confederate soldiers. Generals "Jeb" Stuart and

Fitzhugh Lee cited him, the latter for "Marked bravery and cool courage" in the Kelleysville battle. It was Gilmor who carried gallant Major Pelham's body off the field, swearing it would not fall into Yankee hands.

(*b*) *Marker at Front Royal*

On the road between Front Royal and Bentonville, a Virginia Conservation Commission marker reads, "Near here 'Stonewall' Jackson was met by the spy Belle Boyd and informed of the position of the Union troops . . . May 24, 1862." The date should be May 23.

(*c*) *Prison Correspondence with D. A. Mahony*

Inquiry in Iowa of the *Dubuque Telegraph-Herald* and other sources has failed to locate Mr. Mahony's descendants or his correspondence with Belle Boyd.

(*d*) *Comments on Various Publications*

Swords and Roses. In thirty pages on Belle Boyd, Joseph Hergesheimer shows profound sympathetic understanding that "she gave the cause of the South all the tenderness and passion and belief she possessed," and he discusses her adventures in deeply stirring passages of fine emotional and literary quality.

Reveille in Washington. Miss Leech errs in her biographical sketch of Belle Boyd in giving 1863 as the year the *Greyhound* sailed, in saying the Navy "discharged" Hardinge, in reporting that Belle was imprisoned at Fort Warren and sentenced to death, and in recording that Hardinge died in the United States without rejoining his wife.

Diary of Lucy Rebecca Buck. (Privately reproduced. A copy available in the Library of Congress.) This noted Front Royal record contains at least a dozen entries mentioning Belle Boyd. Miss Buck disliked her and indicated it plainly. But her most critical comments are based more on hearsay and a readiness to believe Belle Boyd always up to something unlady-like rather than on factual knowledge. This interesting instance of unfounded suspicion appears on page 78 of the diary:

> "While we were talking I noticed in the twilight a light female figure coming from down the Mill Road leaning very confidently on a 'blue coat sleeve.' I concluded it was either Belle Boyd or Hattie G. Presently, hearing the gate open, I looked up and saw the figure walk into the yard. 'That's Dr. Gillespie's daughter', said Rouse, and without more ado Nellie and I rose simultaneously and glided upstairs, telling R. that should we be inquired for we were 'not at home.' "

Southern Historical Society Papers. A sketch of "Mrs. Belle Boyd Hardinge," p. 443, Vol. XI, is in error in giving year of birth as 1835, stating her father was a Dr. Boyd, and recording that she divorced in 1868 a Federal officer she married at the end of the war.

The World's Greatest Military Spies and Secret Service Agents. George Barton, in a book dedicated to W. J. Flynn, former U. S. Secret Service chief, outlines adventures of Major André, Nathan Hale, Lydia Darrah, L. C. Baker, Carl Lody, and others, includes a sketch of Belle Boyd based on her own book, and does not question her veracity.

Stonewall Jackson and the Civil War. Col. G. F. R. Henderson, a highly considered English authority, quotes extensively from General Richard Taylor's description of Belle Boyd's rôle in the battle of Front Royal, and does not question it.

The History of Winchester in Virginia. O F. Morton mentions Belle Boyd as the spy who gained the greatest "notoriety" in the lower Shenandoah region, but states she was of magnetic personality, attractive in manner and appearance, possessed dash, energy, and courage, and was a skillful rider. His source of information is Dr. Ashby's *The Valley Campaigns*, and his choice of the word "notoriety" was influenced by Dr. Ashby's unsupported conclusions and inaccurate data.

Secret Service Operator 13. Robert W. Chambers makes Belle Boyd an interesting minor character in a book abounding in historical figures. He describes her parents and her home, weaves her background into his tale, and, not realizing that George Lawrence saw a different prisoner in the Old Capitol, depicts Belle Boyd with the other girl's braids of dark hair and summer toilette of cool, pink muslin. This intriguing story is a promising forerunner of the fascinating spy story that will eventually be written of the actual adventures of Belle Boyd.

Belle Boyd: Famous Spy of the Confederate States Army. A booklet in which Mrs. Leonora Wood made available to the South four years ago a greatly condensed version of Belle Boyd's own story. It has had very wide distribution and has served admirably to combat misrepresentations as to Belle Boyd.

Belle Boyd: Southern Spy of the Shenandoah. A pamphlet summarizing Belle Boyd's story, sponsored by the Warren Rifles Chapter (Front Royal, Va.) of the United Daughters of the Confederacy. It contains several inaccurate statements, the most important being that Belle Boyd's body was "reclaimed by Virginia in 1928 and buried with military honors."

A Virginia Girl in the Civil War. The identity of the "Nellie Grey" who had such intimate experiences with Belle Boyd at Mrs. Rixey's in Culpeper Court House, is suggested by her revelation that her husband was regimental adjutant of the Thirteenth Virginia Cavalry. The war records show that on April 17, 1863 General W. F. H. Lee and Colonel J. R. Chambliss cited "Lieutenant Nash, adjutant of the Thirteenth Virginia Cavalry" for conspicuous gallantry and energy. This Lieutenant Nash was J. V. H. Nash, a Virginian, later a captain on the staff of General Chambliss. Further, Mrs. Myrta Lockett Avary, who wrote this book from reminiscences related to her by "Nellie Grey" states that "Nellie Grey" was the wife of Major Joseph Van Holt Nash of Petersburg, Virginia, and before her marriage was Miss Margaret Bowden of Norfolk, Virginia. Mrs. Avary's success with this work led to her research on the Reconstruction Era which was published in 1906 as *Dixie After the War.* An article on Mrs. Avary (*The Southern Literary Messenger*, Vol. V, No. 1, April 1943, p. 53) also identifies "Nellie Grey" as "Mrs. Joseph Van Horn Nash, wife of a Confederate officer."

The Spy in America. A review of espionage and counter-espionage from colonial days to 1919. Mr. Bryan devotes three and a half pages to a routine and uncritical summary of Belle Boyd's career. It contains several errors, including statements that Hardinge was a lieutenant, that he "left" the Federal service, that Colonel Hammond's name was "John V. Hammond," and so on.

APPENDIX B

To encipher the message referred to on page 34, it is highly probable that Belle Boyd used the variation of the once "indecipherable cipher" of Vigénère which the Confederates thought still good enough.

If Belle used this system, she first wrote down the two words of her cipher key, numbered each letter in numerical sequence, and wrote out horizontally the "clear text" of the alphabet. Next, under this "clear text" she set forth the Vigénère alphabet square, and in the space opposite the left vertical column of the square she placed against each appropriate letter in the vertical column the sequence number or numbers given such letter in the key words. With the following chart before her, Belle was now ready to encipher her message:

KEY:	**C**	**O**	**M**	**P**	**L**	**E**	**T**	**E**	**V**	**I**	**C**	**T**	**O**	**R**	**Y**
	1	**2**	**3**	**4**	**5**	**6**	**7**	**8**	**9**	**10**	**11**	**12**	**13**	**14**	**15**

Clear Text:	**A**	**B**	**C**	**D**	**E**	**F**	**G**	**H**	**I**	**J**	**K**	**L**	**M**	**N**	**O**	**P**	**Q**	**R**	**S**	**T**	**U**	**V**	**W**	**X**	**Y**	**Z**
	A	B	C	D	E	F	G	H	I	J	K	L	M	N	O	P	Q	R	S	T	U	V	W	X	Y	Z
	B	C	D	E	F	G	H	I	J	K	L	M	N	O	P	Q	R	S	T	U	V	W	X	Y	Z	A
1 and 11	C	D	E	F	G	H	I	J	K	L	M	N	O	P	Q	R	S	T	U	V	W	X	Y	Z	A	B
	D	E	F	G	H	I	J	K	L	M	N	O	P	Q	R	S	T	U	V	W	X	Y	Z	A	B	C
6 and 8	E	F	G	H	I	J	K	L	M	N	O	P	Q	R	S	T	U	V	W	X	Y	Z	A	B	C	D
	F	G	H	I	J	K	L	M	N	O	P	Q	R	S	T	U	V	W	X	Y	Z	A	B	C	D	E
	G	H	I	J	K	L	M	N	O	P	Q	R	S	T	U	V	W	X	Y	Z	A	B	C	D	E	F
	H	I	J	K	L	M	N	O	P	Q	R	S	T	U	V	W	X	Y	Z	A	B	C	D	E	F	G
10	I	J	K	L	M	N	O	P	Q	R	S	T	U	V	W	X	Y	Z	A	B	C	D	E	F	G	H
	J	K	L	M	N	O	P	Q	R	S	T	U	V	W	X	Y	Z	A	B	C	D	E	F	G	H	I
	K	L	M	N	O	P	Q	R	S	T	U	V	W	X	Y	Z	A	B	C	D	E	F	G	H	I	J
5	L	M	N	O	P	Q	R	S	T	U	V	W	X	Y	Z	A	B	C	D	E	F	G	H	I	J	K
3	M	N	O	P	Q	R	S	T	U	V	W	X	Y	Z	A	B	C	D	E	F	G	H	I	J	K	L
	N	O	P	Q	R	S	T	U	V	W	X	Y	Z	A	B	C	D	E	F	G	H	I	J	K	L	M
2 and 13	O	P	Q	R	S	T	U	V	W	X	Y	Z	A	B	C	D	E	F	G	H	I	J	K	L	M	N
4	P	Q	R	S	T	U	V	W	X	Y	Z	A	B	C	D	E	F	G	H	I	J	K	L	M	N	O
	Q	R	S	T	U	V	W	X	Y	Z	A	B	C	D	E	F	G	H	I	J	K	L	M	N	O	P
14	R	S	T	U	V	W	X	Y	Z	A	B	C	D	E	F	G	H	I	J	K	L	M	N	O	P	Q
	S	T	U	V	W	X	Y	Z	A	B	C	D	E	F	G	H	I	J	K	L	M	N	O	P	Q	R
7 and 12	T	U	V	W	X	Y	Z	A	B	C	D	E	F	G	H	I	J	K	L	M	N	O	P	Q	R	S
	U	V	W	X	Y	Z	A	B	C	D	E	F	G	H	I	J	K	L	M	N	O	P	Q	R	S	T
9	V	W	X	Y	Z	A	B	C	D	E	F	G	H	I	J	K	L	M	N	O	P	Q	R	S	T	U
	W	X	Y	Z	A	B	C	D	E	F	G	H	I	J	K	L	M	N	O	P	Q	R	S	T	U	V
	X	Y	Z	A	B	C	D	E	F	G	H	I	J	K	L	M	N	O	P	Q	R	S	T	U	V	W
15	Y	Z	A	B	C	D	E	F	G	H	I	J	K	L	M	N	O	P	Q	R	S	T	U	V	W	X
	Z	A	B	C	D	E	F	G	H	I	J	K	L	M	N	O	P	Q	R	S	T	U	V	W	X	Y

Assuming for the purpose of exposition that her key words may have been COMPLETE VICTORY, a key actually used by the Confederates, and that she began her message in clear with the words, "Overheard Shields staff council tonight * * *," her next step was to number all the letters of the clear message from one to fifteen throughout, as follows:

O	V	E	R	H	E	A	R	D	S	H	I	E	L	D	S	S	T	A	F	F
1	2	3	4	5	6	7	8	9	10	11	12	13	14	15	1	2	3	4	5	6

C	O	U	N	C	I	L	T	O	N	I	G	H	T	*	*	*	*	*	*	*	*	*	*.
7	8	9	10	11	12	13	14	15	1	2	3	4	5	6	7	8	9	10	11	12	13	14	15

Now taking the number 1 assigned to the letter O in the clear message, Belle referred to the number 1 opposite the letter C in the left vertical column of the Vigénère square and moved to the right horizontally until she came to the letter in that horizontal line directly under the letter O in the clear text above the square. This gave her the letter Q as the first letter of her cipher message.

Taking the number 2 assigned to the second letter of her clear message, she then referred to the number 2 opposite the letter O in the left vertical column of the square and moving to the right horizontally obtained the cipher letter J under the letter V of the clear text above the square. Continuing, she enciphered her complete message, and its opening words in clear and in cipher read:

Clear **OVERHEARD SHIELDS STAFF COUNCIL TONIGHT** ******
Cipher **QJQGSITVY AJBSCBU GFPQJ VSPVEBZ KMPWSWE** ******

Inevitably, her next step after enciphering her message was to *destroy* all papers used in enciphering so that the key words, the square, the clear message, and the numerical symbols could not be used to decipher the message. Only then was she free to seek Turner Ashby.

The system outlined is a substitution cipher in which the original letters of the clear message are represented by other letters. To prevent quick solution of the cipher by noting the ratio of frequency with which each cipher letter occurs and thus identifying clear text letters because of the known ratio of frequency of each in long messages, the process of substituting cipher letters is scrambled in several ways. One is to use words for the key in which several letters are duplicated and thus insure that such letters will have more than one number assigned. Another is to make certain that numbers assigned letters in the clear message relate directly solely to their sequence and do not, without the key, give a clue to their identity. It will be noted that the key words duplicate the letters, C, E, O, and T, and also that in the first two words of the clear message E appears three times yet when enciphered is consecutively Q, I, and S. MANCHESTER BLUFF, another Confederate key for the same form of cipher, duplicates E and F, and involves suppression of normal letter frequency.

To Major Thomas Parks, Air Corps, U. S. A., is due credit for suggesting that Belle Boyd used the cipher here set forth. Major Parks has furnished a copy of a similarly enciphered message from President Jefferson Davis to General Howell Cobb, and this message, deciphered by Corporal Alan Nemser, Signal Corps, U. S. A., is found to be based on the key word COMPLETE VICTORY. The original message, only partially enciphered, is owned by Mr. Van Dyk MacBride of Newark, New Jersey.

One disadvantage of the Confederates in using this cipher was their bad habit of only enciphering portions of messages and thus providing clues as to the key. Another was the insistence of Confederate Headquarters that for convenience in recognizing word separation such separation be retained in cipher instead of running words together to avoid revelation of individual word length in the message in clear.

Codes and ciphers are far more complex and effective today. However, they owe much to this ancestral form.

NOTES

(For Key to Letters designating Source, see "Sources of Information" immediately following "Notes.")

---

1. The New York Public Library contains more than forty of George Sala's works, including his memoirs.
2. Sources BC, pp. 178, 180, and 190; J, p. 126.
3. Sources AS and CR.
4. Sources DK; BH (see records of descendants of James Reed and James Stephenson, and particularly that of Belle Boyd's sister, Mrs. Rowland, p. 103, Vol. 52); BC, pp. 187-90; DS; C (letter of Adjutant General, Mar. 1, 1943); CB, p. 741, Vol. 13, Ser. 2, and pp. 70 and 96, Vol. 3, Ser. 5; DT; DQ; DV.
5. Sources AP, p. 305; J, pp. 127 and 129; AL, pp. 460 and 920, Vol. 1; U, p. 1565.
6. Source BA, p. 55.
7. For B. R. Boyd's name on company roster, see Source J, p. 228. For Douglas' quotation, see Source BA, p. 6.
8. Source BA, pp. 52 and 157.
9. Source AC (entry of July 12, 1862).
10. All data on James Glenn from Sources BH (see records of descendants of James Glenn, and particularly that of Belle Boyd's sister, Mrs. Rowland, p. 103, Vol. 52); AN, pp. 135-6; AI, pp. 316-17; AK, pp. 245, 246, 252, and 319; C (letters of Adjutant General, Aug. 13 and 24, 1942); AL, p. 460, Vol. 1; DJ; DF, p. 323, Vol. 7; and letter, Aug. 17, 1942, from the Earles of Milldale, Va., connection of Glenn and Burns families.
11. Source BA, p. 6.
12. Source M, July 5, 1861, col. 1, p. 3.
13. Source M, July 9, 1861, col. 1, p. 3.
14. Source CY, p. 86.
15. Source AQ, p. 69, Vol. 1.
16. Source AQ, p. 76, Vol. 1.
17. Sources C (letter of Adjutant General, June 3, 1942, stating "cause of death and place of burial" not of record), and M, July 9, 1861, col. 1, p. 3.
18. Source BY, p. 561, et seq., Vol. 2, Ser. 2, for reports, including that of Major E. J. Allen (Allan Pinkerton).
19. Data on Eliza from Sources DW and DX.
20. Source AL, p. 484, Vol. 1. Source M, July 5, 1861, col. 3, p. 2, shows Gwyn was an assistant provost-marshal.
21. Source DT; DS; BC, pp. 187-90; DV; DR; CB, pp. 44, 105, and 116, Vol. 8, Ser. 1, and p. 130, Vol. 10, Ser. 2; DU; AM, p. 462; U, p. 1452. Source U errs in stating James Randolph Reed was born in 1718.
22. Source AQ, p. 419, Vol. 1.
23. Sources BH (record of Frances Elizabeth Stewart, p. 42, Vol. 38); J, pp. 267 and 281. D.A.R. record errs in giving Mrs. Stewart's year of birth as 1846. Her tombstone in Luray, Va. states it was 1824.
24. Data on J. W. Glenn from Sources E, p. 450, and BY, pp. 248 and 898, Vol. 5, Ser. 1. Also letter, Sept. 17, 1942, from Executive Officer, V.M.I., outlining school record and service with Ashby.

25. Source AH, pp. 77-8.
26. Source CZ, p. 20.
27. Sources AG, p. 286; CZ, pp. 18 and 24.
28. Source AG, p. 286. Source AD for sketch of T. C. De Leon, and Sources CK (Confederate roster, Vol. 3), and CU, issue of Nov. 17, 1863, for status of Edwin De Leon and his letters to President Davis.
29. Source AN, p. 268.
30. Sources CT, p. 135; and DN.
31. Sources O, p. 124, Vol. 1; and CT, p. 227.
32. Source CT, p. 401.
33. Source AC (Entries of Jan. 1 and Mar. 11, 1862).
34. Pp. 43-44, Vol. 2, *Memoirs of John Adams Dix*, Harper & Bros., N. Y. City, 1883.
35. Source AV, pp. 110 and 657.
36. Source AV, pp. 108 and 649.
37. Source AL, p. 587, Vol. 1.
38. Source BY, various orders and communications, pp. 107-214, Part 3, Vol. 12, Ser. 1.
39. Source BY, pp. 536 and 555, Part 1, Vol. 12, Ser. 1.
40. Source AL, p. 977, Vol. 1.
41. Source BY, p. 554, Part 1, Vol. 12, Ser. 1.
42. Source AC (Entry of May 21, 1862).
43. Sources AL, p. 202, Vol. 1, and AV, p. 647.
44. Sources BT, pp. 826, and 837-8, Vol. 1; AJ, pp. 26, 206, and 290.
45. Source C (letter of Adjutant General, May 6, 1942).
46. Source CO, p. 129.
47. General Jackson's Report on Operations in the Valley, May 14-June 17, 1862, Source BY, p. 701, Part 1, Vol. 12, Ser. 1.
48. Source BA, p. 51.
49. Source BA, p. 51.
50. Source AA, p. 51.
51. Source CD, p. 391, Vol. 2.
52. Source AZ, p. 38.
53. Source BA, p. 52.
54. Source AC (Entries of Jan. 1, May 23, and July 5, 1862).
55. For Jackson's plan, Source BY, p. 703, Part 1, Vol. 12, Ser. 1. For Banks' reaction, Source BS, 1st page, issue of June 2, 1862.
56. Source BY, pp. 703-06, Part 1, Vol. 12, Ser. 1.
57. Relevant orders and communications, including Lincoln's wires, Source BY, pp. 626, 643, and 648, Part 1, Vol. 12, Ser. 1, and pp. 219, 220, and 267, Part 3, same Volume.
58. Sources O, p. 311, Vol. 2, and G, p. 52.
59. Source AC (Entry of June 7, 1862).
60. Sources BY, p. 558, Part 1, Vol. 12, Ser. 1, and BS, issues of June 10 and 14, 1862.
61. Source AJ, p. 31.
62. Source DB, p. 140.
63. Source DB, p. 139, et seq.
64. Sources BY, pp. 690 and 697, Part 1, Vol. 12, Ser. 1; and AL, p. 587, Vol. 1.
65. Source CK, p. 179, Vol. 38.

66. Source DB, pp. 17 and 143.
67. Source R.
68. Sources AL, p. 115, Vol. 2; and DB, p. 167.
69. Source AU, p. 249 for Smitley's status, and p. 257 for his story.
70. Source BY, p. 599, Part 2, Vol. 51, Ser. 1.
71. Sources AL, p. 882, Vol. 1, and Y, p. 1029.
72. Source AC (Entry of July 30, 1862).
73. Source DB, p. 167.
74. Source BY, pp. 309-10, Vol. 4, Ser. 2.
75. This Col. Holt cannot be readily identified. Joseph Holt, Secretary of War early in 1861, and creator of military commission jurisdiction over civilians, became judge advocate general with rank of colonel Sept. 3, 1862. Later, as a brigadier general, he conducted prosecution in Lincoln assassination trial. See Sources AL, p. 539, Vol. 1, and AD.
76. Source CF, p. 123, Vol. 3.
77. Source CX, p. 52 (Diary Section), Vol. 5.
78. Sources BF, p. 319, issue of Aug. 9, 1862, and DG, p. 1, issue of July 28, 1862.
79. Sources K, pp. 321, et seq., and CE, p. 26.
80. Sources K, pp. 326-7, and CQ, p. 510.
81. Sources BW, p. 2, issue of April 28, 1865; AL, p. 184, Vol. 1; CV, pp. 282 and 289, Vol. 8; K, p. 322, and AY.
82. Sources BG, p. 104, and CG, p. 458.
83. Source AY, p. 480.
84. Source CE, foot-note on p. 52.
85. Source BG, p. 103.
86. War Department letter and General Wadsworth's report, Source BY, p. 349, Vol. 4, Ser. 2.
87. Source BG, p. 101, et seq.
88. Source DG, issue of Aug. 21, 1862.
89. Source CW, pp. 268, et seq.
90. Source CG, p. 157.
91. Source CE, p. 50.
92. Source CL.
93. Source CJ. See Appendix for comment on book.
94. General Wadsworth's letter and Order No. 175, Source BY, p. 461, Vol. 4, Ser. 2.
95. Sources I, p. 504, Vol. 1, and CY, p. 82.
96. Source I, p. 504, Vol. 1.
97. Source AY, p. 171.
98. Source DH, p. 218, et seq.
99. Source CG, p. 157.
100. Source BY, p. 628, Vol. 5, Ser. 2.
101. Source CK, p. 21, Vol. 43.
102. Source DO.
103. Source H, Chapter V.
104. Source H, Chapter V: "I Meet Belle Boyd and see Dick in a new Light." See p. 337 (Appendix A) for identity of "Nellie Grey."
105. Letter Sept. 17, 1942, from Executive Officer, V.M.I.
106. Source BX, issue of Nov. 27, 1940.

107. Source O, p. 70, Vol. 3.
108. Source BA, p. 203.
109. Source AR; p. 931, East Tennessee Edition, and p. 921, Knox County Edition.
110. Source DO.
111. Source AH, pp. 77-8.
112. Source Q, p. 400 (Journal of S. W. Hardinge).
113. Source AC (Entry of June 9, 1863).
114. Source BP, Vol. 3.
115. Source Y, p. 1661.
116. Source BN lists this officer.
117. Source DW. Item is quoted from a clipping, bearing neither date nor name of newspaper, pasted inside cover of Belle Boyd's personal copy of her book. Believed to be from the *Toledo Commercial.* Belle Boyd toured Ohio extensively in the winter of 1897-98.
118. Source BN, p. 52.
119. Source V, pp. 195-6.
120. Sources AW, p. 405, and AX, p. 480, Vol. 2.
121. Sources BY, p. 992, Vol. 8, Ser. 2, and DG, issue of Oct. 3, 1863.
122. Source AL, p. 975, Vol. 1. For Major Turner's extensive activities, Source BY.
123. Source B (letter of Apr. 6, 1942).
124. Magazine article, Source CQ, p. 507. Col. Colby's record, Sources BY, p. 28, Part 2, Vol. 25, Ser. 1, and BT, p. 3262, Vol. 4.
125. Source Q, p. 425.
126. Source AF, p. 272.
127. Source AL, Vol. 1.
128. Source AT, p. 190.
129. Source AL, p. 734, Vol. 1.
130. Source CA, p. 106.
131. Sources AF, pp. 281-3, and CY, p. 83.
132. Source X, p. 584, general text, and p. 3, Appendix.
133. Source CA, p. 2.
134. Source BZ, p. 613, Vol. 2, Ser. 1, p. 539, Vol. 9, Ser. 1, and p. 214, Vol. 21, Ser. 1.
135. Records of Commander Almy and Lt. Kempff, Source BI, p. 23, and p. 310.
136. Sources CY, p. 86, and AF, p. 283.
137. Source CA, p. 2, et seq.
138. Source BZ, p. 687, Vol. 27, Ser. 1.
139. Commander Almy's report, Source BZ, p. 42, Vol. 10, Ser. 1. Lt. Bier's record, Source BI, p. 57.
140. Source CK, p. 166, Vol. 38.
141. Source DY.
142. Source BI, p. 531.
143. Source BI, p. 458.
144. Hardinge was an Acting Ensign. Source BI, p. 245.
145. Source BI, p. 210.
146. Source BV shows run of play began May 16th.
147. Source DW. Mrs. Michael has a newspaper clipping relating this story which lacks name, town and exact date of paper but gives a Boston, March 8th dateline. Year is probably 1914 as item says incident happened half a century earlier.

148. Source BY, p. 525, Vol. 3, Ser. 4, shows the *Bat* was bought in England about July 1, 1864. Source BZ, p. 547, Vol. 10, Ser. 1, shows it was captured on first westward trip Oct. 10, 1864 by U. S. S. *Montgomery*.

149. Source A (letter of April 17, 1942 from Captain D. W. Knox, U.S.N., Office of Naval Records and Library).

150. Same as Note 149. Further, Source BI, p. 245, states dismissal was July 6, 1864.

151. Same as Note 149.

152. Source BB, p. 167, et seq.

153. Source AD as to James Williams. Source AR, p. 920, (Knox County Edition), shows S. B. Boyd as Asylum trustee and holding other offices.

154. Source AD, and Confederate roster, Source CK, Vol. 3, as to John L. O'Sullivan. Capture and execution of William Boyd, *Encyclopedia Britannica*, p. 993, Vol. 3.

155. Source CQ, p. 508.

156. Source BU, issues of Feb. 8 and 9, 1865.

157. Data on Miss Jones and Mr. Montgomery from various press clippings about them in Theatrical Section, N. Y. Public Library.

158. Data on Belle Boyd's theatrical career from obituary, Source BQ, June 23, 1900. For J. P. Smith, see obituary, *New York Dramatic Mirror*, Nov. 20, 1897.

159. Source BU, Jan. 7 and 8, 1868.

160. Source N, p. 298, Vol. 8. Performance also mentioned Source F, p. 452, Vol. 2.

161. Source S. For text of play, see *Plays for the College Theatre* published by Samuel French, N. Y. City, 1932.

162. Obituary, Source BU, Dec. 18, 1932.

163. Obituary, Source BQ, June 23, 1900.

164. Sources BK, p. 333, Vol. 2, and BM, pp. 53-54.

165. Obituary, Source BU, Dec. 18, 1932.

166. Source C (letter of Adjutant General, Jul. 20, 1942).

167. Source DP (divorce decree), in Mrs. Michael's possession.

168. Communications of Nov. 26 and Dec. 22, 1943 from F. M. Wilcox, State Librarian, Texas State Library, Austin, Texas.

169. Source DW. Wording from existing 1896 handbill.

170. C. K. Bell data, Source U, p. 689, and 1906 Texan gubernatorial campaign records. W. S. Bell data from *The History of Hamilton County and Chattanooga, Tennessee*; Lookout Publishing Co., Chattanooga, Tenn., 1931, p. 304, Vol. 1. For descent of C. K. Bell's mother (Elizabeth Douglass Keith) from Rev. James Keith and Mary Isham Randolph (grandparents of Chief Justice Marshall), see p. 79, *The Keith Genealogy*, by J. Montgomery Seaver; Genealogical Research and Publishing Co., Phila., Pa., 1930.

171. Source DW. Dates of newspaper items cannot be given as material is taken from undated copies in Mr. High's handwriting on reverse side of a "Belle Boyd" letterhead on which he began a letter to his mother Jan. 23, 1898 from Washington Court House, Ohio. Mrs. Michael has this sheet.

172. Source DW. Originals of Kentucky and Ohio testimonials, and handbill quoting Georgia credentials are in Mrs. Michael's possession.

173. Source DW. Clippings in Mrs. Michael's records.

174. Source DW. Mrs. Michael has original telegram.

175. Source DW. Clipping Mrs. Michael has does not give name of paper or date, but refers to death of Belle Boyd "last week."

176. Source T.

177. Source BD, Note 35, p. 374, Vol. 1.

178. Sources I, p. 504, Vol. 1, and BD, pp. 377-78, Vol. 1, including Note 42.

SOURCES OF INFORMATION

(All data concerning Belle Boyd, or statements ascribed to her, and not attributed in the Notes to other sources, are based upon or taken from her original work, Source Q.)

I. Government Agencies

A. NAVY DEPARTMENT.

B. THE NATIONAL ARCHIVES.

C. WAR DEPARTMENT.

II. Printed Works, and Newspapers

D. A FAMOUS COMMAND: THE RICHMOND LIGHT INFANTRY BLUES; by John A. Cutchins; Garrett & Massie; Richmond, Va., 1934.

E. A HISTORY OF THE LAUREL BRIGADE, by William N. McDonald; published by Mrs. Kate S. McDonald, Baltimore, Md., 1907.

F. A HISTORY OF THE NEW YORK STAGE, by T. A. Browne; Dodd, Mead & Co., N. Y. City, 1903.

G. A MILITARY HISTORY OF THE 8TH REGIMENT OHIO VOLUNTEER INFANTRY, by Lt. Col. (Brevet Brigadier General) Franklin Sawyer; Fairbanks & Co., Cleveland, O., 1881.

H. A VIRGINIA GIRL IN THE CIVIL WAR, 1861-65. Edited by Myrta Lockett Avary. Published by D. Appleton & Co., N. Y. City, 1903.

I. ABRAHAM LINCOLN—THE WAR YEARS, by Carl Sandburg; Harcourt, Brace & Co., N. Y. City, 1939.

J. ALER'S HISTORY OF MARTINSBURG, by F. V. Aler; The Mail Publishing Co., Hagerstown, Md., 1888.

K. AMERICAN BASTILE, by John A. Marshall; Thos. W. Hartley, Phila., Pa., 1872.

L. AMERICAN STATE PAPERS, published by Galey & Seaton, Washington, D. C., 1832.

M. AMERICAN UNION. A newspaper issued in July, 1861, by "The Division of the American Army under Major General Patterson."

N. ANNALS OF THE NEW YORK STAGE, by Geo. C. D. Odell; Columbia University Press, N. Y. City, 1927-42.

O. BATTLES AND LEADERS OF THE CIVIL WAR; The Century Company, N. Y. City, 1888.

P. BELLE BOYD, FAMOUS SPY OF THE CONFEDERATE STATES ARMY, by Leonora W. Wood; The Mountain Echo, Keyser, West Va., 1940.

Q. BELLE BOYD IN CAMP AND PRISON, by Belle Boyd; Blelock & Co., N. Y. City, 1865 and 1867.

R. BELLE BOYD, SOUTHERN SPY OF THE SHENANDOAH. Sponsored by Warren Rifles Chapter, United Daughters of the Confederacy, Front Royal, Va., 1936.

S. BELLE LAMAR. Play by Dion Boucicault.

T. BELLE STARR, by Burton Rascoe; Random House, N. Y. City, 1941.

U. BIOGRAPHICAL DIRECTORY OF THE AMERICAN CONGRESS, 1774-1927; Government Printing Office, Washington, D. C., 1928.

V. BORDER AND BASTILLE, by Geo. A. Lawrence; W. I. Pooley & Co., N. Y. City, 1863 (?).

W. BOSTON POST.

X. BUTLER'S BOOK, by B. F. Butler; A. M. Thayer & Co., Boston, Mass., 1892.

Y. COMPENDIUM OF THE WAR OF THE REBELLION, by F. H. Dyer; The Dyer Publishing Co., Des Moines, Ia., 1908.

Z. DAILY REGISTER, Knoxville, Tennessee.

AA. DESTRUCTION AND RECONSTRUCTION, by Richard Taylor; D. Appleton & Co., N. Y. City, 1879.

AB. DIARY OF A SOUTHERN REFUGEE, by "a lady of Virginia" (Mrs. J. W. McGuire); E. J. Hale & Son, N. Y. City, 1867.

AC. DIARY OF LUCY REBECCA BUCK, 1861-1865; privately reproduced; copyrighted 1940.

AD. DICTIONARY OF AMERICAN BIOGRAPHY; Charles Scribner's Sons; N. Y. City, 1928-37.

AE. EVENING JOURNAL, Martinsburg, West Va.

AF. FORGOTTEN LADIES, by R. L. Wright; J. B. Lippincott & Co., Phila., Pa., 1928.

AG. FOUR YEARS IN REBEL CAPITALS, by T. C. De Leon; Gossip Printing Co., Mobile, Ala., 1890.

AH. FOUR YEARS IN THE SADDLE, by Harry Gilmor; Harper & Bros., N. Y. City, 1866.

AI. GENEALOGY OF THE DUKE-SHEPHERD-VAN METRE FAMILY, by S. G. Smyth; New Era Printing Co., Lancaster, Pa., 1909.

AJ. HISTORIC RECORDS OF THE FIFTH NEW YORK CAVALRY, by Rev. L. N. Boudrye; S. R. Gray, Albany, N. Y., 1865.

AK. HISTORIC SHEPHERDSTOWN, by Danske Dandridge; The Michie Co., Charlottesville, Va., 1910.

AL. HISTORICAL REGISTER AND DICTIONARY OF THE U. S. ARMY, (1789-1903), by Francis B. Heitman; Government Printing Office, Washington, D. C., 1903.

AM. HISTORICAL REGISTER OF OFFICERS OF THE CONTINENTAL ARMY, etc., by Francis B. Heitman, The Rare Book Shop Publishing Co., Inc., Washington, D. C., 1914.

AN. HISTORY OF BERKELEY COUNTY, WEST VIRGINIA, by Willis F. Evans of Martinsburg; printed privately in 1928.

AO. HISTORY OF EDUCATION IN MARYLAND, by Bernard C. Steiner; Government Printing Office, Washington, D. C., 1894.

AP. HISTORY OF JEFFERSON COUNTY, WEST VIRGINIA, by M. K. Bushong; Jefferson Publishing Co., Charles Town, West Va., 1941.

AQ. HISTORY OF PENNSYLVANIA VOLUNTEERS, 1861-65, by Samuel P. Bates; B. Singerley, Harrisburg, Pa., 1869-71.

AR. HISTORY OF TENNESSEE (Knox County and East Tennessee Editions); The Goodspeed Publishing Co., Nashville, Tenn., 1887.

AS. HISTORY OF THE BOYD FAMILY AND DESCENDANTS, by Wm. P. Boyd; John P. Smith Printing Co., Rochester, N. Y., 1912.

AT. HISTORY OF THE ELEVENTH PENNSYLVANIA VOLUNTEER CAVALRY, Franklin Printing Co., Phila., Pa., 1902.

AU. HISTORY OF THE FIFTH WEST VIRGINIA CAVALRY, etc., by Frank S. Reader; *Daily News*, New Brighton, Pa., 1890.

AV. HISTORY OF THE FIRST, TENTH, TWENTY-NINTH MAINE REGIMENT, by Major John M. Gould; Stephen Berry, Portland, Me., 1871.

AW. HISTORY OF THE SEVENTH REGIMENT, NATIONAL GUARD, STATE OF NEW YORK, by Wm. Swinton; C. T. Dillingham, N. Y. City, 1886.

AX. HISTORY OF THE SEVENTH REGIMENT OF NEW YORK, by Col. Emmons Clark; The Seventh Regiment, N. Y. City, 1890.

AY. HISTORY OF U. S. SECRET SERVICE, by General L. C. Baker; L. C. Baker, Phila., Pa., 1867.

AZ. HOW A ONE LEGGED REBEL LIVES, by John S. Robson; The Educator Co., Durham, N. C., 1898.

BA. I RODE WITH STONEWALL, by Henry Kyd Douglas; University of North Carolina Press, Chapel Hill, N. C., 1940.

BB. KING COTTON DIPLOMACY, by F. L. Owsley, University of Chicago Press, 1931.

BC. KITH AND KIN, by Anna Eliza Sampson; The Wm. Byrd Press, Richmond, Va., 1922.

BD. LEE'S LIEUTENANTS, by Douglas Southall Freeman; Charles Scribner's Sons, N. Y. City, 1942.

BE. LEGENDS OF THE SKYLINE DRIVE AND OF THE GREAT VALLEY OF VIRGINIA, by Carrie Hunter Willis and Etta Belle Walker; The Dietz Press, Richmond, Va., 1937.

BF. LESLIE'S ILLUSTRATED NEWSPAPER, (Weekly), N. Y. City.

BG. LINCOLN AND EPISODES OF THE CIVIL WAR, by Wm. E. Doster; G. P. Putnam's Sons, N. Y. City, 1915.

BH. LINEAGE BOOK, Daughters of the American Revolution.

BI. LIST OF OFFICERS OF THE NAVY OF THE UNITED STATES, etc., 1775-1900. Edited by E. W. Callahan; L. R. Hamersly & Co., N. Y. City, 1901.

BJ. MARTINSBURG INDEPENDENT.

BK. MASSACHUSETTS SOLDIERS, SAILORS, AND MARINES IN THE CIVIL WAR, by Massachusetts Adjutant General's Office; Norwood Press, Norwood, Mass., 1931.

BL. MCCLUNG HISTORICAL COLLECTION, Lawson McGhee Library, Knoxville, Tenn.

BM. MEMORIAL HISTORY OF THE SEVENTEENTH REGIMENT, MASSACHUSETTS VOLUNTEER INFANTRY, by Thos. Kirwan and Henry Splaine; Salem Press, Salem, Mass., 1911.

BN. MILITARY HISTORY OF THE 123RD OHIO VOLUNTEER INFANTRY, by C. M. Keyes; Register Steam Press, Sandusky, O., 1874.

BO. MIRROR-GAZETTE, Kilbourn, Wis.

BP. NATIONAL CYCLOPEDIA OF AMERICAN BIOGRAPHY; Jas. T. White & Co., N. Y. City, 1898-1938.

BQ. NEW YORK CLIPPER.

BR. NEW YORK DAILY NEWS.

BS. NEW YORK HERALD.

BT. NEW YORK IN THE WAR OF THE REBELLION; compiled by Frederick Phisterer, N. Y. Adjutant General's Office; J. B. Lyon Co., Albany, N. Y., 1912.

BU. NEW YORK TIMES.

BV. NEW YORK TRIBUNE.

BW. NEW YORK WORLD.

BX. NORTHERN VIRGINIA DAILY, Strasburg, Va.

BY. OFFICIAL RECORDS OF THE UNION AND CONFEDERATE ARMIES; WAR OF THE RFBELLION; U. S. War Department; Government Printing Office, Washington, D. C., 1880-1901.

BZ. OFFICIAL RECORDS OF THE UNION AND CONFEDERATE NAVIES IN THE WAR OF THE REBELLION; U. S. Navy Department; Government Printing Office, Washington, D. C., 1894-1919.

CA. OBSERVATIONS IN THE NORTH, by Edw. A. Pollard; E. W. Ayres, Richmond, Va., 1865.

CB. PENNSYLVANIA ARCHIVES.

CC. PHILADELPHIA NORTH AMERICAN AND U. S. GAZETTE.

CD. PICTORIAL HISTORY OF THE CIVIL WAR, by B. J. Lossing; T. Belknap, Hartford, Conn., 1868.

CE. PRISON LIFE IN THE OLD CAPITOL, by J. J. Williamson; West Orange, N. J., 1911.

CF. REPORT OF THE ADJUTANT GENERAL, ILLINOIS, 1861-65; Baker, Bailhache & Co., Springfield, Ill., 1867.

CG. REVEILLE IN WASHINGTON, by Margaret Leech; Harper & Bros., N. Y. City, 1941.

CH. RICHMOND DAILY DISPATCH.

CI. RICHMOND EXAMINER. (Daily)
ROCKINGHAM REGISTER, Harrisonburg, Va.

CJ. SECRET SERVICE OPERATOR 13, by Robert W. Chambers; D. Appleton-Century Co., N. Y. City, 1934.

CK. SOUTHERN HISTORICAL SOCIETY PAPERS, Richmond, Va., printed by B. F. Johnson Publishing Co.

CL. SPECIAL MESSENGER, by Robert W. Chambers; D. Appleton & Co., N. Y. City, 1909.

CM. SPY OF THE REBELLION, by Allan Pinkerton; G. W. Carleton & Co., N. Y. City, 1883.

CN. STONEWALL JACKSON AND THE CIVIL WAR, by Col. G. F. R. Henderson; Longmans, Green & Co., London and N. Y. City, 1936.

CO. STONEWALL JACKSON'S WAY, by John W. Wayland; The McClure Co., Staunton, Va., 1940.

CP. SWORDS AND ROSES, by Joseph Hergesheimer; A. A. Knopf, N. Y. City and London, 1929.

CQ. THE ANNALS OF THE WAR; Times Publishing Co., Phila., Pa., 1879.

CR. THE BOYD FAMILY; compiled and published by Scott Lee Boyd, Santa Barbara, Cal., 1935.

CS. THE HISTORY OF WINCHESTER IN VIRGINIA, by O. F. Morton; Shenandoah Publishing House, Strasburg, Va., 1925.

CT. THE MEMOIRS OF GENERAL TURNER ASHBY AND HIS COMPEERS, by Rev. Jas. B. Avirett, et al., Selby & Dulany, Baltimore, Md., 1867.
THE MORNING POST, London, England.

CU. THE NATIONAL INTELLIGENCER, Washington, D. C.

CV. THE PHOTOGRAPHIC HISTORY OF THE CIVIL WAR, by F. T. Miller; The Review of Reviews Co., N. Y. City, 1912.

CW. THE PRISONER OF STATE, by Dennis A. Mahony; G. W. Carleton & Co., N. Y. City, 1863.

CX. THE REBELLION RECORD, by Frank Moore; D. Van Nostrand, N. Y. City, 1864-68.

CY. THE SHENANDOAH AND ITS BYWAYS, by W. O. Stevens; Dodd, Mead & Co., N. Y. City, 1941.

CZ. THE SIGNAL AND SECRET SERVICE OF THE CONFEDERATE STATES, by Dr. Chas. E. Taylor; Vol. 2, No. 11, North Carolina Booklet; Capital Printing Co., Hamlet, N. C., 1903.

DA. THE SPY IN AMERICA, by Geo. S. Bryan; J. B. Lippincott & Co., Phila., Pa., 1943.

DB. THE VALLEY CAMPAIGNS, by Dr. Thos. A. Ashby; The Neale Publishing Co., N. Y. City, 1914.

DC. THE WASHINGTON NATIONAL REPUBLICAN.

DD. THE WOMEN OF THE CONFEDERACY, by F. B. Simkins and J. W. Patton; Garrett & Massie, Richmond, Va., 1936.

DE. THE WORLD'S GREATEST MILITARY SPIES AND SECRET SERVICE AGENTS, by Geo. Barton; The Page Co., Boston, Mass., 1917.

DF. VIRGINIA CALENDAR OF STATE PAPERS; Public Printer, Richmond, Va., 1785, on.

DG. WASHINGTON EVENING STAR.

DH. WEARING OF THE GRAY, by Col. John Esten Cooke; E. B. Treat & Co., N. Y. City, 1867.

DI. WEST VIRGINIA. A GUIDE TO THE MOUNTAIN STATE. Compiled by Workers of Writers Program, W.P.A. in West Virginia. Published by Oxford University Press, N. Y. City, 1941.

III. Miscellaneous Records and Papers

DJ. Will of James Glenn, Will Book 7, Charles Town, West Va.

DK. Marriage Records, Samuel Boyd-Mary Stephenson, 1798 and John Boyd-Isabella Stephenson, 1803, Martinsburg, West Va.

DL. Family records of Tennessee Boyds from Mrs. C. F. Wayland, (Genealogist) and Mrs. Mary Reed Boyd Birdsong, Knoxville, Tenn.

DM. Letter from Captain R. T. Morrison, Luray, Va., June 30, 1942, regarding Judge and Mrs. James E. Stewart and their daughter Alice.

DN. Letter, May 16, 1942, from Secretary of Equality Lodge 44 (Old No. 136) showing B. R. Boyd a member when Turner Ashby became a member of this Masonic Lodge.

DO. Letter of Mrs. Sue Boyd Barton to Miss Mary Nelson, March 11, 1932, in McClung Historical Room, Lawson McGhee Library, Knoxville, Tenn., relating to Belle Boyd visit in 1863.

DP. Decree of divorce, Mrs. Hammond vs John S. Hammond, November 1, 1884, United States District Court, Dallas, Tex.

DQ. Will of Lt.-Col. James Reed, Dec. 7, 1796, Adams County Court House, Gettysburg, Pa. (Will lists only five sons, but James and Joseph, two additional sons, were then dead.)

DR. Will of Major James R. Reed, probated April 30, 1790, Cumberland County, Pa., Book A, p. 177.

DS. Chart of descendants of James Reed, (1710-1799), drawn in 1933 by William B. Reed of Chevy Chase, Md.

DT. Greenway Genealogical Collection, Maryland Historical Society, Baltimore, Md. (Reed line.)

DU. Miscellaneous Letters, C-H, Force Manuscripts, Hazen vs Reid, 1783; Library of Congress, Washington, D. C.

DV. "Reminiscences of Judge John Reed"; Vol. xx, July 1928, The Reade Record of The Reade Society, Old State House, Boston, Mass.

IV. Individuals

DW. Mrs. A. Michael, daughter of Belle Boyd.

DX. Miss Rebecca Peterman, Martinsburg, West Va.

DY. Lawrence L. Priestman, Peru, Illinois, who has supplied text of letter written by his father, Lawrence Priestman, on May 15, 1864.

ACKNOWLEDGMENTS

IN the preparation of this work, the task of gathering data has been most congenial. No writer has ever had more spontaneous, generous, and helpful coöperation.

In New York, the facilities of the American History Room of the New York Public Library, the Brooklyn Public Library, the New York Historical Society, and the Library of Columbia University were invaluable. And Mrs. Michael, the well-informed daughter of Belle Boyd, contributed much material from her own recollections and her mother's papers.

Elsewhere, the following organizations provided information from their records, and many offered valuable suggestions as to its significance: the State Historical Societies of Maryland, Massachusetts, and Wisconsin, the Historical and Philosophical Society of Ohio, The National Archives, the War Department, the Navy Department, the State Archives of Pennsylvania, the State Libraries of Massachusetts, Texas, and Virginia, the General Library of the University of Michigan, the National Society of the Daughters of the American Revolution, the Simon Harris Chapter of that Society in Knoxville, Tenn., the Old Charles Town (West Va.) Library, the Kilbourn (Wisconsin Dells) Public Library, the Local History and Genealogy Room of the Toledo Public Library, the *Telegraph-Herald* of Dubuque, Ia., the American Antiquarian Society, and the Lawson McGhee Library of Knoxville, Tenn. To Miss Martha L. Ellison, Head, McClung Historical Room, Lawson McGhee Library, the author is particularly indebted for making available Sue Boyd's 1932 letter about Belle Boyd, and for much other gracious and thoughtful assistance.

In diverse ways, the following persons have also made available much useful material: Robert L. Rowland, Esq., of Tulsa, Okla., Miss Rebecca Peterman and Mr. O. L. Snyder of Martinsburg, West Va., Mr. and Mrs. John Burns Earle of Milldale, Va., Mrs. C. F. Wayland (genealogist) and Mrs. A. S. Birdsong of Knoxville, Tenn., Hon. J. Glenn Beall of Frostburg, Md., Mrs. M. S. R. Moler of Shepherdstown, West Va., Miss Elizabeth R. Millar, Hon. Stephen D. Boyd, and Mr. Hugh E. Naylor, of Front Royal, Va., Captain R. T. Morrison of Luray, Va., Colonel Bryan Conrad of Richmond, Va., Mrs. E. G. Wilson of Charles Town, West Va., Mr. J. K. Deming of Dubuque, Ia., Mrs.

C. E. Bilheimer of Gettysburg, Pa., Mr. William B. Reed of Chevy Chase, Md., Mr. Lewis D. Fort of Whitehaven, Tenn., and Dr. John W. Wayland of Harrisonburg, Va.

The courtesy of The University of North Carolina Press, Chapel Hill, North Carolina, owners of copyright in *I Rode with Stonewall* by Henry Kyd Douglas, has made it possible to quote from that notable work as to the rôle of Belle Boyd at the battle of Front Royal. Similarly, as to *A Virginia Girl in the Civil War, 1861-65*, edited by Myrta Lockett Avary, both the D. Appleton-Century Company of New York City and Mrs. Avary have granted permission to use material from the noted memoirs of "Nellie Grey."

LOUIS A. SIGAUD.

INDEX

C